CHINA IN SEVEN BANQUETS

China in Seven Banquets

A FLAVOURFUL HISTORY

THOMAS DAVID DuBOIS

REAKTION BOOKS

Published by
Reaktion Books Ltd
Unit 32, Waterside
44–48 Wharf Road
London N1 7UX, UK
www.reaktionbooks.co.uk

First published 2024
Copyright © Thomas David DuBois 2024

Printed and bound in Great Britain by TJ Books Ltd, Padstow, Cornwall

A catalogue record for this book is available from the British Library

ISBN 978 1 78914 861 9

CONTENTS

6
Franchise Fever
The Price of Efficiency

7
And Beyond . . .

A Note for My Fellow Historians, and for Everyone Else

This is a book for non-specialists, by which I mean pretty much everyone. My fellow historians may find that I have taken a few shortcuts in condensing long, complex processes into a few sentences. Precise scholarly translations have been simplified and different systems of romanization standardized as Pinyin. Detailed footnotes and long-winded diatribes have been pruned with neither mercy nor regret. I hope that this will not take away from your enjoyment of the book.

I have translated everything in the main text into English, adding Chinese characters only when necessary. Unless otherwise noted, most translations are my own. Book titles are hard to translate, so these appear in the Select Bibliography, in a special section on Chinese food writing. Chinese names are written in Chinese fashion, with the surname coming first. Those who need them will find Chinese characters – traditional or simplified depending on the type used in the source – in the book's index.

Recipe instructions use the measurements and kitchen vocabulary of the original Chinese text. Weights and measures that appear only once are converted in text. Ones that are more common are explained in a quick guide at the end of the book.

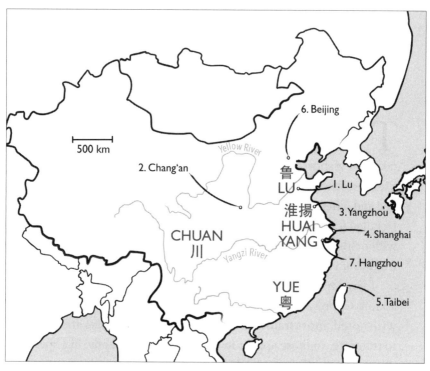

Map of China showing the location of the book's seven banquets
and the 'Four Cuisines'.

Introduction
What Is Food History?

The best way to kill a frog is to throw it hard against a wall. Do it right and the animal dies instantly or at least is stunned long enough that you can quickly swoop in to finish the job with a cleaver. A quick end for the frog, but also pretty physically demanding on the cook. Normally, a kitchen gives this sort of job to its lowest-level apprentices.

Having spent the morning preparing a box of fat croakers brought in from the nearby rice fields, a young cook carries his haul through an open courtyard where, over the years, countless frogs, eels, chickens, ducks and fish have met their end. He crosses into a room packed with pots of pastes, sauces and vinegars and a wall of ovens, smokers and stoves.

What happens next? The skinned and gutted 'water chickens' might be chopped finely, mixed with salt and beans and left to ferment into a paste. They might be destined to be pickled into a medicinal wine. They might be flash-frozen and wrapped in plastic for a journey halfway around the world.

These, however, are being prepared for dinner. A local delicacy, they will be chopped finely and fried quickly with soy sauce, wine, ginger and garlic.

And this is no ordinary dinner. Today's kitchen is brimming
with extra help. In a quiet corner, a troupe of opera
performers sit meticulously inspecting their costumes. Servants
inside the house are busy arranging flowers and preparing
paper and tables for displays of calligraphy.
But the centrepiece will be the food. The master of the
house is a well-known gourmand and everyone feels
the pressure to perform.

Tonight's meal is not just dinner. It is a banquet.

China's Food History

I first saw this method of stunning frogs during the early 1990s in
the coastal city of Xiamen, but this scene could have taken place
at almost any point in China's long history. Our young cook might
have been employed in the household of a wealthy merchant or
retired local official. Let's say that he worked for the infamous
gourmand Yuan Mei. That would place us in the late 1700s, right
in the heart of China's wealthiest region. But swap out a few of the
details and we could be anywhere in China, at almost any point
from prehistory to the not-so-distant future.

This book is a quick tour through that long history – 5,000
years of food in China. Making sense of this much time is a tall
order. We'll have to keep our eye on the grand scheme of what
changed and why, when new foods and techniques appeared and
what parts of this vast transformation, if any, can be considered
essentially Chinese. That's the big picture, but seeing only that is,
as the saying goes, like 'viewing flowers from horseback'. We will
also need to get close up to see the way that food has influenced
countless lives, generation after generation. Who was our kitchen
apprentice and how did food shape his world? What did he eat
at the end of a long day of cooking lavish meals for the wealthy?

How similar was his cuisine to anything we would recognize as Chinese food today? Had he ever seen a tomato? What did his distant descendants think the first time they saw a refrigerator or tasted chocolate?

Before going any further, let's first acknowledge that we are in some very good company here. The field of China food studies has produced some excellent scholarship over the years, and we will be standing on the shoulders of generations of historians and anthropologists. Some of these scholars appear in the brief bibliography at the end of the book. Much of the best writing on China's food comes from outside academia. Some of my favourites are Sean J. S. Chen's outstanding translation of Yuan Mei's *Recipes from the Garden of Contentment* and of course anything by Fuchsia Dunlop.

This is just a drop in the vast ocean of Chinese-language food writing – scholarly and historical, amateur and professional – going back thousands of years. Food appears in novels and films, scientific and medical texts and farmers' almanacks. We will be mining centuries of sources, from tomb frescoes to market segmentation reports.

So, with all that has been written, let's start by thinking about what *hasn't* been done. For one thing, it is time for an update. Some of the classic writings on food in China are already a few decades old, leaving us out in the cold for all the big changes since China's economic opening. For another, the anthropologists and the historians need to talk to each other. By this, I mean that the process we use to understand the present – interviews and patient observation of occasions like banquets – needs to be grounded in questions of long-term historical change.

We need to think big, because food is just so fundamental to . . . everything. There is no part of our world that food doesn't touch. Food is universal. I'll go out on a limb and assume that you, dear reader, eat food, and probably wouldn't be very happy if you were asked to live without it. The French gastronome Jean-Anthelme Brillat-Savarin famously challenged readers to 'tell me what you eat, and I will tell you what you are.' If anything, he was underselling his point. Food is civilization. The first thing any competent government will do is to make sure that its people never miss a meal. Any two people eating together immediately constitute a tiny little society. Food marks taste and status and cuisine is no less an art form than painting or poetry. Food is a driving force of history, arguably *the* driving force.

What all this means is that the history of food in China can't just be about the food itself. This book looks at famous dishes and kitchen techniques, but just as important, it shows the backstory: the ways that economic and social changes shaped how food was produced, prepared and eaten. To really understand food in China, we need the big picture and intimate detail, both of the food itself and of the society that consumed it – over a span of fifty centuries.

We will find our way to seven historical banquets. When I say 'banquet', what I really mean is a meal, big or small, lavish or humble, real or invented. Our seven banquets are drawn from a variety of sources. Two are actual events recorded in original sources. One comes from the pages of literature, another from film and yet another is a delivery menu that I read on my phone. The book's first banquet sprang from an ancient philosopher's imagination. The last one from my own.

Each banquet is a snapshot in time, one that embodies a specific moment in China's mosaic of food. Each reveals a unique facet of food in society: how and why people ate together, who was invited and who sat at the head of the table.

As for the food itself, we will be deconstructing each meal using something akin to the 'history in objects' approach that is beloved by museums worldwide. Every object, say for example a Roman coin found buried in the mud of the Thames, has a story.

Find someone who has the skills and patience to learn where that coin was minted, where its metal was mined, whose face is now barely visible on its weathered surface and how it came to rest in the spot where it was discovered and that one coin can end up telling you a lot about the spirit of a time.

In her 1986 classic *Much Depends on Dinner*, Margaret Visser famously takes this approach to food. Visser examined seven ingredients of a typical American meal – corn, butter, rice, chicken, olive-oil-and-lemon (dressing) and ice cream – tracing each item from prehistory to the present and relating the efforts that brought them into hundreds of millions of homes. Visser not only tells a good tale, but does us a service by highlighting the stories and controversies behind objects that are so vital they are almost invisible. Entire books have been written on the global travels of individual ingredients: sugar, salt, milk, beer and cod and goodness knows how many on tea and coffee.[1]

We're doing something similar, at least as a starting point. We'll definitely need to know how and when China first encountered ingredients like onions, chillies or soy sauce, red wine or instant coffee. We will also keep an eye on how food was prepared. Just like new ingredients, cooking skills and styles leave a footprint as they move from place to place. We'll be following tastes as they change along with the times, new ones coming into vogue and old ones fading away – often coming back into fashion a few generations later. This focus on technique also means trying to reverse-engineer actual recipes.

But before that, I want to briefly step back and look into two fundamental questions that drive the study of food history: *what was the food* at any given place and time and *what did it mean* to the people who made, sold, desired or consumed it? A bit of background on these questions may give perspective on what's at stake in our sprint through China's culinary past.

The Food

Any food item has a distinct journey from 'farm to table', changing hands from growers to processors, middlemen, retailers and cooks, before finally appearing on our plates. Tracing that journey often starts with understanding who stood to make a profit. Why did ancient Romans eat wheat? How did some foods become global staples? Why did farm labourers eat wheat bread before the Black Death and white bread after? How did milk end up in cans or tea in tiny single-cup bags? How did whittled-down carrot pieces become 'babies'?

Different questions, same answer: money. Changes happened when someone discovered the cheapest way to solve a problem (for example, how to feed a city), when market realities changed (workers could demand better food when labour was scarce) or because someone at some point in the process saw the chance to make a profit by cornering an existing market or creating a new one.

Let's not be completely cynical about this. Consider the sweet potato. Starting in the sixteenth century, a wave of new foods began to spread throughout the world. Reliable, calorie-rich crops like cassava, breadfruit and sweet potatoes would become daily staples, rescuing millions from endemic hunger. They still make up the foundation of diets and cuisine across much of Africa, the Pacific and the Caribbean.[2] But let's not be naive either. These foods followed in the wake of imperialism, which was not exactly a humanitarian enterprise. High-calorie crops like sweet potatoes displaced native food systems, but they also saved land and time, which in turn translated into higher output of a market product – rubber, indigo, coffee, lumber, tin or whatever it was the people in charge were *really* interested in producing.

Keeping a close eye on the details of production, processing and transportation tells us why some new food arrived, and the form it arrived in. One food that we will be seeing surprisingly often is dairy. In the past few years, China has gone dairy crazy and is now one of the world's largest milk consumers. Why do Chinese people today drink so much milk? Because they can. Modern cold-supply chains are a marvel. They can stock a supermarket in Wisconsin with raspberries from Chile, fresh-cut flowers from Ecuador or lamb shanks from Australia – and we don't even notice them. In China, the process of bringing fresh milk to a supermarket is a miracle of precision timing that allows consumers in almost any major Chinese city to buy fresh, cold milk.

But the miracle of fresh milk delivery is a relatively new one, the result of decades of investments, technology transfers and trade agreements. Like most modern food industries, China's milk industry is fully globalized. The country has millions of dairy cows, but a lot of what those cows eat comes from overseas – that's the price for making the industry ecologically and financially feasible. It also relies on technology. As milk spoils quickly, the network that transports it from farm to dairy and from dairy to shop has to be quick, cheap and reliable. Just twenty years ago, fresh milk delivery was simply not possible and much of China had to settle for shelf-stable UHT-processed milk. Before that, there was milk powder or tinned condensed milk, and before *that*, it was the luck of the draw. If you had a ration coupon, you might get some of the milk that was trucked into the city each morning, poured directly from a metal pail into a jug that you brought from home. Or you might not, since there was a fair chance that the milk would have spoiled during the time that you and your jug were patiently waiting in line.

In other words, milk is not a single thing. The backstory of how a product like milk is made, processed, shipped and stored completely changes not just how much people consume, but *how* they will consume it. Fresh milk is great for drinking, but since

UHT-processed or reconstituted milk doesn't taste as good, makers learned to mask the difference with loads of sugar, which naturally appealed to children.[3] Milk powder needs to be dissolved in boiled water, so people raised during that era developed the habit of drinking it hot or mixing the powder into porridge. And if refrigeration wasn't an option, you'd have to save the dairy protein by processing it into yogurts and cheeses, which is exactly how people in China – or at least parts of it – consumed milk for centuries.

We're focusing on physical production technology here, but you could say the same thing about any of the other economic factors – like the consumer scarcity that is built into planned economies or the culture of mass marketing – that shape what food people are actually able to buy and how they buy it. Growing up in 1970s Indiana, there was a lot missing from my childhood, culinarily speaking. Not that I would have known it at the time, but the coffee was terrible. Bread was strictly of the mass-marketed, pre-sliced variety, bleached to the colour of snow and blissfully free of either taste or nutrition. Ethnic foods . . . simply didn't exist. I remember my favourite aunt making the occasional supply run to the Middle Eastern groceries in Chicago, returning with a trunk full of supplies – jars of tahini, bags of flatbread, canned chickpeas, tubs of kalamata olives and, above all, gallon tins of olive oil, which she distributed in the church parking lot like she was handing out war relief. That was then. My same small town now boasts three megastores, each of which keeps all of these once rare items in stock. Oh, and each one has a Starbucks on the premises.

Food fashion can be a self-fulfilling prophecy. When I was working in my college cafeteria, I decided it would be a pretty hilarious trick to collect and cook the decorative plants that we used to cover the ice around the salad bar. These plants looked pretty and stayed fresh forever, but nobody thought of them as food. Imagine my surprise when I discovered that this mystery vegetable was actually pretty tasty. Over time, I learned to steam it with rice, roast it with chicken and stew it with pork. The one thing I could not do was *buy* it. I never saw it in a shop, except being used as decoration for *their* cold displays. As far as I knew, this exotic treat could only be obtained through petty theft. That is, until years later when it came into vogue and started to appear in produce sections. It turns out that my magic vegetable was none other than kale.

Tracing the flow of commodities reveals variations on these same processes playing out across history. Long before we had to consider the complexities of supermarket retail, other factors determined what food might be available. The opening of a new trade route might introduce new exotic foods or it might supply existing foods more cheaply. The ancient city of Rome never could have grown to its size and complexity without seaborne imports of grain, a trade that in turn relied on a large body of politically connected merchants.[4] Creating a new way to market a waste product generates new demand. Long before I learned to eat the salad bar decorations, this same sort of innovation repurposed leftover tea dust in convenient tea bags or shaped broken carrots into adorable 'babies'. The logic of abundance also works in reverse. Lobster was once so common in the North Atlantic that workers stipulated in their contracts that work meals would *not* include lobster.[5] Scarcity changed all that. But *over*-exploit a sea species like lobster, herring or cod and you will sooner or later affect or even lose the fishing communities that depend on them not just for livelihood but for food.[6]

History shows numerous foods traversing the arc from exotic to mundane all because someone found a way to match supply to demand. A classic example is the European spice trade. While the often-heard claim that Europeans craved Asian spices to cover the taste of rotten meat is clearly nonsense (especially when you consider that fresh meat was a whole lot cheaper than the spices themselves), the part about wealthy Europeans having been willing to shell out large sums for commodities like nutmeg and pepper is very true – at least at the outset, a time when pepper was known as 'black gold'.[7] It didn't take long for all that money to grease the wheels of trade: routes switched back and forth between the Atlantic and the Mediterranean, trading countries developed new alliances and new trade structures, commercial centres – Malacca, Aden, Istanbul, Venice – rose and fell, the seas became safer for trade and ship design allowed for longer voyages holding more cargo. The end result is that prices went *down* and by the eve of the American Revolution, items like pepper, nutmeg and cloves had all become fairly commonplace in Western kitchens.[8] It wasn't a straight line – history never is – but in the long view, two things are true: fashion plus scarcity equals demand, which on its own has the power to drive up prices almost without limit, and when there is money to be made, *someone* will find a way to outwit their competition, bringing more product to market and eventually lowering the price along with it. Replace the story of pepper with any other luxury commodity – sugar, tea, coffee, chocolate or vanilla – and the same holds true.

Skills and techniques behave in a similar way, circulating across space and deepening over time. As far as food-related technologies go, nothing is more fundamental than agriculture. Historically, higher yields on the farm could let you do more with less land. Unlike today's extensive, mechanized model, agriculture through most of human history was small-scale and intensive. Land was the limiting factor and the goal was to squeeze as much as possible out of however much you had. Crops like wet rice really responded to this – the more care you put into a field of rice, the more you will get out of it. But efficient rice agriculture had a steep learning curve. Disseminating wet rice cultivation wasn't just a matter of showing up with seeds; it also meant mastering the complex cycle of caring for seedlings and ensuring that the transplanted rice plants get the optimal schedule of air, water and manure. This is not something that could be learned overnight, especially since you would have needed to adapt existing techniques to suit the unique soil, water, altitude and climate of your little patch of land.

No less important are the techniques for storage and processing. It doesn't matter how good a farmer you are if half your harvest gets lost to mildew or rats or sneaky neighbours. Processing isn't just about preventing loss. Brewing grain into beer, turning milk into cheese or curing pork into ham also adds taste and value. Ancient cultures across the world developed all of these techniques and some have spent millennia perfecting them. One of the most important types of processing is sauces. The fermented fish sauce known as garum added protein and flavour to the cuisines of the ancient Mediterranean. The creation of sauces made from fermented and pickled meat, fish, beans and grains was a fundamental innovation in early cuisines across Asia, later influencing such global favourites as Worcestershire sauce and ketchup.

The mention of flavours brings us to the most visible food technique – cuisine. We will spend a lot of time on this final stage of food preparation, learning in detail the different ways that Chinese cooks boiled, steamed, fried and baked food. Anyone expecting to see a 'timeless' Chinese cuisine will be surprised to learn just how radically Chinese cooking techniques have changed over time. One reason for this is changing tastes. Fashionable diners in the Song dynasty (tenth to thirteenth century) had a special penchant for *hui*, a style of marinated raw meat that probably influenced Japanese dishes like sashimi. Other reasons include material change, the introduction or innovation of new foods and also new designs for basic equipment like stoves and utensils. Culinary sophistication rose and fell and some traditions have been lost forever. The delicate aesthetic of the Song was swept away by the Mongol invasions, which also ushered in new ways of eating. By the time the Mongols left, tastes had irrevocably changed. During the revolutionary extremism and material austerity of the mid-twentieth century, the very *idea* of high cuisine was debased as a vice of the corrupt bourgeoisie. When carriers of China's culinary arts departed the scene, they took much of their collected knowledge with them.

The Meaning

As far as what food means, let's start with etiquette. Good table manners have always been a marker of status and the upper classes are the ones who set the standard. Society often ties the way someone eats to assumptions about that person's values or mindset. Good etiquette might mean keeping the genders separate, not allowing children at the table, not eating or drinking to excess – all variations on the basic virtues of modesty and propriety – but in practice, the rules applied very unequally to those in power and to the unwashed masses that they aimed to keep at bay. The ancient Greeks considered it uncouth to spit at the table, but made exceptions for those of status. And as social lines shifted, the circle of people who were expected to chew with their mouths shut expanded outwards, from lofty lords to the rising bourgeoisie and eventually to us regular ol' commonfolk. It is not unreasonable to view the long-term evolution of Western society as a democratization of the demand that everyone should behave like a 'civilized person'.[9]

Foodways give us a sense of belonging. Think about dietary restrictions. Some dietary taboos share practical origins. Irish folktales warned against eating certain livestock for fear of offending the fairies in nature. Look closer and you'll see that the stories actually allude to conditions like bovine spongiform encephalopathy, better known as mad cow disease. Butchering an animal that died from wandering off a cliff might seem like a good bet

– until you learn that the animal was infected and that eating its meat could be deadly. As this disease only popped up every few decades, turning this knowledge into folk tales about vengeful fairies and cursed cattle made it easier to remember and pass on.[10] Religious dietary practices build a sense of inclusion, binding the most intimate act of eating to sacred moments in history. There is real power in being able to envision your co-religionists through time and across the globe sharing the same meal.

People imagine a lot about food, linking certain foods to the groups and values that they find meaningful, and pairing different tastes and dishes with human personalities. We all describe certain people as sweet, spicy or bland, even if we have no actual intention of eating them. Medieval Europeans tied tastes to status – earthy garlic was suitable for the labouring classes, who ate it raw for a burst of strength. But society's elites were better served by aromatic herbs, which flourished in the air and were literally closer to God.[11] For most of history, that loaf of rustic wholegrain bread was peasant food. Anyone who could afford it wanted their bread smooth and white. When population events like the Black Death made labour more expensive, workers demanded the upgrade.

Advertising culture has made food identities ever more tribal. Four decades ago, humourist Bruce Feirstein told us that *Real Men Don't Eat Quiche*. Update that same sentiment with veggie burgers or Hawaiian pizza and you can probably call to mind people who you know wouldn't be caught dead with the stuff. Ask people for their idea of the typical 'man's man' diet and you're likely to hear steak. Popular imagination tells us that beef is more masculine than chicken, even if it doesn't know exactly why. Ask what kind of person eats organic kale, processed cheese, unsweetened oatmeal or chop suey and you're likely to hear all sorts of responses that include assumptions about that person's politics, income, educational background and, certainly, ethnicity.

Some assumptions are grounded in actual consumption patterns, but just as often they are created when a kernel of fact erupts into a stereotype. Americans do indeed eat a lot of hot dogs and apple pie, but that is different from the idea that these foods embody the 'spirit' of America in some mystical sense. Yet that is exactly what the idea of a 'national cuisine' wants us to believe, without even taking into account the sort of product marketing that explicitly ties a personality to a brand and then saturates the public with images of what kind of person drinks Coke versus Pepsi, Budweiser versus Heineken or Del Monte versus Tropicana juices.[12]

Finally, people everywhere crave novelty and they always have. Food fads have always existed and getting in on the ground floor of the next big thing has its own inimitable appeal. Add in rare ingredients and the gatekeeping function of good taste and you have a recipe that makes food a perfect arena for social competition. The entire ballet of choosing, opening and ceremoniously serving a bottle of rare Scotch whisky is in fact an elaborate display of the ability to obtain and appreciate fine things, uniting host and guest in a shared bond of connoisseurship but also separating them along the same lines – since only one of the two is in the position to show off. We see much the same thing on the tables of the wealthy, from ancient Rome to *Real Housewives*. This trinity of forces – scarcity, taste and community – spans time and cultures.

You have by now no doubt also noticed that the two big questions of food studies – food and its meaning – are in fact two sides of the same process. Social meaning interacts with demand; production creates or solves scarcities. Food is never just a matter of farm-gate prices, marketing schemes or finding new ways to fry a fish. It's all of these influences and many more interacting, and they are all universal.

Sources

This book is about China, so let's get down to details, starting with our sources. As food is so important in so many different ways, we need to draw on numerous different perspectives.

Official sources like political records give us a skeleton of facts. Statecraft starts with food, and dynasty after dynasty kept a close eye on harvests and grain prices. Sometimes governments took direct action: distributing famine supplies, building up strategic food industries, banning grain exports or lavish feasts. Commercial records from China's merchant houses, importers and food makers present the perspective of the business world, telling us how trade worked and how far goods travelled, and showing the scale of planning that went into sending a merchant ship to the Spice Islands or a caravan across the Gobi Desert.

Other sources put meat on these bones. Archaeologists have uncovered tombs and treasures, including whole kitchens frozen in time. Biological remains like bones and seeds can tell us about the natural and human environment for which no written records exist. Paintings, frescoes and sculptures depict how food was produced, sold, prepared and consumed. They show us how grain was stored, how animals were slaughtered, what table settings looked like, whether men and women ate together and how shop fronts were decorated. Literature depicts food in a social setting: a story about two friends chatting over tea might focus on the content of their conversation, but the details that fill out the scene – what they were eating, how the shop was laid out and the price of their meal – are a snapshot of the time. Religious texts recount the role of food in rituals and the complex social ethics behind what and how we eat.

Food Books and Recipes

The source we will use most is writing about the food itself. Agricultural texts like the sixth-century *Essential Techniques for the Common People* include instructions on how to pickle, dry or preserve meat, fruits and vegetables. Memoirs like the twelfth-century *Dream of Splendour in the Eastern Capital* recall, street by street, market by market and dish by dish, the foods of medieval Kaifeng in the years before the city was sacked by Jurchen invaders. Medical books like the early fourteenth-century *Principles of Eating and Drinking* describe the therapeutic properties of different foods and prescribe recipes to maximize both effect and appeal. And gastronomic classics like the eighteenth-century *Recipes from the Garden of Contentment*, a loving account of Jiangnan cuisine, introduces dozens of dishes, along with descriptions about where certain dishes were supposedly invented, praise for the local produce, tea and wine and a critic's-eye view of what separates good from mediocre cuisine.

We will use a good number of recipes, which are reproduced pretty much exactly as they appear in their original sources, including original measurements and technical instructions that might occasionally be less than clear. The reason for keeping close to the original is that historical recipes are more than just instructions. Books like the *Essential Techniques* are written in a kind of terse shorthand. They skip obvious steps and include instructions to add 'enough' salt to a brine mixture or cook a fish until it 'feels done'. These books are written for a reader who already knew their way around a fermenting vat. They are completely different from the precise descriptions and measurements of the modern, idiot-proof cookbook. This new style of recipe reflects a changing readership – China's first generation of modern cookbooks was written for the 'busy housewife', one who didn't have time to cook and presumably came to the task with little or no knowledge. Recipes tell us what food was available, what techniques were considered common knowledge and what sort of equipment existed in a standard kitchen. Commercial food magazines are aspirational; they hint at a life that we want to have, even if all we do is look at the pictures. We'll be using a lot of these, especially for the new food culture of the 1980s.

Which brings us to the food itself.

We will be spending a lot of time recreating historical foods, either by coaxing detail out of vague descriptions or in some cases actually preparing the dishes. More than just fun (although let's be honest . . . it is pretty fun), we need to understand and experience the completed dishes to fully appreciate the evolving art of cuisine. Not seeing the food – in a book *about food* – would be like reading about Renaissance art without seeing a single painting or reading about music theory without ever hearing a note. Technically accurate, but perversely sterile.

Culinary recreation is quite big in food history. For her 1980 classic, food historian Karen Hess forensically reconstructed the collection of eighteenth-century Anglo-American recipes known as *Martha Washington's Booke of Cookery*. Making the actual dishes helped her to correct misconceptions about individual techniques and puncture the commonly held conception of the time being populated by culinary primitives. Others have done this for the often-maligned cooking of the European Middle Ages and for the ancient world. There are numerous YouTube channels devoted to recreations of historical cuisine and some of these are really worth checking out.[13]

Reverse-engineering historical recipes requires some creativity. There will be gaps in what is actually written down. For example, if we intend to recreate a recipe for brined fish in the *Essential Techniques*, we first need to know what kinds of fish were swimming around in sixth-century China. If ingredients are unavailable, we need to find analogues. Assuming that we don't have access to exotic meats like muntjac (a small species of deer), long-lost flavouring pastes or the unique red rice grown only in one particular mountain valley, we need to make a good guess as to how these would have looked, smelled and tasted. Often this means combining sources. For example, dishes described in the eighteenth-century novel *Dream of Red Mansions* can be cross-referenced against techniques described in food texts like the *Recipes from the Garden of Contentment* from roughly the same time. I have drawn liberally on the generous advice of chefs and home cooks, amateur and professional food scholars, as well as from China's growing legion of history junkies and culinary cos-players that meet in kitchens, banquets and in cyberspace, united by their love of food heritage.

But the payoff makes all the trouble worthwhile. Beyond the inherent thrill of recreating a dish from one, three or twenty centuries past, you may find lost techniques making their way into your own culinary bag of tricks. Cooks in the past had time to spare, but we moderns possess everything but patience. Most of us leave techniques like pickling and fermenting to industrial producers, who might prefer a shorter (and cheaper) process, relying on artificial smoke, alcohol or MSG to mimic the taste of time. Having never experienced the real thing, most of us wouldn't even know that a difference exists.

Seven Banquets

Now that we have set up the scale of the book, we have to back-track a bit and say that we won't go through everything evenly. China is too big and its history is too long to cover it all. Instead, we will focus on six big transformations: the formation of a distinct philosophy of food in ancient China; the arrival of new ingredients and techniques from neighbours near and far; the perfection of techniques during China's later imperial era; the introduction of Western cuisine and industrial food production during the early twentieth century; the rapid-fire appearance of new foods and fads during the economic boom of the 1990s; and the effect of tech-driven globalization since 2000. The last chapter offers a glimpse into the future, extrapolating from trends already set in motion.

You might have noticed that the pace of change speeds up, which in turn means that the chapters slow down. The first chapter strides quickly through 2,000 years, the last historical one just twenty. But what a busy twenty years they have been.

Following a more or less roundabout path, each chapter eventually comes to focus on a banquet that captures the spirit of the time. The chapter on ancient traditions presents a meal that was once served to honour the elderly. The one on new foods takes us to court banquets of the Tang, Yun and Qing dynasties. For the high cuisine of the later empire, we look at the foods that appear in novels of the eighteenth century. The encounter with Western cuisine takes us to 1920s Shanghai for a New Year's Day set-course meal. For the go-go '90s, we will look to the comforting homestyle foods in the food cinema classic *Eat Drink Man Woman*. For global China's love affair with convenience, we take apart a home-delivery hotpot dinner. Finally, our glimpse into the future ends with not one, but *three* meals, each corresponding to a different path that the coming years might take.

1

Of Meat and Morality

The Eight Treasures of Zhou

Our first banquet takes place in the garden of a palace.
A group of elderly men is seated on reed mats, surrounded
by a ring of younger attendants. The atmosphere is
decorous. Barely a word is spoken, the silence broken only
by the sound of ringing chimes.

One by one, the attendants bring in a succession of eight
bronze vessels, each containing an elaborate dish: Clay-
baked suckling pig; sheep cured with cinnamon and
ginger; dog liver grilled in its own fat; pickled, marinated
and macerated meats; fried cakes made of rice and mince.

Nobody knows when or where these dishes, the 'Eight Treasures of Zhou', were first served, but we do know who first recorded their existence. They are mentioned in the second-century BCE *Book of Rites*, one of the classic texts of Confucianism.

The author wasn't describing a meal that he had enjoyed himself. Nor was he using food to recount the life of Confucius, who had lived hundreds of years earlier. This was a meal from a much more distant past.

Confucius himself was born 26 centuries ago, so we might think of him as a fairly ancient figure. But by the time he arrived on the scene, Chinese civilization had already been evolving for millennia. In his own telling, this deep antiquity was a golden age. Confucius always thought of himself as born too late.

The Eight Treasures banquet epitomized the moral society of the early Zhou kingdom, the lost age that the Confucians loudly pined for. The description also reflected some of the ways in which food had already come to shape China's ancient civilization. Over millennia, the land that we now know as China had emerged gradually as hundreds of Neolithic cultures coalesced into a series of Bronze Age kingdoms. This was a formative age, recalled by later generations as a time of wise princes, sage philosophers and crafty tacticians. Even without the benefit of nostalgia, this was the time in which Chinese civilization began to take shape, when the foundations of its unique science, philosophy and religion were laid. It was also the time that China developed comprehensive theories of food and a distinct set of culinary techniques, both of which are on display in the Eight Treasures banquet.

Ancient Origins

As anyone who has spent time crossing the country will attest, China is vast, at least within its current borders. From north to south, the country extends from tundra to tropics. From west to east, it gradually descends in altitude from the Himalayas to a string of teeming coastal cities.

The historic cradle of Chinese culture is considerably smaller, but still covers an area that is remarkably diverse in both topography and climate. At its core, it is centred on two rivers that created the conditions for cultures to bloom.

In the north, the Yellow River begins in the stark, arid mountains of Qinghai and descends on a snaking path through Gansu, Inner Mongolia, Shaanxi and Shanxi, lumbering into the northern heartland of Henan and Shandong before disgorging into the creatively named Yellow Sea. The Yellow River is a river of mud. More brown than yellow, it carries tons of fine sand from the western mountains into the sprawling expanse of the North China Plain, which every year grows just a little bit larger as a result.

Just like the Nile and Tigris, the rich floodplains of this muddy river proved an ideal site to start a civilization. Eight millennia ago, people of the Houli culture located along its banks created stone houses and tools and elaborate pottery.[1] They also left behind evidence of a rich and varied diet. Carbonized seeds show a diet based on millet, a dryland grain that looks like couscous. They grew herbs and greens, and foraged for wild beans, apricots, dates and nuts. Charred bones confirm that the Houli people raised and hunted a wide variety of animals: pigs, chickens, dogs, wild deer and foxes. They fished the rivers for black and glass carp. Similar cultures further inland hunted an even wider variety of game. Those closer to the sea enjoyed all manner of mussels and clams.[2]

Further south, the Yangzi (sometimes written as Yangtse) River starts in the Himalayan snowcaps. Unburdened by mud, the Yangzi flows clear through the mountainous terrain of southern China, forming a lifeline that today connects riverine ports in the lush basin of Sichuan, moving on to Hubei and Anhui before emptying into the sea near the city of Shanghai. The Yangzi is one of many rivers that feed the region known as Jiangnan ('south of the river'). Enriched by trade and agriculture, this region was traditionally known as a 'land of fish and rice'. And indeed, it has long been precisely that. Neolithic sites near the river, such as Hemudu in the north of today's Zhejiang Province, show the early cultivation of wet-field rice and evidence of a diet that included a wide array of river fish, shellfish and turtles.

The handful of Neolithic sites that have actually been discovered intact is just the tip of a much larger and much older iceberg. Besides Houli and Hemudu, there are dozens more, each named after the contemporary village where artefacts were uncovered and each giving name to a distinct culture: Qijia and Majiawo in the northwest, Hongshan and Xiajiadian in the northeast, Shanbei in the southeast and Baodun near modern Chengdu. These represent only the smallest glimpse of what must have been thousands of small settlements and micro-cultures scattered across the landscape of today's China. The earliest clusters date to about 8,000 years ago, but at least one is a full 2,000 years older than *that* and the earliest domestication of grain earlier still.[3]

But brief though it is, this peek into China's prehistoric past can show us a couple of things. The first is a broad divide between two types of agriculture, millet-based in the dry north and rice-based in the warmer, wetter south. This basic divide between dry and wet farming systems would shape diets for centuries and remains very evident today.

The second is that these scattered cultures were all communicating – talking to, learning from and probably trading with each other with ever-greater frequency. Precious objects like carved jades were carried over large distances, eventually to be discovered hundreds of kilometres from where the raw stone was first pulled from the ground. Trading objects also meant exchanging ideas: the aesthetics of design motifs, the techniques of carving and often something more profound. Jade pieces were carved into

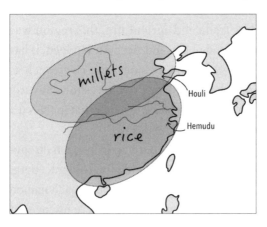

Millet and rice zones, c. 3000 BCE. The basic divide between northern and southern grain crops remains visible today.

objects of personal adornment but also into objects with ritual value, such as flat discs that represented the shape of the universe. As these prehistoric cultures came to know and understand their physical world, they also encountered and learned from each other. Extended over millennia, this communication created the foundation of what we would know as Chinese civilization.

This includes knowledge of food. Across this wide area, such objects as the pottery vessels used to store, ferment or cook food all started to take on a few characteristic shapes, such as ewers,

Bronze *fuzeng* grain steamer. This item was unearthed in Shanxi, but steamers using this basic design have been found across China.

broad basins or the three- or four-legged pots known as *ding*. Early methods of processing grain included smashing it with a grinding stone or heating it over a hot rock, but these gave way to the techniques of steaming and boiling. Unlike Southwest Asia, where grain was already being milled into flour, ancient China preferred these wet methods.[4] About 4,000 years ago, southern areas developed characteristic pot-bellied steamers called *fuzeng*. Within a few generations, these steamers were being used across the entire region.

Part of this cultural exchange was learning what to eat and how to eat it. Seeds of domesticated crops were carried over long distances. People also shared knowledge about which plants were useful for flavouring and medicine. One Neolithic village in Shanxi was found to have a vast trove of stored herbs, many of which are still part of the Chinese pharmacopoeia.[5]

Spread across a wide and diverse landscape and still many millennia away from any thought of political unity, these hundreds of Neolithic cultures were nevertheless developing a common toolkit of techniques, tastes and customs around food. These roots would further deepen as China entered its classical phase.

Culture and Cuisine

The gradual transition from hunting to settled agriculture meant that more people could live together, and that's when things got complicated. Five thousand years ago, northern agriculture had mastered a farm economy based on the combination of millet and pigs. Southern rice-growing areas had already developed into specialized communities. Archaeologists have unearthed evidence of craft centres, canals and defences. They also discovered elite graves, which is a fairly sure sign that society is starting to stratify.[6]

Give or take a few thousand years, something similar was happening all over the world. A new wealth of food was allowing ancient societies in places like India, Egypt and Mesopotamia to support new classes of people: rulers, bureaucrats, priests, artisans and of course a military, none of whom spent their time farming. The emergence of complex societies also gave rise to a new sort of introspection about what it all meant. It was the global flowering of religion and philosophy.

In China, this period gave rise to a succession of kingdoms, remembered as Xia, Shang and Zhou, over a span of about 2,000 years. That's of course vastly oversimplifying it, since there was still no idea of a unified China and each kingdom actually consisted of more or less peaceful component states. When the ruling kingdom was weak, existing rivalries broke into open warfare. But whether one kingdom or many, the place that would one day be China was united by a growing sense of common civilization.

Both parts – the rivalries and the civilization – gave rise to China's great ideas. The school of thought that we now associate with Confucius (but which actually existed centuries before him) taught that a strong ruler should cherish ancient traditions and prize a strict standard of correct behaviour. There was also a budding idea of what made the universe work. All phenomena, natural and human, were powered by the interaction of basic forces of change, represented in the flowing of yin and yang. Since these forces were universal, they could explain any sort of dynamic system, including cycles of change in politics, in the planets and seasons and within the human body. These basic civilizational foundations also included a comprehensive theory of food and a suite of characteristic kitchen techniques.

Classical China knew that it was advanced. It was intensely aware of cultural achievements that by that time already included writing, bronzeworking and philosophy. But nothing was more important than farming. Folk tales attributed the invention of agriculture to a mythical figure known as Shennong, the divine farmer. It was Shennong who taught primitive humans how to plant, harvest and store grain. In order to know which wild plants were edible and helpful, Shennong went out and tried each one. Shennong invented the plough, the calendar and medicine. In a fundamental way, Shennong marked the beginning of everything. He remains an important figure in folk religion, especially among farmers.

While farming let communities settle down and live stable lives, it was cooking that marked the dawn of civilization. Later sources recall this transformation in semi-mythical terms:

> In ancient times, people were few and animals were plentiful; people could not overcome the birds, beasts, snakes and insects . . . People ate fruits, mussels and oysters and raw meats that stank and hurt their bellies, making them sick. A sage appeared and taught people how to drill flint for fire and how to cook meat. His name was Sui Ren and the people said he was the king of the world.[7]

It was the Yellow Emperor, China's mythical sage king, who taught man to cook grain using water. As a later source remembers it: 'The Yellow Emperor created the *fuzeng* and the way of eating cooked grains,' and just in case the point wasn't clear, added, 'the Yellow Emperor ate his grain steamed.'[8]

Meat and Morality

China's early philosophers had a great deal to say about food. For political thinkers like Confucius, the central issue was to eat correctly: the right food, in the right season, in the right way and in the right company. This should be no surprise, as his entire school of thought was all about social propriety, which basically meant acting according to one's own station. The other reason is that food was part of a complex, moving cosmos. Each season, every physical condition had its own food; the idea was to eat in a way that mimicked nature's own cycles.

Like most areas of Chinese thought, the theory of eating couldn't escape the influence of politics. Given that much of the ancient world was at war, it was fairly important to know the secret to making your own kingdom peaceful and prosperous. Great minds flitted between royal courts offering counsel. Confucius was one of these would-be advisers.[9] So, in their way, were many of ancient China's great thinkers – even the ones who spoke solely in mystical or other metaphors.

What did these early philosophers have to say about food? As it turns out, quite a lot. Historical accounts show real and mythical kings being laid low by food.[10] Banquets were a frequent setting for royal assassinations – one king was done in by means of a dagger hidden inside a fish. Even without the danger of tableside violence, a king's diet was a fairly transparent metaphor for his fitness to rule. An undisciplined royal table indicated a weak moral core. Such was the fate of the former Shang kingdom, which the official history recalls as ending in a drunken stupor, the stench of dissipation offending heaven itself.

Mindful of this decline, the moralistic Confucians advised subsequent rulers to be models of straight-backed propriety, intensely mindful of etiquette and moderate in all things, including diet. Later generations would hold up Confucius himself as a paragon of correct eating habits. Neither glutton nor ascetic, Confucius' dining habits were portrayed as having been above reproach, indicating respect to heaven and gratitude for the bounty of the earth. He is shown eating simply and deliberately, avoiding rich tastes, but having a special fondness for ginger. He refused the hospitality of a prince who offended him, but gladly shared the humbler table of a poor village host who understood the value of propriety.

When the Confucians talked about food, they were often talking about meat. The story of Confucius rejecting the prince does not concern an invitation to a cooked meal, but rather a gift of meat. Meat clearly had a special meaning – according to these texts, Confucius was reportedly unmoved by other gifts, but for a gift of meat he would stand and bow in respect.[11]

This was more than just Confucius being a hungry philosopher. The rulers of the Zhou kingdom (the time that Confucius lived) were called 'meat eaters' not because they were especially carnivorous, but because they embraced a custom of sharing sacrificial meat between superior and vassal. There was even a special term that was used specifically to mean meat that was given as a gift. By refusing the gift of meat, Confucius was stating that he did not accept this relationship and would not work for the prince. Meat was also offered *up*, as a ritual sacrifice to heaven and to the ancestors. This is one of many ways that dining customs and religious rituals were mirrors of each other. It is also why royal tables featured meat at every meal – because ritual demanded a meat offering to heaven in all but the most desperate circumstances (such as times of famine or periods of mourning).[12]

Meat was especially important for the elderly; it nourished the waning strength of age and showed deference at table. Confucian propriety was essentially a matter of treating people according to their station, including respect for the aged. Just as a good child cared for his parents, a good society showed respect to its elders. Confucian thinkers sought proof of such ideals in the more enlightened past. They dwelled particularly on the early days of the Zhou kingdom, which was held up as a golden age of perfect government and social harmony. A trilogy of Confucian texts (written and rewritten over centuries) explains every aspect of how these enlightened forebears lived and died, including the special treatment they afforded to people as they advanced in years. According to these texts, the young in ancient times ate simply, but those over the age of sixty were given rations of meat that increased over each subsequent decade of life. Those lucky few who lived to ninety were basically followed around with trays of food.[13]

A Cup for Heaven

If we are talking about food in classical ritual, the other big factor is wine. The story about drunkenness destroying the late Shang kingdom was not a form of ancient puritanism, but rather a criticism of excess. Alcohol was in fact a fundamental part of ancient Chinese society.

Like the domestication of crops, the earliest evidence of brewing comes not from historical records but from physical finds. Archaeologists had long suspected that the pottery found in Neolithic sites may have been used for brewing. Recent finds have included a 5,000-year-old 'brewing kit', consisting of a pottery stove, funnel and fermenting jars, complete with residue that confirms the recipe: broomcorn millet, barley, Job's tears and tubers. Other sites reveal fruited wine made from honey, peaches, plums and dates, as well as medicinal recipes containing seeds of sweet clover, jasmine and hemp.[14]

The actual method for ancient brewing is not known precisely – there were probably a number of different methods in use at the same time. Looking around Asia and the Pacific, there are many different ways to convince grain to ferment: using a starter of germinated grain, the natural enzymes found in wild grasses or tree bark or the so-called chewed-grain method that uses human saliva. (And that's not even counting the many ritual methods that grow out of a perceived connection between fermentation and the supernatural world.)

A writer from the fourth century recorded a process that by that time was already thousands of years old:

Mix ground rice and assorted grass and leaves together with the juice of the ko [ge] plant, make the dough as large as an egg, put it in the shade of reeds for a month and will become fermented. Then mix this [ferment] with rice and produce wine.[15]

In other words, the earliest methods may simply have replicated the pleasant surprise of discovering that badly stored grain ferments on its own. The contents of the Neolithic brewing kit – two pots and a stove – suggest that the first 'beer' may have been made from cooked grain, a process known as 'solid-state' fermentation, identical to the method used to make the sweet fermented rice known as *lao zao*. The commercial starter available at my local supermarket contains the fungi *Rhizopus nigricans* and *Rhizopus oryzae*, both of which are found extensively in nature, especially on grasses and harvested grains. You may know them as the sheen of powdery black mould that forms on leftover bread.[16]

Using the *lao zao* fermentation method, I tried making a batch of the mix found by archaeologists, using broomcorn millet, barley and Job's tears. For the tuber, I grated the long, thin yam known as *shanyao*. I was pleasantly surprised by the results. Since the ancient mash had less natural sugar than glutinous rice it took longer to fully ferment, but the final product had the sweet smell, distinct taste and smooth texture of fermented *lao zao*, or the millet-based 'sour porridge' made in parts of China today. The result would not have made anyone drunk, but the fermented mix would have brightened up ancient palates, held its own against spoilage and been easy to digest.

Fermented Grains (Prehistory)

Soak equal parts (½ cup each) of broomcorn millet, barley, Job's tears and shredded yam for 3 hours.* Discard the

soaking water, rinse and steam the mixture in a flat pan
for 30 minutes or until the largest grains are soft enough
to crush between finger and thumb.

When the steamed grain mash is cool enough to handle, stir
in a commercial rice leaven starter (one packet per 2 cups of
mash) and pack into a glass or porcelain bowl, forming
a large hole in the centre to add air. Cover with plastic wrap
and leave in a warm spot for about 48 hours, occasionally
adding a few drops of water if needed to maintain an
oatmeal-like consistency. Fermentation time will depend
on temperature and humidity.

A perceptible wine smell tells you it's ready. A skin of black
mould means that you have gone too far. Completed *lao zao*
can be refrigerated in a loosely covered jar that allows gas to
escape.

*Fermentation is a biological process and works best using
organic grain and non-chlorinated water. The fermented
grain can be added to porridge or used as a starter for
steamed bread.

By the late 1000s BC, ritual bone inscriptions, China's earliest written records, already distinguish between different kinds
of wine: herbal *chang*, sweet rice or millet-based *li* and *jiu*, a filtered, fully fermented wine with a 10–15 per cent alcohol content
(similar to a non-fortified grape wine). As clay pottery gave way
to cast bronze, drinking kit became more and more elaborate.
Bronze drinking vessels were made to resemble earlier pottery
shapes – tall cups, wide-bottomed jars and bulbous tripods – but
the new material was far rarer and more expensive, literally the
stuff of royalty. Royal graves are full of these precious bronzes,

Bronze cauldron, Shang dynasty, 13th–11th century BCE. Besides this classic three-legged shape, bronzes were cast into a variety of different pots for cooking and serving food, as well as wine cups and ritual vessels.

indicating how wine culture was not just socially important, but significant to status and court life.

Like meat, wine had a vital role to play in ritual life. Wine and meat were the two indispensable offerings to heaven and to ancestors. Wine also featured prominently in secular rituals to mark marriage and funerals. Like the offering of meat, formal drinking ceremonies displayed status and fealty. This description of ceremonial drinking protocol between friends comes from *Etiquette and Rites*, one of the three key Confucian ritual texts:

> The host and the guest salute each other three times. When they reach the steps, they concede to each other three times. Then the host ascends. The guest also ascends. The host stands under the lintel, faces north and salutes twice. The guest ascends from the west of the steps, stands under the lintel, faces north and returns the salutation. The host sits down and takes the chü-eh [jue] cup from the tray and descends to wash. Guest follows host. The host sits down again and pronounces words of courtesy and the guest replies.[17]

Contrast the importance of wine with the official contempt for drunkenness. Having overthrown the Shang, the Zhou kingdom gleefully took every chance to badmouth their drunken predecessors, especially the final Shang king:

> He was obsessed with drinking and refused to refrain from pleasure. He had a perverse and cruel heart with no fear of death. He behaved badly at Yin [Shang's capital] and cared not about its fall. No fragrant sacrifices ascended to Heaven; only the people's grievances and the rank odour of the drunken officials.

Thus, Heaven showed no love for Yin and sent down destruction.[18]

This quote comes from the Zhou's own restrictions on drink. Later commenters suggested that the elaborate drinking rituals were not intended to ban alcohol altogether, but rather to imbue drinking with a sense of formality, claiming somewhat unrealistically that paying close attention to ritual slowed the pace of consumption and allowed everyone involved to drink all day without losing control.[19]

But so much for theory. In fact, China's early drinking culture was widely pervasive. Confucius himself was said to enjoy his drink, but not to the point of excess. Others openly sought out the freedom of inebriation. Folk poems collected in the *Book of Songs* place feasting and drinking on the same plane and revel in wine as a celebration of life and friendship and a balm to soothe the pain of loss and longing.[20] First-century writer Xu Shen captures this dual nature in his pun-heavy definition of wine:

'Alcohol' (*jiu*) means 'to achieve' (*jiu*). It is what brings out the good and evil in human nature ... It also means 'to produce', since it is what produces good and bad fortune.

In ancient times Yi Di invented unfiltered ale. King Yu tasted it and found it excellent.

Then he exiled Yi Di.[21]

Five Tastes

Alongside morality and ritual, a final element is the idea that food mirrors the nature of the universe, producing a complete theory of what to eat and when. The foundational idea of early Chinese cosmology is that the universe is driven by the interaction of unseen forces. We see this in the cycling between different sets of opposing forces: yin and yang, dark and light, female and male, cold and hot. Represented in the black and white swirl of the taiji (aka the yin-yang symbol), these opposing forces are in balance and in motion, each creating the other. The same logic relates to the Five Phases, also known as the Five Transformations – Wood, Fire, Earth, Metal and Water. Each state creates and flows from the other in cycles of growth (for example, wood gives birth to fire) or destruction (water rusts metal). Just as yin and yang govern universal binaries, the Five Phases correlate to other phenomena that divide into five: five planets, five internal organs of the body, five colours, five cardinal directions and so on. The theory of the Five Phases is why each new dynasty would adopt a new official colour to signify that it had lawfully overcome the previous one.[22] The same idea can be expressed as patterns of eight, patterns of sixty-four, and so on, all following this idea of natural, predictable cycles of change.

Food was fundamental to this expansive cosmology. The five grains – rice, millet, broomcorn millet, wheat and soybeans – relate to different times of the year and to different ailments. The 'five flavours' – sour, bitter, salty, acrid and sweet – appear in Chinese medicine, not as flavouring agents but as ways of stimulating the five organs, channelling forces and restoring balance within the body. The *Rites of Zhou* relates these forces of nature to a medicalized diet:

> Each season has its pestilence. Spring has gastritis, summer has itches, autumn has chills and fevers and winter coughs and rising vapours. Use the five flavours, five grains and five medicines to cure them. Use the five forces, five sounds and five complexions to see each one rise and fall.[23]

The same texts that discuss social etiquette also outline the role of the court dietician, one of four doctors to attend the king. More than rousing the king's appetite, his job was to maintain balance in his diet and thus in the man himself:

> [The dietician] cares for and harmonizes the six grains, six drinks, six meals, hundred medicines and hundred pastes. Grains should dominate in the spring, geng in summer, pastes in autumn and beverages in winter. All tastes are to be in harmony: spring with sour, summer with bitter, autumn with hot, winter with salty. All to be properly matched: beef with glutinous rice, sheep with glutinous millet, pig with broomcorn millet, dog with large-grain millet, wild goose with wheat, fish with wild rice.[24]

The task of the dietician shows how Chinese medical theory had already developed around the conception of the body as a mirror of the cosmos. Just like the change of seasons, the human body sought a state of active equilibrium. Early medical texts like the *Yellow Emperor's Book of Internal Medicine* understood the body as a vortex of circulating qi energies, each sort of qi flowing along a set path. Maladies arose from excesses, deficiencies or blockages of these forces. Eating the right food at the right time could help to maintain this equilibrium; the wrong food could throw it all out of balance.

The ideal of healthy dietary balance was also a metaphor for a well-run kingdom. Just like the dietician adjusts flavours for the well-being of the royal patient, the ruler seeks to maintain balance among the different social forces within the realm. Even if the solution to political problems wasn't as literal as changing the taste of a dish, the metaphor of 'five flavours in harmony' is a common way to express the political ideal of fairness and balance.[25]

Technique and Cuisine

All this theory is fine, but what did people actually eat?

Luckily for us, the birth of China's cuisine coincided with another great invention – writing. The great flowering of China's classical cuisine gave birth to a vocabulary of foods, with new characters being created to represent basic foods and techniques. Some of these are more literal than others. The character *shi* 炙 refers to spit roasting, a technique that was used for beef, pork, sheep and fish, and is composed of meat (肉) on top of a fire (火). This form of roasting displaced an earlier method called *pao*, a technique that cooked meat inside its own skin, burning off the fur in the process.

Geng 羹, a character originally written as a young sheep (羔) plus the character for delicious (美), was stewed meat, with or without grain or vegetables. Now used to mean any thick soup, the original meaning was much more meat-centric. A later source defined *geng* simply as 'meat with its liquid'. Other explanations get a little slippery. The linguist Wang Li compared *geng* to today's dish of braised pork. Another source defines *geng* as the meat broth itself. Yet another draws the line by saying that *geng* has broth, while meat with less broth is a different dish called *chuai*.[26]

The character for *hai* 醢 was composed of a hand, a dish and a jar. Similar to Roman garum, Thai fish sauce or the impossibly pungent shrimp paste used in Indonesian cuisine today, *hai* was made by pickling dried meat with a grain starter, after which both were used as foods. The liquid, known as *tan* 醓, was valued as a condiment.

Second-century writer Zheng Xuan described the process of making *hai* as follows:

> To prepare hai and sanluan, first dry the meat and then cut it fine, mix with grain, starter and salt. Soak it in fine wine, close up the jar and it will be ready after 100 days.[27]

In other words, *hai* is a fermented product, an early ancestor of the myriad bean pastes that enrich Chinese cuisine today. A recipe from the twelfth-century book, *Mrs Wu's Records from the Kitchen*, uses bean paste as a starter and provides a clearer explanation of the process:

Prepared Meat Sauce (Song)

Take 4 jin of good meat, remove the bones and tendons [and chop fine]. Prepare 1½ jin of bean paste, 4 liang of good crushed salt, 1 bowl of crushed onion whites, 5 or 6 qian each of Sichuan peppercorns, fennel and orange peel. Mix all of the flavourings with the meat and wine until it reaches the consistency of porridge, place in a fermenting jar and seal the opening. Let the jar sit under the sun during the hottest time of day for 19 days and then open. If the meat looks too dry, add more wine. If it lacks taste, add salt. Reseal the jar with mud [over paper] and continue to sun.

Similar forms of fermented meat are much harder to find today. One reason is that time-consuming fermentation has been replaced by faster methods, such as starting dry-cured meat in an alcohol marinade. A dish called *tanzi rou* ('meat in a fermenting jar') appears on restaurant menus today, but that dish is actually made by steaming large chunks of pork belly in sauce. Today's *tanzi rou* is indeed a time-consuming dish, but one that takes three hours, not three weeks. But the original point of *tanzi rou* was preservation. One traditional method used in Sichuan preserves large chunks of deep-fried pork in a shell of rendered fat that ages the meat in an oxygen-free environment but without fermentation. Other forms of wet-vat fermentation – including a paste made by fermenting pork bones and chillies – are still preserved by ethnic minorities in the mountainous south and southwest. I managed to get hold of the hundred-day fermented 'sour pork' made in Guizhou – the taste and texture have a complexity that shorter-term salting or pickling cannot match, akin to the difference between salted cabbage and fermented kimchi.

Which meat was used to make *hai* in ancient China? The more the merrier, it seems. One book of palace protocol mentions keeping a standard of '120 vats of *hai*', each containing a different sort of pickled meat, including pork, beef, sheep, chicken, dog, rabbit, deer, muntjac and fish, as well as a large variety of snails and molluscs. The highest-prestige *hai* were made from the largest animals: the *haishishi* made of cooked or raw pork sliced into large chunks, the *hainiushi* made of cooked or raw beef, or the *hai* that used the meat from along the spine of the deer or muntjac. In addition to these, there was a recipe for *hai* that combined rabbit meat with vegetables, a sour-tasting *hai* made of fermented vegetables in animal broth, the *hai* made with snail meat and the *hai* made of pickled fish eggs. Fans of sushi may be interested to know that one of these ancient preparations was fermented slices of raw fish called *zha,* which was similar to early versions of Japan's signature dish.

Meat that was completely dry was called *fu* if it was prepared whole, or *xiu* if it was first sliced into thin strips. *Fu* could be made from any large game: deer, elk, wild boar or muntjac. Meat, vegetables and fruit were all dried using basically the same method of sunning on a ventilated rack or a tile roof. Sources mention spicing air-dried *xiu* with ginger and cinnamon paste. Ancient teachers once received their salaries as strips of *xiu*, which is why graduating students across much of Asia still present teachers with gifts of dried beef.

That's a lot of meat. Why so? Since we are talking about elite – even royal – tables, meat was more than a luxury. It was a ritual necessity. A blood sacrifice was the proper offering to heaven and official functions were inseparable from ritual. Protocol for serving guests dictated not just the amount of meat, but the number of different animals. The quantity of *hai* served at a banquet was a mark of prestige directly proportional to the status of the guest. For the king's meal, sixty different *hai* were set out. For an honoured guest, that number was fifty.[28] Like other matters of royal dining, the strict protocol of serving *hai* was maintained by a dedicated arm of the royal household staff.

Vegetables most often appeared as an accompaniment to balance meat dishes but, significantly, the types are often left unspecified. Making a *geng* without meat was unusual enough to warrant a mention, as when Confucius stopped at a farmhouse for a modest meal of meatless *geng*. Having just refused the lavish hospitality of a prince (whom we will remember had just offered a symbolic gift of meat to coerce him into service), Confucius professed that this humble family understood the meaning of propriety well above their station and gladly partook of their meal.

There were other roles for vegetables. Chopped fine and pickled in wine, they were called *ji*. Pickled whole they were called *zu*.[29] But however you did or did not slice them, vegetables were secondary.

Order and Opulence

The importance of proper eating to early Chinese society has left us with a lot of real and imaginary meals to look at. Ritual handbooks dictate with painstaking precision the protocol of food in formal state occasions: what greetings are to be offered, who is to stand where and facing in which direction and of course how the food is to be served. Here's just a small portion of a section outlining the rules for the table:

> In all cases the rules for bringing in the dishes (for an entertainment) are as follows: Meat cooked on the bone is set on the left, and the sliced meat on the right; the rice

is placed to the left of the parties on the mat, and the stew [geng] on their right; the minced and roasted meat are put on the outside and pickles and sauces on the inside; the onions and steamed onions at the end, and the wines and broths are placed to the right. When slices of dried and spiced meat are put down, where they are folded is turned to the left with the ends put to the right. If a guest is of lower rank (than the host), he should take up the rice, rise and decline (the honour he is receiving). The host then rises and objects to the guest's (request to retire). After this, the guest resumes his seat.[30]

After some time, we finally see the rules of etiquette for the diner:

Do not roll the rice into a ball; do not bolt down the various dishes; do not swill (the soup). Do not make noise when eating; do not crunch bones with your teeth; do not put back fish you have been eating; do not throw bones to the dogs; do not snatch (at what you want). Do not spread out the rice; do not use chopsticks to eat millet. Do not gulp down broth, nor add condiments to it; do not keep picking your teeth, nor gulp down sauces. If a guest adds condiments, the host should apologize for not having had the food better prepared. If he refuses the sauces, the host will apologize for his poor hospitality. Soft and juicy meat may be torn apart with the teeth, but dried flesh may not.[31]

Official records provided witness to posterity that the number, order and placement of dishes were all properly followed. They also show the behind-the-scenes operations needed to feed an ancient court. Besides the royal dietician and the royal brewer, there were another 3,000 people tasked with preparing food for the Zhou kings. Of these, nearly five hundred were employed in the kitchen.[32]

These numbers might sound excessive until you realize the magnitude of the task. Ritual demanded that formal visits be accompanied by massive amounts of cooked food and raw flesh. At the highest level, this would include:

A *tailao* [an entire ox, sheep and pig] and one set of cooked animals, to be presented in nine *ding* [ceremonial bronze vessels]. The *ding* are to be placed at the west steps, lined from north to south in order of importance: ox, sheep, pork, dried fish, intestines and stomach, fresh meat, fresh fish and freshly dried meat, along with three additional ding of beef *geng*, sheep *geng* and cooked grain. A gift of seven ding uncooked meat (consisting of the same animals as the cooked, minus the fresh fish and dried meat) is placed along the east steps. These are joined by eight dishes of pickled *hai*, eight dishes containing different grains and six tureens of animal broths, all precisely arranged.[33]

This quote comes from *Etiquette and Rites*, another of the three Confucian ritual texts. The passage continues with precise detail about how this lavish gift should be presented and received: who should bow and who should remain still, how many steps the host should descend to receive his guest and who should enter the hall first. When it does get around to the actual dining, the focus is on dictating the ritual behaviour at the table: who should sit where, which dishes should be placed to the left and which to the right, who should hold their cup with one hand and who with two and what phrases of welcome should be uttered at each stage.

What's never mentioned is who actually *ate* all this food, much less how it might or should have tasted. The value of the

Kitchen scene, 1st century BCE. This tomb carving shows sheep, cattle, pigs and dogs being slaughtered, along with cooks cutting, mixing, cooking and drying food. Pickling vats make up the bottom row. A turtle, bird, fish, rabbit and pig's head hang on hooks across the top.

food was in the propriety of the gift, not the lavishness or conviviality of the feast that presumably followed. Other than separating cooked food from raw meat, there is barely any indication of how food should be prepared.

Was dining all so . . . tasteless? It's hardly fair to expect manuals of ritual protocol to focus on cuisine, but some other menus do show just how extravagant China's early gourmets had already become. For all the talk of modesty at the table, China's classical cuisine itself had become highly elaborate.

The first of these menus comes from a funeral custom of calling back the souls of the departed by reminding them of their favourite things – including food. This 'Summons of the Soul' comes from a book of folk songs from the southern kingdom of Chu and the inclusion of such foods as turtles reflects these southern tastes:

> O soul, come back! Why should you go so far away?
> Your household is here to honour you; all kinds of good
>   food are ready
> Rice, broomcorn, early wheat and wheat, all mixed with
>   yellow millet
> Bitter, salty, sour, hot and sweet: dishes of all flavours.
> Fattened beef ribs cooked tender and succulent
> Wu-style *geng* blending sour and bitter
> Stewed turtle and roast kid, served with yam paste
> Goose in sour sauce, stewed duck, fried crane
> Braised chicken, stewed tortoise, seasoned without
>   spoiling the taste
> Fried rice-flour honey cakes, malt-sugar sweets
> Honey wine served in winged cups
> Ice-cooled liquor, strained clear
> Painted spoons and sparkling wine.[34]

Another menu from this same southern kingdom of Chu comes from slightly later in the form of an allegorical conversation with a dissipated prince who is ill and responds to no medicine. Hoping to revive his spirits, his guest reminds the prince of the seven great pleasures of the world: music, carriages, palaces and gardens, hunting, the comfort of watching the waves and literature. Food comes near the beginning of the list, but there is a sting in the tail, since the visitor's true purpose is to convince the prince that these exaggerated pleasures are in fact the source of his woes and that the only true cure is to embrace a more enlightened lifestyle. But, along the way, we get a glimpse of a truly extravagant table:

> The fat underbelly of a young ox served with bamboo
>   sprouts and reed shoots
> Fat dog meat stewed with mountain lichens
> Rice from Miao Mountain, wild rice from An Lake
> Rolled into a ball it does not crumble; but with one bite
>   it dissolves
> Yi Yin fries the meat, Yi Ya blends the seasonings
> Bear paw *geng*, well-spiced paste
> Thin roasted dorsal fins, a *hui* of minced fresh carp
> Autumn-yellow thyme, white-dew madder
> Orchid blossom wine to rinse the mouth,
> A course of pheasant, the foetus of a tame leopard
> A small bite or large drink, it is like hot water melting
>   snow.[35]

Keeping in mind that both menus are imaginary (although leopard foetus was an actual delicacy[36]), these two poems still show the growing sophistication of China's food culture and a culinary ideal of rare ingredients, artfully prepared and served in abundance. Look past the exaggerated opulence and you can still see the same preoccupation with balance. There is a certain elegance in how the poems match the five tastes with the five grains, how they pair the produce of lakes and mountains, and how they balance the seasonality of autumn wine and spring orchids.

Even in the midst of indulgent luxury, there is taste and logic.

Eight Treasures of Zhou

It's now time to reconstruct our Eight Treasures banquet.

Let's start with who was there. According to the *Book of Rites*, the text that records it, this was a meal that ancient kings served to honour the elderly.[37] Not the virtuous or deserving elderly, mind you. The only qualification was the number of birthdays. Commoners were served in one banquet and retired state officials in another.

Other Confucian truisms about food can help us to recreate something of the atmosphere: Confucius himself was said to have eaten in silence, so we can imagine that there probably wasn't a great deal of conversation. Since music was prized, we can add some decorous melody from the bronze chimes nearby.[38]

What about the physical setting? Murals from the time show diners seated on mats, around a low table. Food and wine might be served in bronze vessels or in cheaper pottery versions cast in the same characteristic shapes. Or they might use natural materials like the lavish lacquer place settings that archaeologists recovered from the Mawangdui tombs.

Whatever the plates are made of, there are a lot of them. Unlike today's 'family style' method of presenting dishes to be shared by a table of diners, formal settings consisted of small, measured servings in individual plates and bowls. Chopsticks were already in common use.

Finally, our eight treasures are brought to the table. Each dish is described in detail:

Chun ao

> Fry hai and serve over dry-field rice. Ladle with rendered
> fat. This is called chun ao.

We know that *hai* can mean a lot of things, but here we seem to
be talking about pickled meat, either chopped fine as in the fermented meat sauce above, cut into small cubes or pickled whole,
producing a texture similar to corned beef. The type of meat is
not specified, but the showiest choices would have been beef,
pork, deer or wild game. The pickled meat is fried in rendered
fat, which is then added to the dish before it is served. The recipe
specifies the type of dry-field rice that would have grown better
in the north.

Chun wu

> Fry hai and serve over broomcorn millet. Ladle with
> rendered fat. This is called chun wu.

Chun wu is the same dish as *chun ao,* but served over glutinous
millet.

Pao

> Remove the organs of a young pig or a young lamb and fill the
> cavity with jujubes. Wrap the animal with reeds, encase it in
> clay and roast it over an open fire. Once the clay is completely
> dry, break off the outer covering and use wet hands to peel off
> the charred skin. Slather a paste of rice flour on the outside
> and fry in melted fat deep enough to cover the whole animal.
> After it has been fried, remove and cut into slices, prepare
> the seasonings and place into a bronze ding vessel, which is
> immersed into a large pot of water. Simmer for three days and
> nights and serve with hai and vinegar pickles.

The *pao* shares the same name as the earlier method of roasting a whole animal in its own skin. In this upgraded version, the skin is protected from charring by a casing of reeds and clay, while the stuffing of fresh jujubes adds flavour and moisture. The roasting is sufficient just to remove the skin, but the meat is further cooked by deep-frying and three days of slow braising in a double boiler. The meat is served with *hai*, here referring to the pickling liquid and preserved vegetables.

Dao zhen

Take equal-sized pieces of beef, sheep, elk, deer and muntjac, using only the fillet from just beside the spine. Pound on all sides and remove the membranes. Cook the meat, remove the skin and soften the meat.

This 'pounded treasure' is the only dish that specifies which cut of meat to use: lean flesh that has been thoroughly cleaned of any connective tissue and cooked, although by what method is not specified. Later authors interpreted these instructions to mean that the cooked meat would be thoroughly crushed with a pestle while mixing in *hai* pickling juice.[39] I think that a closer approximation may come from a preservation method from the sixth-century *Essential Techniques*.

Autumn Dried Meat (Northern Wei)

Best made in the *la* [twelfth] month, although the first, second or third months are also fine. Use lean pieces of beef, sheep, roebuck or deer. Meat that contains fat or impurities will not stand up to preservation. Cut into slices and wash in water to remove the blood, stopping when the water runs clear. Wash a clay pot with salt, add fresh salt, crushed Sichuan peppercorns and the meat. After two days, take the meat out and partially dry it out of direct sunlight. When it is partially dried out, take the meat out and beat it with a stick just enough to tighten it up, but not enough to pulverize it. Sheep or cattle that have starved to death are good for this method, as is the meat of calves and lambs that have little fat. For a sheep, wash the entire animal in warm water until the gamey smell is gone.[40]

The similarities include the repeated warning not to allow any fat into the meat (which is why the dish is best prepared using lean animals from winter and early spring or even ones that have died of starvation) and the instruction to pound the meat. The insistence on lean meat only makes sense for pickling or drying, not for heat-based cooking, which would certainly require some fat to work. Using this later recipe as a reference, we can reinterpret the cooking instructions of the *dao zhen* as follows:

> Take equal-sized pieces of beef, sheep, elk, deer and muntjac, using only the fillet from just beside the spine. Pound on all sides and remove the membranes. When the meat is cooked, remove any dried bits and soften.

The obvious omission here is any reference to salt. More than just a matter of flavouring, salt would be vital to breaking apart the meat fibres before subjecting it to open-air drying.

> Take meat from a freshly slaughtered cow, slice it thin, remove all fibres and marinate it in fine wine. The next morning it can be eaten flavoured with hai, vinegar and plum juice.

Unlike the long process of pickling *hai*, this dish sits long enough only to soften and flavour the meat, which the recipe stipulates must be fresh. Since this recipe predates distilling, the effect was less to kill bacteria than a light-touch fermenting, similar to marinating meat in beer. The meat is served uncooked.[41]

Ao

Take beef, pound it and remove the membranes. Place it on a reed rack and spread with a paste of cinnamon, ground ginger and salt and allow it to dry. Sheep, elk, deer and muntjac can all be prepared in this same way. To eat the meat wet, moisten it with hai. To have it dry, pound the meat before eating.

This basic *ao* method of drying meat is fairly universal, with only the spices being relatively particular to this dish. The method of preparing the dried meat is seen today in Yunnan and Southeast Asia, where sheets of dried beef are pounded to loosen the fibres, torn into shreds and mixed with chillies and spices.

Gan jun

Wrap a dog liver in its own caul fat and grill it over a fire. When the outside is cooked, the dish is complete. The dog liver does not require any seasonings. Make a porridge using soaked rice and the fat from a wolf's breast.

The caul is the netting of fat that covers the internal organs and is used in this same way in French and other cuisines to moisten terrines. The pairing of dog and wolf meat is no doubt more about symbolism than anything else.

San

Mix equal parts of beef, sheep and pork. Chop fine and mix with twice the amount of rice. Shape these into cakes and fry.

Another dish called *san*, consisting of rice porridge cooked with beef broth, is still eaten today in parts of Shandong – which is where Confucius actually lived. In the original dish, the rice cakes might have been served in soup.

Given everything we have seen so far, nobody will be surprised that the Eight Treasures banquet consists almost entirely of meat. After all, meat was traditionally given as a gift and served to the elderly. A royal banquet honouring the elderly could hardly serve anything else.

The Eight Treasures aren't just meat, they're the most valuable sorts of meat – deer, pig, sheep and especially beef, cattle being the 'first among animals'. Even more notable is what isn't mentioned: there are no fowl or fish, and few plants or grains. But beyond that, the banquet itself is not especially lavish. We hear almost nothing about spices or tastes. There is no mention of side dishes, barely any mention of prepared *hai* and no wine. (This is not to say that these weren't present, just that they weren't worth writing down.) Unlike the state protocol of giving gifts, the number of animals is not important. In most recipes, one meat could be substituted for another. Altogether, these show that this feast was much less a social occasion than a ritual one. The aim of this banquet was to stuff these old people with as much fine meat as possible. Beyond that, the details were less important.

In a very tidy way, the Eight Treasures of Zhou sums up everything we have seen about China's ancient food culture: the way that gifts of food expressed the moral ties within society; the cosmological theory that dictates what to eat at different stages of life; and the distinct tastes and techniques that would develop into the world's great gastronomic traditions. But one major question remains. Did it ever happen? We can have no idea. The book that records it had been edited and re-edited over the course of centuries, and was repeating hearsay that was already centuries old.

The legacy is much clearer. Long after Confucius had departed the scene, subsequent governments gradually came to accept his thought as political orthodoxy and honouring the elderly became something that a moral society was expected to do. Later dynasties did hold annual banquets for the aged. Sometimes it was the custom for the emperor himself to roll up his sleeves and serve the food and sometimes it was the custom just to throw a party and leave the locals to pick up the tab.[42] But regardless of how the actual event changed, the idea of holding a banquet to honour the elderly had clearly taken root.

We can still see this sort of sentiment expressed in ceremonial settings. The recent fashion for reviving 'authentic' Chinese culture (leaving aside the problem of exactly what point in China's long history that was) has included lavish stagings of ancient customs like the Village Wine Ceremony. Some of these events consist of enthusiasts dressing in period costumes to perform the pronouncements and movements of the ceremony and then

The Eight Treasures of Zhou was an expression of high etiquette and propriety. But many of the guests likely just saw it as a free meal.

uploading the video to social media. For some participants, the appeal of these rituals is limited to the romanticism of playing historical dress-up. Others, notably among the young and well-educated, have created new rituals, not to emulate the look of Confucian China, but rather to recreate what they see as its essence – the reverential sense of gratitude to nature and society.

The same values can be found in more traditional village religion. I once visited a huge three-day temple ritual in the far southern peninsula of Leizhou, thousands of kilometres away from where Confucius lived and wrote. The highlight of the event was an immense procession that snaked around for hours. There were kids in costumes, two marching bands, hundreds of people burning incense and statues of the village temple gods being carried in sedan chairs. Near the front walked a group of very old men, all wearing matching fedora hats and dark blue robes. When I asked an onlooker what their special status or function was, the answer came back, 'They are very old.' And that was reason enough. At the temple banquet, the old men were seated and served first.

Another legacy is one that most readers might have seen, if not ordered, themselves. Long after the Zhou banquet had faded into history, the 'Eight Treasures' format lived on. Eight being an auspicious number, 'eight treasures' became a stock phrase for any rare and precious collection. Millennia after Confucius, Chinese writers were using the term to talk about the Eight Northern Treasures, Eight Treasures of Hangzhou, Eight Treasures of Beijing, and so on, except that they were referring to famous dishes, with no other implications, certainly no connection to ancient ritual. Even now, if you order a dish of 'treasures' (such as tofu or porridge), the number you receive will certainly be eight.

2

By Silk Road and High Sea
New Foods Come to China

We are again at a formal function in a palatial setting.
A group of guests stand at nervous attention as they wait to
be shown to their places at a low, long table. These men –
young, middle-aged and old – are here to have their tails
burned off.

Since the first banquet, we have jumped forward ten
centuries. Hairstyles and clothing have changed. So has
the decor. This room is laden with delicate porcelains and
heavy earthenware statues, rich textiles, gilt buddhas and
flower-shaped bowls of wrought silver. The musicians are
playing new types of music on a completely different set
of instruments.

But no change is as dramatic as the food.

Our banquet consists of 58 dishes, brought out one by one.
A few dishes of *geng* connect us to a now-distant culinary
past, but almost everything else is new. Mounds of butter
and plates of honey-soaked pastries. Birds stewed in
milk, sausages stuffed with marrow, breads, noodles and
dumplings. Some are sculpted into elaborate designs –
hearts, mandalas and a row of dough servants moulded
into lifelike poses. And tea.

This 'Tail-Burning Banquet' is a snapshot from right in the middle of two millennia of culinary evolution. Imperial China was reaching out to the east and west and absorbing new waves of culture, each one bringing new ingredients, new techniques and new aesthetic influences to the country's changing cuisine. Our second banquet would have been inconceivable to people at the time of Confucius and its de-tailed attendees would have been equally unable to recognize the food served just a few centuries later.

Wave after Wave

China was first unified in 221 BCE. After nearly seven centuries of warfare, a kingdom called Qin came out victorious. The Qin was quickly overthrown, lasting just long enough to leave us the name used for China in most Western languages. But the idea of a unified China had taken root.

From their early cradle along the Yellow River, China's restless empires quickly reached out to trade and conquer. As they did so, they adopted new foods and new ways of eating. This chapter introduces three successive waves of culinary influence: the Silk Road to Central Asia and the Mongol world, seaborne trade with Southeast Asia and the arrival of 'New World' crops in the sixteenth century. These cultural exchanges carried Buddhism, Islam and Christianity to China. They also brought tea, high-yield rice and chillies, as well as an entire garden of new vegetables, spices and techniques that today's Chinese cuisine could scarcely do without. These exchanges radically expanded China's food horizons – new ways to make food tasty, healthy and profitable, the world of food growing larger with each new contact.

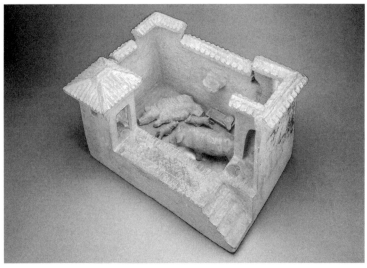

Clay miniatures of granaries and livestock pens that were placed in tombs for rituals and to ensure that the dead were well fed in the afterlife; Han dynasty, 206 BCE–220 CE.

Silk Road

The conquering Qin was quickly overtaken by the Han, a dynasty that lasted for roughly as long as the Roman Empire. The Han dynasty also marked the beginning of China's long relationship with Central Asia, including the series of cultural and trade links romantically known as the Silk Road. But dreamy images of spice-laden camel caravans aside, this relationship was not always a positive one. From China's perspective, the western frontier was a vital source of military horses, but for that same reason, it was also a constant threat. It shouldn't be a surprise, then, that the Han moved a significant military presence to the west, creating fortifications and settlements deep into Central Asia.

This influence went two ways. While the Han empire was reaching west, the cultural influence of Central Asia was also moving in the other direction. This was when Buddhism first began to trickle into China, carried by intrepid missionaries who travelled east from Buddhist kingdoms in today's Afghanistan, bringing with them a new universe of science, art and medicine. Long after the Han dynasty had come and gone, these western links would continue to wax and wane with China's commercial and military power, reaching a peak during the Tang, the dynasty (618–907) that is today synonymous with the Silk Road.

The Silk Road brought new ingredients to Chinese cuisine. Sources from the Han dynasty record these new additions to the Chinese garden. Crops like grapes, pomegranates and walnuts reached China during this time, as did new varieties of gourds and melons. This was also the source of new vegetables like alfalfa, mustard greens, turnips and the starchy tuber known as taro, all of which would become vital to Chinese cuisine.

Perhaps most vital was the new spices. This was when China first encountered onions, spring onions (scallions) and garlic. These were culinary game-changers. Until this point, Chinese

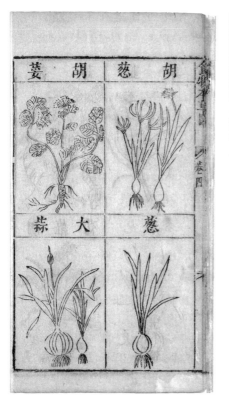
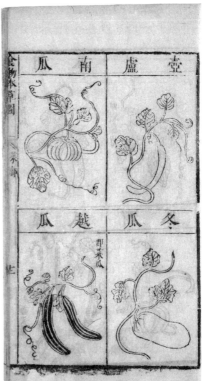

China's ever-expanding garden: this 1803 encyclopedia of edible plants and animals (*Shiwu bencao huizuan*) features plenty of onions, melons, beans and garlic, but, at least as of this printing, still no chillies.

cuisine had relied largely on pastes and vinegars for flavour; the spices most frequently mentioned were ginger and the numbing spice known in English as 'Sichuan peppercorn'. (Incorrectly so on two accounts, since it's neither unique to Sichuan nor is it a peppercorn.) Onions and garlic quickly became an absolute necessity of the Chinese kitchen and their arrival brings us significantly closer to something we would identify as Chinese cuisine.

This is also the first mention of coriander, which is identified as *husui*. That 'hu' prefix is sometimes translated as 'barbarian' but really just means foreign, specifically from the regions that lie beyond China's far west. Seeing something marked as 'hu' – such as the two-stringed musical instruments known as *huqin* (western fiddle) – is a pretty clear giveaway of Central Asian origin. This is very true for food. Sources from the time sometimes refer to grapes (*putao*) as *huputao*. Translated directly, carrots are 'western turnips' (*huluobo*), walnuts are 'western peaches' (*hutao*), pepper is 'western pepper' (*hujiao*). (*Hushuo*, 'hu-speak', means that you are talking nonsense.)

Another 'hu' custom was the new habit of consuming dairy foods. Influenced by neighbours to the north and west, Chinese farmers learned how to dry, ferment and sour milk from different animals, including mares, cattle and sheep. We don't often associate these sorts of foods with China, but they were very important in this period for two reasons. First, the imperial families of some of these early dynasties were themselves of mixed ancestries. Royal marriages and diplomacy brought Uighur, Tibetan and Sogdian customs and tastes into the palace. Government officials recognized the value of dairy foods and actively sought to spread these techniques to the people. Second, just as Confucian-era ritual demanded meat sacrifice, the ritual use of dairy is identified in Buddhist scriptures and this was a time of intense Buddhist piety.

The complexity of the Chinese garden continued to grow. Over the following centuries, new melons continued to be added – winter melons, pickling melons and cucumbers (initially called *hu* melons) – as well as aubergine, lotus root and an ever-growing variety of beans and greens, including cabbage, which was first known as *su*. The Tang Taizong emperor was partial to a dish of celery in vinegar.[1] Spinach may have come from Persia. Sunflowers were a reliable food for the poor. New fruits first seen in the Tang – mango, pomelo, coconut, olives, palm dates, sweet melons, tangerines, longan and lychee – mirror medieval China's march to warmer climes. Another of these ingredients was sugar cane, which by the Tang dynasty was being refined into white sugar using a technique that came from India in the mid-600s.

But not every change came from far away. Each dynasty introduced policies that transformed the foodscape. Recognizing rice as the most reliable grain, the short-lived Sui dynasty commissioned a canal to ship southern rice to the troops and cities in the north. For the next fifteen centuries, that canal would be China's main north–south highway. Other dynasties would expand the frontier of rice cultivation into northern provinces, a policy that didn't just increase production but raised the population level.

The development of internal trade also encouraged new varieties of existing foods. The *Essential Techniques* shows how far the ancient idea of the 'five grains' had evolved by the sixth century. This one short text mentions over 150 different varieties of these basic grains, including 97 distinct kinds of foxtail millet and 36 types of wet rice. In addition to grain for eating, new varieties included seeds that could be pressed for oil. There was a specialized market for plant oil in the Tang capital and probably a lot of other cities as well.

There were also new ways to eat grain. While ancient China had exclusively used wet methods of steaming and boiling, this new exchange brought flour milling and with it a universe of breads, cakes and pastries, all under the general heading of *bing*. This originally foreign taste quickly became a Chinese staple. The one that was actually called foreign – *hu bing* – was probably a baked yeast bread that was shaped into large rounds and topped with sesame. Bing could be rolled flat and spread with different flavourings and meat – these were called *tan*. One street food known as the 'old tower' piled a *jin* of uncooked lamb on top of a large *hubing* that had been moistened with butter and spread with bean paste and Sichuan peppercorns. The whole thing was then baked in an oven until the meat was cooked. In homes, it was a custom to greet guests with one plate piled with *bing* and another with fresh vegetables. *Bing* could be baked, fried, steamed or boiled. There were crispy *bing* made with butter, savoury *bing* stuffed with meat and sweet *bing* that were dyed and soaked with honey or sugar.[2]

Most of the early *bing* were not leavened and were instead made as thin pancakes or softened with copious amounts of oil. This Qing-era recipe for crispy *bing* was similar to other variations that included sesame, meat, mint or chives:

Cooks with a tray of breads, noodles and dumplings, tomb painting from the Liao Kingdom, 10th–12th century.

Selling *mantou* in 1930s Shanghai.

In the Mouth Crisps (Qing)

1 jin white flour, 1 jin sesame oil, 7 liang sugar; melt and mix together. Shape into long strips and pinch into short pieces, adding a pine nut on top of each piece. Place in the oven and roast on a low heat.[3]

The exception was the steamed bread known as *mantou*, or in the early sources as *fa mantou* or leavened *mantou*. Today these snow-white breads are a staple across northern China, the simplest and most common recipe consisting of flour, water and a small amount of sugar to activate dried yeast. The original recipe, recorded in the same Qing source, used something even more familiar – rice fermented into *lao zao* using the ancient process discussed in an earlier chapter.

Changshu Mantou (Qing)

1 dou white flour, 1 jin fermented rice, ½ sheng of glutinous
rice half cooked into porridge. Add a bowl of warm water
and mix. Cover and keep cool or warm to maintain at body
temperature. After one night it should have already risen.
Use a winnowing tray to drain off the clear liquid and use a
stick to stir the mixture. Stir only in one direction, without
reversing. After stirring, divide into three parts and give to
three people to knead. As the dough gradually begins to rise,
form into shapes and fill. Place the mantou into a steamer
and cover [to rise]. After a quarter of an hour take one out
and dunk it in water. If it floats then they are ready to steam
at any time.

Another gift of the flour-milling revolution was 'soup *bing*',
otherwise known as noodles. There were many of these around
by the Tang; the *Essential Techniques* explains several. Flat, wide
botuo noodles were not rolled, but pressed by hand, similar to a
Shanxi speciality dish called *jiupian*:

Botuo (Northern Wei)

Roll into the shape of a thumb, 2 cun long, fill a plate with
water and press the dough against the side of the plate until
it is very thin. Cook in rapidly boiling water. These are not
only shining white and attractive, but also have a good taste
and texture.[4]

A smaller, more delicate noodle called *shuiyin* was made the
same way, pressed to the length and thickness of a chive. Others
were made by deftly tearing a cake of steamed flour into bean-
sized pieces, probably similar to Hungarian *csipetke*. There were
cold noodles and long noodles and noodles that were especially

Cutting noodles by hand, Beijing, 1930s. The method of shaping and cutting is essentially the same one described for sixth-century *botuo*. This image is part of Hedda Morrison's documentation of Beijing crafts.

for birthdays. The filled dumplings known as *huntun* are mentioned by name, but the ones now called *jiaozi* were not. Both sorts have been discovered intact in Dunhuang caves.[5]

Other than wheat flour, there were 'noodles' that were made from thinly sliced sheepskin and another recipe that combined flour with starchy *shanyao* yam for what could accurately be called Chinese gnocchi:

Yam Noodles

6 jin flour, 10 egg whites, 2 ge fresh ginger juice, 4 liang bean flour. Add these to 3 jin of shanyao that have been boiled and mashed into a paste. Slice into thin noodles and cook in boiling water. Separately prepare three large pieces of sheep breast, cut into cubes and cook the noodles with good meat stock. Adjust the taste with onions and salt.[6]

There were also new ways to prepare milled rice flour into *gao*, sticky cakes that were steamed with dates or other fillings. This is also when starch extracted from tubers like lotus root made its way to the table, not only as a thickening agent, but as starch cakes and noodles.

This era also marked the arrival of tea, which is native to China, but was first popularized during the Han dynasty. Tea drinking probably originated in the southwestern province of Sichuan and for centuries retained the aura of a local specialty. Its national spread was initially associated with Buddhism; monks famously drank it to stay awake during meditation and marathon scripture-chanting sessions. As a drink, it was initially brewed with accompanying flavours like orange peel, roasted rice and even onions. But not sugar. If anything, China's new tea habit came served with salt.

By the Tang dynasty, the aesthetic of tea had come to focus on the drink itself. The association with Buddhism gave tea an aura of purity, as did an endorsement from the scholar Lu Yu, whose eighth-century *Book of Tea* initiated the genre of tea appreciation. Not just an exotic commodity, Lu's writing made tea – from source to sip – an art. Equally important was the proper preparation of the leaves, as well as the moment of brewing, the choice of water, and the tools, utensils and setting.[7]

This profound level of aesthetic appreciation for tea further bolstered its association with monks, Daoist recluses and free-spirited poets, creating a mystique around tea as an almost otherworldly pleasure. In the work of Tang poets, tea is more than just a break from daily life, it is the antidote to it. Just like wine (which we will see more of later) tea represents a kind of artistic escape from the muck of the world. Note the contrasting images in the closing lines of a work by the early ninth-century poet Liu Yuxi. After drinking tea with Buddhist monks on a mountain, Liu contemplates the tragedy of taking a parcel of tea home with him:

The monks say the divine flavour befits quiet seclusion.
The abundant fluttering leaves become a welcome guest.

They would send a package to my prefectural office,
But the brick well and copper stove would ruin its
character.
Worse yet, the spring teas from Meng Mountain and
Guzhu
Sealed in white clay, stamped in red, they travel dusty
roads.
If you want to know the pure cooling taste of milky buds,
You must be one who sleeps in clouds and squats on rocks.[8]

All these earthbound metaphors: the white clay, the dusty road and the brick well in his office symbolize the weight of daily life. Like the Buddhist metaphor of the world as 'red dust', these are all vanities that ultimately come to nothing. Like the poet, tea is made to thrive in the free air of nature, its true essence known only to those who have renounced the cares of this world.

Perhaps unsurprisingly, such refinement did not come cheap. In his *Food and Drink of the Cloud Forest Hall*, fourteenth-century painter Ni Zan outlined the process for making and brewing scented lotus-flower tea. The silver vessels and laborious instructions belie the idea that this was the unspoiled world of the simple recluse:

Lotus Flower Tea (Yuan)

At early daybreak, before breakfast, pick lotus flowers from the middle of a pond. Remove the pistils by hand, pack each flower full of tea leaves, bind with a help string and leave overnight. The next day, remove the tea leaves and dry them on paper. Do this three times. On the third day pack the tea into a silver jar with a tight lid.

To make the tea, heat water in a silver kettle, waiting until the water forms small bubbles like the eyes of a crab. Place the tea into a separate pot, add a small amount of water from the kettle and quickly cover. Return the kettle to the fire and heat until the sound of boiling water is heard, and then add the water to the teapot. Remove the kettle from the fire and again reheat the water slowly. This taste is exquisite.

Tail-Burning Banquet

The new ingredients, tastes and techniques of the Silk Road all come together in the Tail-Burning Banquet. Served at the Tang court, this was originally a banquet to welcome high-level officials coming to present themselves for the first time to the emperor.

Let's start with the obvious question: why 'Tail Burning'? Apparently, the reason for the banquet's unusual name was not entirely clear even then. An eleventh-century writer described a few possibilities:

> One saying is that when a tiger is to be reborn as a human, only the tail does not change and it must be burned off before he can become a person. It is also said that when a new sheep is introduced to the herd, the other sheep will not accept it as one of their own until its tail has been burned. Others say that when a fish jumps through the dragon gate to be reborn into a dragon, its tail is burned off by lightning for it to transform.[9]

So regardless of which story we choose to accept, the 'tail burning' represents a sort of rebirth and induction into greatness. For the new officials being feted at the Tang court, it meant joining the ranks of the uppermost circle of scholarly elites, the culmination of a lifetime of aspiration.

Apart from the name, little else about the banquet is recorded. Since this was an initiation for new officials of the highest rank, the centrepiece would undoubtedly have been a ritual swearing of fealty to the emperor. For all of the other details – whether there was music, how the food was served, how and where people sat – we can rely on general knowledge of the Tang aesthetic as it is preserved in ceramics, paintings and frescoes.

The artists of the Tang left us plenty of these. Paintings on the walls of tombs and the caves of Dunhuang show banquets of diners, most often surrounded by male and female musicians playing a variety of flutes, reeded instruments, lutes and zithers. Other images show robed dancers in a characteristic pose of jumping on one foot and swinging one long sleeve into the air. The banquet meal itself is served on a low table laden with small dishes, with diners seated not on mats, but on long, low benches. Like the food, many of these accoutrements – the instruments, the dance, the furniture – were all heavily influenced by centuries of contact with Central Asia.

Most important, one actual menu does survive. In 709, a guest named Wei Ju recorded a Tail-Burning Banquet consisting of 58 dishes. Although the names are occasionally artistic to the point of being unintelligible, later comments give us some idea of their content.[10]

Tail-Burning Banquet (709)

'One-tray gold', either a butter pastry or fresh cheese, cooked in individual trays

'Mandala', baked, filled pastry shaped like mandala flowers

'Black sesame crisp', a deep-fried pastry soaked in honey

'Brahmin high cake', a steamed or layered pastry of Indian origin

'Crimson concubine', a red-dyed pastry

'Seven folds', probably a layered pastry

'Golden bell', baked butter pastry in the shape of a bell

'Yellow queen mother', rice or millet cooked with eggs
and animal fat

Tonghua soft sausage, sheep marrow stuffed into a cow-
intestine casing and steamed

'Bright roasted' shrimp, cooked live over a fire

Shengjin 24 dumplings, individually coloured and shaped
to match the 24 solar terms

Noodles in duck soup

Meat sliced into the shape of a knot and air dried. This is a
test of the cook's knife skills

'Melt in the wind' oil cake, a delicate fried pastry
Unrelated to the medicinal plant of the same name

'Gold and silver flower slices', roll of crab meat and crab
roe that is steamed in a tube and cut into slices

Deep-fried glutinous rice balls

Clam *geng*, served cold

Tang'an cake, a type of filled *bing* from Tang'an County

'Crystal dragon and phoenix', sticky rice stuffed with
dates, steamed until the filling comes out

Double-mixed cake, shaped like flower petals

'Jade dew', crisp cake carved in the shape of a flower

'Han palace chess', unclear but possibly a flour noodle the
size of a chess piece

'Long-life porridge', a medicinal soup, possibly medicinal
herbs or sesame paste

'Heaven flower *biluo*', a Central Asian stuffed bread with
tianhua mushrooms

'Cifei hanxiang', spiced dumplings made of red glutinous
rice steamed in bamboo leaves

'Sweet snow', probably a crispy honey sweet

'Eight-sided' moulded sweet, like a mooncake

'Suzheng yinyuebu', flour sculptures of a Penglai immortal
and her servants

'White dragon', *geng* made from katsura fish

A yellow-coloured millet bread stuffed with fish eggs

Phoenix foetus, possibly fish milt, or chicken egg cooked inside a whole bird

Sheep stomach cooked, sliced very fine and served cold

Xunpao sauce fish, fish or fish sauce cooked inside a roast sheep

Whole fish stuffed with sheep milk cheese

Salted meat or fish drizzled with clove oil and vinegar

Onion vinegar chicken, roasted live in a cage. The bird was intended to drink the vinegar as it grew thirsty

Wuxing salted fish

'West river' spiced pork shoulder, made into meatballs and steamed

'Red sheep' hoof with sheep meat

'Shengping grill', dish made of three hundred sheep and deer tongues

'Eight Immortals', cold goose platter

'Snow babies', a dish of deboned frogs, coated in bean flour and fried

'Immortal' chicken, cooked in sheep milk (one explanation suggests that the dish used human breast milk)

Cold dish (or possibly porridge) made of chicken and deer

Salted and steamed bear meat or bear paw, hunted in winter to retain hibernation fat

'Early morning' rabbit *geng*

'Cooling meat broth', civet meat cooked, frozen, thawed and served cold like an aspic

'Chopstick spring' quail diced to the width of a chopstick

'Warm and cold' donkey meat soaked in wine and steamed until extremely tender

Boiled whole calf

'Five animals', plate of sheep, pork, beef, bear and deer –
or any other mixture of five

'Patterned dish' of sheep meat, intestines and organs
roasted with bean flour

'Smell from the street', a selection of foods sliced thin and
briefly cooked in boiling oil

'Cuanhua Yunmeng', meat, fat and spices rolled, weighted
down and roasted

'Red *luo*', cold dish of cubed chicken blood and sheep's
and cow's milk

'Brocades abound', crab or fish, cooked with duck egg
yolk, sheep fat and roasted turtle

'Fantijian lübao xianggan', probably a dish of shaped
animal livers

'Splendid' meatball of minced meat and chicken eggs,
braised in soup

Influenced by the tastes, techniques and culinary culture of Central Asia,
the Tail-Burning Banquet was the Silk Road on a plate.

These romantically named dishes may have been the set menu customarily served at every Tail-Burning Banquet or they may have simply been chosen to create a sumptuous feast on that one occasion. Reflecting the mixed ancestry of the Tang royal family, this banquet is radically different from anything that someone from the time of Confucius would have imagined. It shows just how profoundly contact with Central Asia had completely changed the face of Chinese cuisine.

First the new ingredients: the most striking feature of this banquet is the huge amount of dairy. Nearly half the dishes feature dairy prominently, either as butter pastries or food cooked in sheep's or cow's milk. As far as meat is concerned, this is a menu straight out of the pastoral north. Pork has almost disappeared – instead, the main meats are sheep, supplemented with cattle and game like deer and bear, as well as a few chickens and geese. There is a small amount of seafood, some of which is preserved. As far as grains go, old standbys like millet and rice appear in supporting roles – the real hero here is the milled wheat that appears in the large number of pastries, cakes and noodles.

This feast was visually extravagant. Dishes were served shaped into flowers, hearts and Buddhist symbols. Many of the animals were roasted whole, no doubt with the sort of dramatic flair seen in other contemporary dishes like *hunyang*, a turducken-adjacent banquet dish consisting of a deboned goose stuffed with glutinous rice and then roasted inside a whole sheep.[11] And it was colourful. Tang cooks loved to play with colour, using flowers and leaves to create different layers within a single dish. The pastry dish called 'crimson concubine' was probably dyed deep red with powdered persimmon. But what can we say about the taste? The names of dishes give little indication about flavours, and since the commonly used spices – Sichuan peppercorns, ginger, cinnamon, nutmeg, dill seeds and orange peel – were used as much for medical as gustatory purposes, it seems unlikely that any one dish would have been overdosed with any one taste. In its instructions for roasting the whole leg of a cow or sheep, the normally precise *Essential Techniques* does not mention flavourings at all. For the brisket, it recommends only a brief marinade in chopped onions, bean paste and salt.[12] All indications are that this gorgeous meal was also somewhat bland.

By Sea

The other direction of expansion was towards the south and towards the sea. Seafood had long been a part of Chinese diets. Neolithic communities along coasts and rivers collected shellfish and fish and advances in preservation and trade brought the seafood frontier ever further inward. Texts refer to dozens of different kinds of fish, each identified by the radical for fish 魚 that appears in their name. The character 鱣, for example, refers to a large fish, possibly a sturgeon, that a tenth-century source describes as 'weighing hundreds of *jin*, with bones soft enough to eat' and living in the rivers of Jiangyang in Sichuan.[13] The insect radical 虫 signifies crustaceans (shrimp 蝦) and molluscs (oysters 蠔), identifying them essentially as bugs of the sea. As the internal market became more advanced, the gastronomic appreciation for seafood grew.

The sea was also a route of trade, one that was no less important than the overland Silk Road. During outward-looking dynasties like the Tang, seaborne commerce connected China to the Korean peninsula, Japan and Southeast Asia. Cultural flows followed, allowing Japan to imbibe large amounts of continental culture (not just from China, but also Korea), including characters, Buddhism and fashion.

Just like the overland routes to the west, the seaborne trade with Japan, Korea and other oceanic routes also influenced China's food. Romaine lettuce, eaten not for its leaves but for its stem, came from Japan. The traditional Chinese name is thus 'Japanese lettuce' (*woju*), referencing an old name for Japan. Trade to the south linked China to the islands of present-day Indonesia and from there to ports along the Indian Ocean littoral and eventually to Persia. Along these routes, Chinese traders plied ships loaded with precious metals, ceramics and silk. Among the valuable goods they brought back were exotic woods, fragrant incense and spices. These foreign products were firstly medicinal and there were enough of them to fill a tenth-century book on *Foreign Pharmacopoeia*.[14] The Chinese spice trade ebbed and flowed depending on how different dynasties felt about the sea frontier, but at its peak in the 1400s, Chinese demand for spices rivalled anything in Europe. Chinese merchants bought Sumatran pepper in the port city of Melaka and sold it back in Hangzhou for three times the price.[15] Cloves, mace, nutmeg and fragrant incense woods drew Chinese merchants to the Maluku 'spice islands', and to such trade centres as Banten, Ambon and Aceh, long before the Dutch and Spanish showed up and started fighting to keep each other out.[16]

But the biggest change came from something much more ordinary: rice. Rice was of course nothing new to China. Millennia before the first written records, Neolithic villages were already planting tidy patchworks of rice fields. As rice is generally more productive than dry-field crops, successive governments were keen to see it spread, encouraging the southern crop to move farther and farther north.

While images of verdant rice terraces in places like Bali may give the impression that rice belongs to the tropics, all the crop really needs is water – enough to flood the field during the early part of the growing season. As the muddy seedlings grow to waist height, the water drains away and, by harvest time, you are walking on hard, dry ground.

There are hundreds of different strains of rice. Some are bred to thrive in particular soils or to be more resistant to drought or insects. Short-grained *Japonica* rice is dense and sticky enough to roll into a ball. Thai jasmine rice is long-grained and fluffy. Glutinous rice (*nuomi*, which also happens to be the name of my neighbour's Jack Russell) can be milled into flour and shaped into chewy desserts.

Perhaps the most fundamental question for rice is how long it takes to grow. The sixth-century *Essential Techniques* explains that a crop of rice should take eighty days to sprout and another seventy days for these sprouts to ripen – 150 days or just under half a year in total. But by the tenth century, farmers were planting a strain called 'hundred-day gold', and, not long after that, varieties that ripened after sixty days.

This early-ripening rice and the techniques to grow it both originated from Champa, a medieval state in what is now Cambodia. Palace records explain how the new crop first came to China:

> Emperor Zhenzong (998–1022), being deeply concerned with agriculture, came to know that the Champa rice was drought-resistant and that the green lentils of India were famous for their heavy yield and large seeds. Special envoys, bearing precious things, were dispatched [to these states], with a view to securing these varieties. From Champa they procured twenty shi [bushels] of [rice] seeds, which have since been grown almost everywhere. From central India, two shi of green lentil seeds were brought back. It is not exactly known whether the green lentils now being grown were originally planted in the imperial garden. When the first harvests were reaped in the autumn, Zhenzong called his closest ministers to taste them and composed poems for Champa rice and Indian green lentils.[17]

There is no way to overstate how massive this change was. New strains of fast-ripening rice shortened the growing time for

Illustrations from *Tiangong kaiwu* (The Exploitation of the Works of Nature), 1637, depicting the laborious process of tilling, planting and irrigating a field of rice.

our main food crop from 150 to 60 days. That essentially meant that farmers could potentially get two and a half times more food out of the same piece of land – or alternately use that land for growing more of something else. This in turn meant that cities could grow twice as big, and that twice as many people could engage in pursuits other than growing food. Fast-ripening rice was one of the reasons that China's centre of population shifted from the dry northern plains to the moist and mountainous south. It is one of the reasons behind the often-heard claim that medieval China was the wealthiest, most sophisticated and most advanced place on Earth.[18]

Columbian Exchange

The last big wave of change came in two parts, one commercial and one political. The commercial change was that China finally became connected to Europe. This contact came by sea. A trickle of European traders and missionaries had reached China via the overland Silk Road, but real trade would depend on a seaborne passage to the East. When Europeans did start to arrive in serious numbers, it was from the other direction: travelling west through the new Spanish colonies in the Americas and thence to the Philippines, Malacca, Japan and finally to tiny Macao (then an island, now a peninsula).

European trade brought a lot of things to China: silver, Christianity and of course opium. (All of these existed before; what the Europeans did was to vastly expand the supply.) Less visible, but no less important, than these was maize, the life-giving plant that had sustained centuries of civilization in Mexico. Maize was transplanted by the Spanish to Manila, where it was initially used as animal feed. Chinese traders in the Philippines quickly brought the new crop back to their home provinces on the southwest coast, where it was perfectly suited to the hilly terrain. Other New World crops – potatoes, peanuts, squash, sweet potatoes – all followed a similar pattern of being transplanted and spreading, slower or faster, across the countryside.

The reason that these New World crops were accepted with such enthusiasm was that they were dependable. Chinese farmers knew how to prepare for disaster by diversifying – growing emergency crops on some leftover patch of unusable land.[19] And maize can be grown almost anywhere. It thrives just as well in soils that are salty or sandy, on the side of a steep hill or on a plain that is prone to flooding. The crop might not always be bountiful, and I can say from experience that a diet based on cornmeal is plenty tedious, but the fact is, that if you plant maize, you are much less likely to starve. The giant stalks also make ideal animal feed, and in a pinch, they even make a tolerable bed (again, voice of experience here – it's amazing what you can learn over decades of fieldwork). That was enough to convince hundreds of millions of Chinese farmers to plant maize in every clime, from the subtropics to the arid northwest. By 1800, corn was being grown in almost every province. Unglamorous sweet potatoes

– which could mean the difference between life and death during a drought – followed a similar path. New crops fuelled another massive growth in China's population – which tripled during the eighteenth century. But it didn't stop there – new crops and population growth also expanded the frontiers, to southern mountains, internal highlands and the vast plains of Manchuria.

How was corn used in cooking? As a graduate student back in the late 1990s, I spent a year in a northern Chinese village where the whole agricultural year revolved around corn. Families planted it in the spring and harvested it in the late summer. By late autumn, every courtyard was a sea of golden corn cobs laid out neatly to dry in the sun, and by early winter, most of that corn had been milled into fine flour. Each morning started with a bowl of corn porridge: unsalted, unflavoured and adorned only by a couple of chunks of sweet potato or some of yesterday's rock-hard *mantou*. Over the course of a year, I progressed through the whole range of emotions regarding my corn-based existence – ambivalence gave way to loathing and, just as suddenly, to a profound love of all things corn. When I returned to Tianjin, I carried a backpack full of notebooks and a giant sack of cornflour.

Since corn has no gluten, it won't hold together on its own. Perhaps because of these limits, it does not appear in any of the major recipe collections. An extensive nineteenth-century collection called *Flavouring the Pot* has recipes for every type of grain, bean and tuber imaginable, but not for corn.

Nevertheless, because corn was so universal, every locale developed its own way of preparing cornflour into cakes and breads. Local corn specialities were adaptations from much older recipes. Across northern China you can find *wowotou*, a dense, cone-shaped cornbread (sometimes made with bean flour or other grains). Steamed on top of a stick, *wowotou* comes out of the steamer looking like a giant yellow lollipop. Just like steamed wheat *mantou*, traditional *wowotou* is completely unflavoured with either salt or sugar. (Very recently, home cooks have started adding sweetened milk powder to improve nutrition and taste.) Other variations fill pan-fried or steamed corn cakes with dates, pumpkin, salted vegetables or meat. Corn mixed with wheat flour can be steamed into *gao* or fried into *bing*. The chewy *baba* cakes seen in the southwest provinces of Guizhou and Yunnan are made by mixing cornflour and glutinous rice (or by using the local variety of glutinous corn) and either frying the sticky dough into oily cakes or steaming it inside corn husks.

If corn was the new crop that fed China's growing population, it was another New World import that was destined to change the face of cuisine – the chilli pepper. Chillies had already travelled the world by the time they reached China. Early sources called them 'sea peppers', meaning that they entered by the coast as opposed to the older overland route. (With the two routes, the terminology starts to get complicated. Instead of 'hu', imports from this period use 'fan', a word that originally referred to India. Tomatoes, another import of the time, are thus *fanqie*, 'foreign aubergine' – despite the fact that aubergine was itself foreign.)

Chillies were first valued as medicine that could dry up excess moisture from the body, and as an 'extender' that could sort of replace the taste of expensive salt. Following the trail of where they are mentioned in local sources, historian Cao Yu reckons that chillies travelled from the coastal province of Zhejiang and gradually moved inland to the west and south. Fresh, dried and powdered chillies made their way into the cuisines of Hunan, Guizhou, Jiangxi and, of course, Sichuan, but remained associated with the diets of non-Han minorities or of labourers like cart pullers or the dockhands in Chongqing. Just like garlic, chillies would only gain mass social acceptance during the twentieth century.[20] The late nineteenth- or early twentieth-century *Thoughts on a Vegetarian Diet* gives one of the first written recipes for what must already have been an extremely common condiment:

Chilli Paste (Late Qing)

With the chilli peppers of late autumn, pick out the red ones and hang them to dry. The ones that are light red, half yellow or slightly green are really good for making into paste. Mix 7 jin of chillies, 3 jin of finely chopped carrots and 12 liang of fried salt until even, adding water according to your desired thickness. Use a mill for making tofu to crush the mixture into a paste. Stored in a ceramic bottle, it will last for a long time without spoiling. Add this to porridge; it will greatly increase the piquant taste.[21]

Eating the Frontier

The second – political – sort of change arrived by land: successive invasions from across the northern frontier. China has twice experienced periods of extended rule by foreigners, first the Mongols and five centuries later the Manchus. (There were other, smaller, hybrid kingdoms, which we won't get into for the moment.) These two invasions eventually transformed themselves into two fully Chinese dynasties – the Yuan (1271–1368) and Qing (1644–1911) – and together they remained in power for a total of three and a half centuries. Each one left a deep and lasting impression on the country they ruled, including, of course, its food.

Foreign rule integrated China into the culture of its conquerors and of any other people who might have been subjugated along the way. The Mongol Yuan built their capital at Dadu, today's Beijing, combining the talents and aesthetics of Chinese designers with engineers and craftsmen from across the Islamic world.[22] Centuries later, the city again became a dizzying array of customs, temples, costumes and languages, representing the people under the expansive rule of the Manchu Qing.

Each of these dynasties remained aware that they were a small foreign minority ruling a much larger Chinese population – a task they accomplished by bringing in more outsiders, in the form of garrison troops, merchants and officials. Each of these foreign populations brought its own language, customs and tastes. Nowhere more so than in Beijing. Besides being the capital of a vast empire, Beijing sat at the intersection of three worlds: Chinese agriculture, Manchurian forests and vast Mongol pastures. The capital ate from all three. Two centuries before the Yuan, the city was part of a northern kingdom called the Khitan Liao. The semi-pastoral Liao ate a diet that included fish and fowl, milk in all its forms and a sour fermented bean soup called *douzhi* that is served in Beijing today and embodies the concept of 'an acquired taste'. (I hasten to add that I absolutely love the stuff – imagine thick sauerkraut juice served hot.) But the mainstay was overwhelmingly meat – steamed and dried, herded and hunted; bear, sheep, pig, rabbit, wild boar, fish and goose. At the top of the Liao food pyramid, a large fatty rodent called *pili* was so rare and delicious that it was forbidden to serve it at non-royal tables.[23] Qing dynasty Beijing was a huge market for meat, including tens of thousands of cattle and sheep that were herded in vast drives from the grazing fields of Mongolia. Large trade houses earned vast profits from this 'golden road' to Beijing. For most animals entering the city, the final stop was 'Cattle Street', the slaughtering grounds in the Muslim quarter.[24]

Beijing's cosmopolitanism wasn't just the food, but the way of eating it. In his 'Old Beijing in the Vernacular', the writer Xu Lingxiao connected Beijing's mutton hotpot to these pastoral origins: 'Sheep hotpot is the most common delicacy in the cold season; it is best to eat it at a butcher's shop. This way of eating is a local speciality and is a more refined version of the customs of the northern herdsmen.'[25] The city's street food bore other marks of this influence, from yoghurt and milk tea to sweets like *sachima*, a cake of fried flour noodles soaked in honey syrup.

Zhama Feast

So how did the Yuan court eat? Like any other dynasty, the Yuan had its apex-level banquet, this one called the Zhama Feast. First the name. The 'ma' in Zhama means horse, leading to the fairly logical assumption that this event had something to do with horses. After all, the Yuan themselves were pastoral. Their military and their whole way of life were built on horseback. The feast was held outside, so we can assume that the entertainment would have included displays of horsemanship. The first syllable, the 'zha', is more of a mystery. The word could be interpreted to mean handsome, but most current and past meanings are all based around the idea of cheating or fraud.

But like the Yuan themselves, the name of this event was actually foreign. Some scholars contend that the name comes from the Persian word *jāmah*, meaning bright clothes, as wearing clothes of matching bright colours was indeed one of the customs associated with the feast. Others claim that it comes from Mongolian *juma*, meaning an animal that has been cleaned of fur and organs and is ready to cook. Whichever is true, most scholars agree that the name is *not* Chinese and that the 'cheating horse' in the name is just a coincidence.[26] This is regrettable, as I had really been looking forward to calling it the 'Sneaky Pony Picnic'.

In fact, the Zhama feast was a kind of diplomatic event that the Mongols used to court the loyalty of their northern princes. Since part of the aim was to impress, we can be sure that everything was planned on a big scale: imagine a scene of open grassland dotted with hundreds of yurts and tens of thousands of horses, cattle, camels and sheep.

The event is recorded in the writings of contemporaries like the poet Zhou Boqi. According to these depictions, the Zhama feast was a massive three-day affair, with thousands in attendance: high-ranking officials, allied princes and any other honoured guests whom the emperor wished to win over and intimidate with an unparalleled display of wealth and power. The event began with a solemn reading of the Yasaq, Genghis Khan's sacred law of the land, which was carried to the site in a golden casket. After that, the fun began. There were dancers, acrobats, competitions and feasting on a monumental scale. In verse, Zhou Boqi records:

A thousand officials gather from near and far,
Drunk for three days at a great feast,
Ten thousand sheep eaten clean, ten thousand jugs
of wine.[27]

While in Chinese the term 'ten thousand' is often a simple euphemism for 'a lot', in this case it actually may be fairly accurate. To match the massive displays of wealth in imperial gifts, resplendent horses decked out with pheasant feathers and coloured silk ribbons, the emperor laid out a spread that included tens of thousands of cooked animals: camel hump, bear paw and roasted sheep, as well as mare's milk wine and grape wine served in ice-chilled urns. One new addition was *shaojiu*, 'cooked wine', China's first hard alcohol. Yuan Shizhen describes the new process of distillation:

Shaojiu is not made in the old way. This method only comes from the Yuan. Place strong wine and dregs into an urn, steam to bring out the vapour and use an apparatus to capture the dew. You can even do this with wine that is old and sour. This kind of wine is made with glutinous or normal rice, yellow or broomcorn millet or wheat, fermented in a vessel for seven days and then steamed. It is clear like water, extremely strong tasting and covered with dew.[28]

Complete Manchu-Han Feast

The Qing dynasty lasted longer than the Yuan, and its Manchu rulers expended significant effort to bear themselves as proper Chinese monarchs. But they also strove to maintain their separate identity, retaining their own language and court dress and mounting months-long imperial trips to tour their Manchu homeland.[29]

While the Yuan was happy to rely on foreigners to staff its bureaucracy, the Qing was scrupulously careful to balance the interests of the Han Chinese, instituting quotas for the numbers of Chinese and Manchu officials in its government and military, and using both languages in court documents. Important imperial pronouncements, the ones literally carved in stone, often added Mongolian and Tibetan.

These two tendencies to integrate and maintain a distance created the event known as the 'Complete Manchu-Han Feast'. As we will see, this event has been highly mythologized. Some have imagined it as a metaphor for racial harmony – the formation of a 'fusion cuisine' to represent the coming together in a great nation. This is, of course, complete nonsense.

The roots of the Manchu-Han Feast are fairly evident. Just like the Mongols, the Manchus had long used feasting as a go-to tool of diplomacy, both at home and abroad. The early Qing Kangxi emperor was especially adept at exploiting the spectacle of a grand banquet. As a young emperor of a new dynasty, he initiated annual feasts to secure the allegiance of the Mongols on his northern frontier. These events were modelled on the 'meat-ups' that were customary among the Manchus,[30] a style of entertainment that suited the Mongol guests just fine:

When the Mongolian princes came to the Capital, they always carried some food back with them, saying that it will bring good fortune back to their home. If they lacked the proper vessels to carry the food, they would not hesitate to wrap the food in fine garments. They did not seem to mind the food and its juices soiling the elaborate stitches and the threads of their robes.

In 1713, the Kangxi emperor celebrated his own sixty-first birthday with a massive banquet for a thousand guests, all aged sixty and over. You'll no doubt recognize from a previous chapter this idea of feting the elderly. More than just a reference to his own advancing years, satisfying the basic Confucian directive to revere and care for the aged was a way of advertising his own fitness as a Confucian monarch. That message was directed to his Chinese subjects.[31]

Two distinct cultures, two completely different events. Qing rulers knew very well how to use food to win the loyalty of groups within their sprawling and diverse empire – by hosting according to the guests' own customs. A palace event called the 'Manchu-Han Feast' could only mean *two* menus.

Nobody knows when the first Manchu-Han Feast was held. Palace records talk about holding separate 'Manchu and Han' feasts as early as 1687 and refer back to one event from 1763 that apparently set the standard.[32] One of Yuan Mei's contemporaries mentions a Manchu and Han Feast held in Yangzhou and describes separate menus for Manchu and Han officials.[33]

As these official court banquets were matters of palace protocol, they were handled with high precision. The 1839 *Protocols of the Court of the Imperial Kitchen* presents the first known record of an official menu, outlining six levels of formality with each one having separate dishes for the Manchu and Han banquets. Each description begins with exact instructions for decor and table settings, the number of plates and ewers to be used, as well as the allocation of tents, cloth and firewood calibrated to the level of the event. Each menu then outlines the dishes and ingredients.[34]

Han Feast, 1839

The top-level Han feast is a selection of familiar dishes: stewed chicken, goose and duck, exotics like abalone, medicalized ingredients like deer tendon and shitake mushrooms, and a variety of fresh fruits and pickled vegetables – squash, aubergine and turnips. But the overwhelming ingredient is pork. The Han banquet includes dishes of pork fat, salted pork, kidneys, trotters and stomach, as well as pork balls and pork buns. Two different preparations of stewed pork belly – *fangzi* pork and Dongpo pork – represent tastes of the north and south, respectively. All the cooked vegetable dishes, bamboo shoots, seaweed and long, thin *shanyao* yams were cooked with pork, or rather the reverse, as the ingredient list confirms that all these dishes contained more meat than any other ingredient.

Han Banquet (1839)

White stewed goose: 1 goose per 3 places
White stewed chicken: 1 chicken per place
Small pavilions: 1 pig intestine, one jin pork, 6 liang bean flour
Roasted pork: 1.8 jin pork
White pork: 1.8 jin pork
Sea cucumber with meat: 1 liang sea cucumber, 7 liang pork
Pork stomach: ½ jin pork stomach
Duck geng: ½ duck, 1 qian melon seeds, 1 qian apricot kernels, 1 qian pine nuts, 2 liang bean flour
Pork trotter: 1 pork trotter
Abalone with meat: 1 liang abalone, 1 liang pork
Bamboo shoots with meat: 4 liang bamboo shoots, 6 liang pork
Seaweed with meat: 2 liang seaweed, 6 liang pork

Dongpo pork: 12 liang pork
Deer tendon with meat: 2 liang deer tendon, 6 liang pork
Meatballs: 6 liang pork, 2 liang bean flour
Pig kidneys: 2 pig kidneys
Shanyao with meat: 1 jin shanyao, 4 liang pork
Steamed egg gao: 5 chicken eggs
Stewed chicken: ½ chicken
Fragrant mushroom duck: 1 liang shitake mushrooms,
   ½ duck
Salt-fried meat: 12 liang pork
Fangzi pork: 12 liang pork
Fish: 1 fish, weight 1 jin
Red and yellow pears, 12 of each
Tang pears, 15
Fresh grapes, dried persimmons, sun-dried dates,
   red dates, chestnuts: 1 bowl of 2 jin each
12 baozi: each 2 liang flour, 5 qian pork
12 huajuan: each 2 liang flour, 3 qian sesame oil
12 mantou: each 2 liang flour, 3 qian sesame oil, 3 qian
   white sugar
Preserved aubergine: 1 liang
Preserved cucumber: 1 liang
Preserved kohlrabi: 1 liang
10-flavour herbs: 1 liang

In addition to the main ingredients mentioned above, the strict economy of the palace kitchen quartermaster has left a record of every other food, in some cases measured to the fraction of a *qian*:

Han Banquet Ingredients

Proteins

9.4 jin pork
1 pig intestine, 1 trotter, 2 pig kidneys, ½ pig stomach
1 duck, 1½ chickens, ⅓ goose
1 fish (1 jin)
5 eggs

Vegetables

1 liang: abalone, shitake mushrooms
2 liang: deer tendon, seaweed
4 liang: cabbage, water bamboo shoots
1 jin: shanyao, carrots

Starches and Flours

1.2 jin bean flour
4 liang water powder (starch)
1 qian: melon seeds, apricot kernels, pine nuts,
    fermenting rice
4.8 jin white flour

Flavourings

5 bunches of yellow chives
1 jin onion
5 heads of garlic
1 qian Sichuan peppercorns
4 fen pepper
5 fen star anise
7.2 liang sesame oil
4 liang coriander
1 liang ginger

6 liang salt
4 liang bean paste
8 liang vinegar
3.6 liang sugar

Other

½ sheet smoking paper
1 qian red flower petals
Preserved aubergine, melon and kohlrabi

This ingredient list for the cooked dishes gives us a clear idea of the taste of this feast. Overwhelmingly, this meaty spread is flavoured with onions, chives and garlic, and secondarily ginger. Salt is not overwhelming – about ⅔ of a cup of salt and ½ cup of bean paste for a table piled high with at least 9 kilograms (20 lb) of meat. Dishes like the 'white stewed' goose and chicken come to the table completely unflavoured. (Another recipe from *Flavouring the Pot* confirms that 'white stewed' simply means boiled in clear water.) No doubt, many people ate these together with the preserved vegetables and coriander that were provided on each table. Spices for this Han feast are vanishingly rare – the total allocation of one *qian* of Sichuan peppercorns comes to just about one teaspoon for the whole table. Pepper is just half of that.

This detailed description has one omission – a fairly important one – and that is exactly how many people this lavish spread is supposed to serve. As they appear in the *Protocols*, these ingredients are the allocation for one '*xi*' 席, a word that might mean an entire event, or might mean a single place setting. The question of which it is has much more than just menu planning at stake. These state occasions have always been an exercise in ritualized decorum. Remember the fifty kinds of *hai* that ancient kings were obliged to serve to high-level guests? It seems that this sort of formalized largesse was still very much the ideal. A bit more poking around the original source confirms that these ingredients are in fact the allocation *per guest*.[35]

Manchu Feast, 1839

The Manchu feast was completely different, consisting almost entirely of small cakes and fried flour dishes:

Manchu Feast (1839)

Four-colour jade frost pastries – 48
Four-colour stuffed white crispy pastry – 48
Four-colour stuffed white pastry – 48
White honey egg pastries – 48
Egg pastries – 48
Yellow and white treats – 50
Pine nut cakes, 2 plates – 48
Red and white sanzi, 3 plates – 8.8 jin
12 plates of dried fruits, 6 plates of fresh seasonal fruit

Like the Han feast, this menu also came with a precise list of ingredients:

Manchu Feast Ingredients

Proteins

100 eggs

Oils

12 jin butter
15 jin 'crisping' [clarified] butter

Starches and Flours

1.2 jin white flour
8 jin bean flour
3 sheng millet

Flavourings and Colourings

18 jin white sugar
3 jin white honey
10 jin fine apricot kernels
2 jin red flower water
10 bunches spinach
8 liang gardenia flowers
2 liang indigo
1 liang alkali
8 liang green salt
6 qian brick salt

Other

5 pieces smoking paper
15 pieces table paper

Of course, Manchus did not normally subsist on a regime of dainty sugared treats. The traditional diet of the Manchus was heavy on meat, especially pork, but also fish and deer. Their annual feasts were orgies of meat, where it was considered impolite to do anything other than gorge. After the dynasty was established, the imperial clan's home region of Jilin continued to supply the palace with an annual tribute of fresh and dried deer meat, tails and tendons.[36]

Rather, this Manchu feast is banquet food and like the Tang Tail-Burning Banquet eleven centuries earlier, it uses a truly awesome amount of butter: 27 *jin* per person. The protein for the feast comes not from meat, but from eggs – a hundred per place setting. The main taste would have come from over 9 kilograms (20 lb) of sugar and honey. Chopped fine and pressed for juice, the spinach and flowers add colour. Flower water may also have been for fragrance, similar to the way that rose or orange blossom water are used in Middle Eastern sweets. The single largest item consists of nearly 13.6 kilograms (30 lb) of deep-fried noodles known as *sanzi*.[37]

The cakes themselves were variations on the Manchu speciality known as *Bo bo*. With some adjustments for sweetness and fillings, the central dishes at the Manchu banquet would have resembled the following recipe from *Flavouring the Pot*:

Manchurian Bo bo (Qing)

For the outer layer, mix 1 jin of white flour, 4 liang of pork oil, 4 liang of boiling water until even. Use force to knead the dough, the more the better. For the inside, mix 1 jin of white flour with ½ jin pork oil (use more if the dough is stiff) and knead until it is extremely smooth, neither hard nor soft. Combine the two into a large block, folding the outside layer in. Cut into small pieces and use to wrap around a filling (such as walnuts) and bake until done. Just like moon cakes. Can also fry the cakes in sesame oil. Use both methods to make some that are heavy and some that are light.

Over time, the Manchu-Han Feast changed from a precisely managed diplomatic event to a *type* of cuisine. Just as the name 'Eight Treasures' took on a life of its own, the 'Complete Manchu-Han Feast' came to mean *any* two set menus of contrasting but equally opulent delights.

There have been many other versions of this feast – those concocted by local governments, hotels, tourism boards, television shows and famous chefs – but let's focus on one that appears in the

1868 recipe collection *Flavouring the Pot*. Like others, this book of recipes divides the feast into Han and Manchu tables and further into first and second grades of importance. As the *Flavouring the Pot* menu appears in a handwritten version of the text, it can be considered authentic to the nineteenth century, if not as a court banquet, then at least as a very fancy one. This text also includes recipes, which will be important given that many of our dishes are no longer intelligible from the names.

Manchu-Han Feast, 1868

We'll begin with the Manchu feast. Far from the table of dainty butter pastries that we saw in the previous version, the Manchu feast has now become a veritable butcher's shop. The 25 listed dishes include a whole pig, whole sheep and suckling pigs served roasted, steamed and steamed in lees. We also have chicken and duck, both roasted and steamed, as well as fragrant duck, white (steamed) and roasted *harba* (pig spine) and steamed *wucha* (roasted sheep). Perhaps reflecting the dining practices of the Qing court, beef is notably absent.[38]

Manchu Feast (1868)

Whole pig: red or white [that is, roasted or steamed], served with head and trotters

Whole sheep

Whole roasted piglet: 8 jin live weight

Hanging roasted ducks: 1 pair

White steamed piglet, served with oil cakes

White steamed ducks: 1 pair

Crawling piglet

Fragrant duck with soy sauce, Sichuan pepper, cumin, cloves, sausage

Piglet steamed with lees, served with oil cakes

White [boiled] harba: 6 jin, can also dry steam [bake?]
Hanging roasted chicken, or butterfly chicken
Roasted harba: 6 jin, can also dry steam
White steamed chicken
White steamed wucha: half or whole
Chicken simmered with pine nuts
Red and white brisket (xiongcha): 5 jin
Roasted ribs: 6 jin per piece
Boiled ribs: 6 jin
House shrew (soulou), red or white: 4 jin
Red or white offal: liver, intestines, 'dragon strips'
   [pig marrow]
Sheep zhaoshi[39]
Sheep brains, [with] meatballs, ham, sea cucumber
Roasted pig brains: as above
Sheep stomach fried with garlic, bamboo and meat
   [presumably ham]
Sheep tail with lees

And the taste? As this menu is not dictated by court protocol, it does not come with the same precise ingredients list as the
earlier version. Instead, we have the actual recipes preserved in
Flavouring the Pot. Like other books from the time, these recipes
are descriptive and rely on the experience and judgement of
the cook. But it is clear that compared to the bland dishes of the
earlier version, the standard here is as much taste as it is opulent
presentation. Note the elaborate preparation behind the simple
idea of 'roasted meat':

Hanging Roasted Meat (Qing)
Mix 2 jin of short ribs, 1 bowl of bean paste, 2 qian of crushed
star anise and vinegar as needed into soy sauce. Place four
iron bars on top of a pot. Use the vinegar paste to paint the

meat and rest it on top of the bars. Add 4 or 5 onion whites and cover the pot with a plate so it is airtight. Once smoke and oil start to escape, turn the meat over and apply more of the paste, vinegar and onions. Do this several times until the skin is golden. To improve the taste, spread some fine salt at the end.

For chicken, goose or duck, first boil the meat until it is cooked. Spread with sugar syrup or honey. Add fat or sesame oil to the pot and fry until golden. As with hanging meat, sprinkle some salt over the meat and spread it evenly. Let the boiled meat cool before frying and then add the sugar or honey. Fry at a low temperature to ensure that the insides are warmed.[40]

The transformation of the Han menu is no less striking. From an early focus on all things pork, this lavish menu has turned definitively to the exotic: the dishes mentioned include four different types of swallow's nest, five dishes of shark fin, as well as sea cucumber and snails. Pork is still present, although far less prominent. We still have pig stomach and other pork dishes like Wenwu pork. Plus we now have numerous ducks and chickens, and two dishes of stewed sheep.[41]

Han Feast (1868)

'Gold and silver' swallow's nest [with egg yolk, chicken skin, ham, bamboo, quail egg, salted fish]
Shark fin with wild duck [with sliced pork]
'Hushua' shark fin [stewed with thin-sliced ham and chicken broth]
Swallow's nest [with chicken geng]
Shark fin stewed with brassica, duck tongue, ham and chicken

Swallow's nest balls [with abalone]

Shark fin with crab cake [with pork, ham and bamboo]

Ten brocades swallow's nest [with thin-sliced pork and ham]

Shark fin with thin-sliced meat [pork, ham, bamboo and chicken skin]

Swallow's nest with 'snails' [wild chicken or duck slices, ham, chicken skin, white fish balls, farm duck slices – rolled into a snail shape]

Eight treasures sea cucumber

Roasted turtle skin with pork and ham

Thin-sliced sea cucumber

'Jiasha' duck

Thin-sliced sea cucumber, with chicken, ham and fried tofu strips

Eight treasures duck [with ham, Job's tears and lotus seeds]

Sea cucumber and wild duck geng

Wild and farmed duck deboned and stewed together

Sea cucumber balls [with cubed shanyao, pork, chicken and bamboo]

Stewed salted and fresh duck

Shredded chicken braised with Job's tears, ham and thin-sliced pork

Duck tongue stewed with brassica [with duck tongue, ham and chicken]

Stewed, thin-sliced chicken [with pine nuts]

Guandong chicken [with ham and winter bamboo]

Stewed sheep with pumpkin

Duck stewed or fried with garlic

Pot-stewed lamb

Red stewed chicken

Swallow's wing chicken

Chicken deboned and braised with bamboo
Baisu [Suzhou style?] chicken
Ham hock stewed with pork hock
Pine nut chicken
'Gold and silver' pork hock [crisped skin and meat]
Lychee chicken
'Huankuai' [boiled and resalted] ham
Sliced ham, river fish, bamboo and abalone
Anchovy fishcake
Stewed mock bear paw
Boiled, fried or braised sturgeon
Slices [of what?] cooked briefly in soup
Stewed mock turtle
Noodle fish with bamboo and ham
Braised deer tendon with dried shrimp and winter melon
White fish dumplings
White fish balls [deep-fried fish belly]
Abalone fried with pork and bamboo shoot slices
Pot-braised crab
Crab fried brassica
Wen-Wu pork
Fried pork served with starch noodles
Qunzhe pork: sliced pork, dried tofu and deep-fried pork
   all steamed together
Pork hock with lotus seeds
Ham stewed with pork tendon and skin
Stewed, sliced pork belly
Fresh mussels stewed with ham, sliced pork, bamboo
   and chicken
Dried mussels stewed with pork, carrot and pork balls
Braised mussels with pork
Dried mussels fried with pork, chicken and bamboo
Tofu dumplings

Tofu balls with pine nuts and cubed ham

Tofu braised with pine nuts, ham and pork

Tofu braised with almonds, ham and chicken

Mushroom tofu braised with ham, bamboo and chicken
skin

Swallow's nest stewed with frozen tofu

June frozen tofu [braised to mimic the texture of frozen
tofu]

Scrambled tofu braised with minced pork and dried
shrimp

Dried tofu strips with salted peppers

Courgette strips with salted peppers

Like the dish of hanging meat, many of these dishes also appear as recipes in *Flavouring the Pot*, suggesting how they would have been understood in a nineteenth-century kitchen:

Wen-Wu Pork (Qing)

Cut ham and fresh pork into cubes. Simmer (in liquid) over a fire.

Lychee Chicken (Qing)

Cut a chicken breast into pieces the size of eyes and shape to resemble lychees. Cook briefly in salted water with onions, wine and pepper and remove. Add slices of fermented ginger, cubes of shanyao and bamboo according to season. Mix and dip briefly in the boiling water. Before serving again return briefly to the water and serve with bamboo and tonghao leaves.

[Unlike today's dish of the same name, this does not include any actual lychees]

Braised Deer Tendon Cubes (Qing)

First, beat the dried tendon with an iron bar, boil to soften and remove any yellow skin. Deer tendon has tough and soft parts together. Cut away the hard parts and continue to cook.

To braise, cut the cooked tendon into cubes. Stew with cubes of chicken, bamboo and carrot, pork oil, soy sauce, wine and fatty pork.

Beyond the tastes, this menu is a trove of information about newly available ingredients. First on the list is swallow's nest, which is slowly boiled into a glutinous soup. These are actual nests, which are collected from sheer cliff faces where the swallows make their homes, and came into medical fashion during the Ming dynasty. Then, as now, the best swallows' nests are imported from Southeast Asia.[42]

There is a variety of exotic seafood – shark fin, sea cucumber, crab, dried mussels – where the palace Han feast had almost none. The absence of seafood in the palace menu may be a remnant of the Qing's early history, a time when their conquest was not entirely complete. The invaders had swept in from the north, driving their opponents to the south and especially to the coast, where they proved difficult to eradicate. To alleviate the problem, the new dynasty had simply closed the coast, which in turn cut off much of the supply of seafood. By the time of the second menu, this policy was already a distant memory. In fact, the seafood on this menu covers the full length of China's coastline. Sea cucumber and mussels come from the northern waters of the Bohai Gulf, while crab, shark and dried shrimp probably come from farther south. Saury swim in north China's rivers, while sturgeon is famously found in the rivers of Manchuria. *Flavouring the Pot* has recipes for two dozen different types of fish, arranged by when they come into season. Large fish like Yellow River carp can be braised, roasted, fried and preserved in grain brewing lees. There are also numerous recipes for the 'noodle fish' that appear on the Han menu. Small and oily, similar to sprat, these fish are most often seen deep-fried. Seven recipes in *Flavouring the Pot* show both the versatility of preparation and the economic shorthand style of recipes in this generation of cookbooks:

Noodle Fish: Seven Ways (Qing)

Noodle fish are available from the eighth month through the second month of the next year.

Braised 煨: Braise with strips of ham. [or] Cut into thin strips and braise as a sauce. [or] Cut into pieces and braise with pig trotter or duck. [or] Cut into pieces and braise with vegetables.

Steamed 蒸: Wash clean and steam with soy sauce, wine, vinegar, ginger juice, onion and pork fat.

Fried 炒: Cut into strips, stir-fry with pork fat and thin dry strips [of dried pressed tofu?].

Grilled 烧: Wash clean and dry, dredge with baijiu [a strong, distilled liquor] and bean flour, stir-fry in oil, wine, salt and pork fat. Grill with ham strips and chicken strips.

Deep-fried 炸: Remove the heads and tails, dredge in flour and fry. [or] Remove the bones, dredge in bean flour, salt and wine and fry. [or] Fry with vinegar and oil.

Sliced 膾: Remove the heads and tails, serve in soup with winter bamboo and thin chicken strips.

Drunken 醉: Briefly deep-fry to cook out the water, remove the bones and use baijiu brewing lees, fried salt and onion flower to pickle [lit. intoxicate].

The 1868 menu is just the beginning. Just like the idea of 'Eight Treasures', the Manchu-Han Feast would evolve from a set menu to a type, an empty box that restaurants or local cuisines could fill in any way they saw fit.

After All, What Is 'Chinese' Cuisine?

Cuisine is an endless battle between innovation and authenticity. Purist voices today will reject out of hand the very idea of putting pineapple on pizza or adding chorizo to paella, regardless of whether people think it tastes good. No doubt, many would be happy to add border-crossing Chinese diasporic cuisine – dishes like the much-maligned General Tso's chicken – to this list of perceived culinary abominations. But apart from how you feel about these particular dishes or about the ownership or appropriation of cultural tradition more generally, we can't deny that food is always evolving, and for that reason the quest for culinary authenticity is fundamentally a fool's errand.

Nearly everything we would today recognize as Chinese cuisine – foods, flavours and techniques – originally came from somewhere else. Some foods, like 'hu' melons and 'fan' tomatoes, keep a vestige of this origin in their name, but other imports like onions, noodles or chillies are so fundamental that it seems ridiculous to call them anything other than Chinese.

3

Gardens of Delight
Imperial China's High Cuisine

We open upon a scene of refined wealth, a family home of manicured courtyards, graceful palisades and richly decorated sitting rooms. Inside one of these rooms, we find a small family gathering, about a dozen relatives and their maids and a busy stream of kitchen servants coming and going. The family matron forms the tranquil centre, the forces of affection and propriety holding the proceedings firmly in orbit around her.

After stopping by to toast the New Year, the younger men withdraw, leaving the family matron holding court over a room full of female relatives and their servants.

This is an event for the women.

There are opera singers and professional storytellers, gossip and riddles and a drinking game where a flower is passed around and whoever is left holding it when the music stops has to take a drink and tell a joke.
The Dowager is first to be chosen and tells a joke about the Monkey King pissing in hell.

A hamper of delicate cakes and dried fruit is sent
to the servant quarters. Hot food is ordered for the
exhausted performers.

We eat and drink at a refined pace. Cups of wine and
pots of hot tea are brought in to ward off the cold. Plates
of snacks and various cooked dishes follow us through
the night. Our refined winter menu includes seasonal taro
pressed into cakes, winter bamboo prepared with cured
ham and cabbage, stewed quail and steamed deer. Plates
of dumplings bring in the New Year.

As the night draws on, we warm up with bowls of hot duck
congee and sweet almond soup before going out to enjoy
the evening fireworks.[1]

China's Late Empire

Historians divide China's 2,000 years of empire into a few major parts, the last of which we have creatively named 'late' imperial China. The earlier periods peaked with the Tang dynasty and ended roughly around the year 950. China's late empire was substantively different in many ways, with sustained changes to politics, economy and culture. During that time, China's food grew progressively more elaborate, and before too long a gourmet culture was in full bloom.

We might start with the question of why China's new food culture developed at that time and in that particular way. The answer, as you might have guessed already, is money.

The fall of the Tang dynasty was more than just a change of rulers. Under a new dynasty known as the Song, China entered the beginning of an economic and commercial revolution that lasted, give or take, for the next eight hundred years. Energized by changes to the tax system and money supply, the Chinese economy continued to grow. So did the population, from 60 to 100 million, aided by the new high-performing crops we talked about in the previous chapter. Late Imperial China was a triumph of pre-industrial technology – with sophisticated farming, metal-working and finance. It wasn't all smooth sailing – this period still endured the chaos and bloodshed that accompanied the rise and fall of four separate dynasties – but over the long term, the trajectory of progress still made late imperial China an extremely prosperous place.[2]

These changes had two long-lasting effects on China's food. The first was the growth of trade, both inside and outside of China. Farmers and artisans produced for a growing internal market and traders brought in more and more exotic goods from distant lands. Specialized trade houses created reliable trade networks to ship tea, fermented condiments, wine, dried hams, fruits, rice and aromatic spices within and into China. Every step that made food trade easier, wider or more profitable also brought new foods into Chinese diets.

The second was how all that wealth fed a culture of consumption, one in which being a gourmand was not only socially acceptable but a sign of sophistication. The combination of new ingredients, new techniques and a new class of culinary sophisticates who were willing to pay for luxury supercharged the development of China's high cuisines – not one but many, as most of these new tastes and new cooking styles were very local.

A Dream of Splendour

Our first stop is the central city of Kaifeng. Known as Bianjing (also Bianliang), this city was the capital of the Song dynasty, a teeming metropolis of over a million people, and a centre of learning, wealth and sophistication.

The end came in the twelfth century, when the city was captured and looted by invaders from the north. Not long after, a refugee named Meng Yuanlao recorded a nostalgic description of the city in his *Dream of Splendour in the Eastern Capital*. Meng had probably fled Bianjing and now found himself residing in the Song's new southern capital of Hangzhou. With the nostalgia of a man who can never return home, he recalled each of the city's districts, temples, palaces and customs. He also remembered Bianjing's food, dish by dish.

Food in Bianjing was entertainment. Walking us through the glittering entertainment district, Meng shows us a city that took its entertainment seriously. The rows of wine- and teahouses had their own specialized vocabulary. The shop owner in charge of sales was called the 'Master of Provisions', and his young assistants were 'uncles'. The girls who wrapped themselves in layers of fine silk and moved among the wealthy guests carrying pots of tea water were known as 'lamplighters'. The young men on hand

The bustling heart of Bianjing, 12th century. This detail of the Song capital from a scroll by Zhang Zeduan shows a grain merchant, animal market, fruit and pastry vendors, and a two-storey restaurant.

to run errands or entertain the drinkers were called 'roustabouts' and *sibo*. 'Needles' were the lower-level singers, the ones who came even when they weren't summoned. Those called *sazan* – a word that translates roughly to 'temporary peace' – would move from table to table accepting money by 'selling' a simple item like a radish until customers would buy it to make them go away.[3]

But of course, we are there for the food. We can imagine the exiled author looking back to recall the culinary delights of his youth.

Remember *geng*, the thick soup that the ancients equated with stewed meat? Meng recalls a dozen types: hundred-flavour *geng*, top *geng*, new-style quail *geng*, three-crisp *geng*, gathered fairies *geng*, golden tripe *geng* and stone tripe *geng*. There was two-colour kidney *geng*, shrimp mushroom *geng* and chicken mushroom *geng*. Smaller houses served plum juice blood *geng* and powder *geng*.

Bianjing also had vast markets for meat, grain, vegetables, sauces and wine. *Dream of Splendour* mentions dozens of different kinds of fruits, vegetables and fish, representing tastes from north and south. Pork was still king – the market even had its own guild of pig slaughterers. A pig sacrifice was required for almost any ritual occasion, a situation that naturally produced a great deal of pork. But there was also sheep, beef, quail, chicken, goose, wild and domestic duck, deer, tiny water deer, fox and badger. There was a whole section of the market just for mushrooms, with nearby farmers cultivating new strains to satisfy the city's demand for novelty.[4]

There was also a range of sauces – each one a distinct combination of fermented beans, spices, dried meat, seafood or vegetables. We have already mentioned one meat-based paste that appeared in the twelfth-century *Mrs Wu's Records from the Kitchen*. That version combined meat with a basic yellow or black soybean paste as a starter and flavouring agent, for a result that may have been similar to the *hai* that appears in ancient texts. Other books from the same time introduce a wide world of pickles, including recipes for pickled pork face or trotters, melon or vegetables like melon or aubergine preserved in brewing lees, for a result that was undoubtedly similar to the Japanese sake pickles called *kasuzuke*.

Lees-Pickled Aubergine (Song)

5 jin aubergine, 6 jin lees, 17 liang salt and 3 bowls of river water. Mix the ingredients together with the lees and the flavour will naturally become sweet. This will require some time before it is ready.[5]

A word here about the rabbit hole that is fermentation. As any sensible person will agree, fermentation is neither craft nor science. It is sorcery. Do it right and you get beer. Make one innocent mistake and you are punished with a room full of exploded bottles and a vocally annoyed room-mate. That is because fermentation is not one single process. It can use bacteria, mould or yeast, with oxygen or without. Bacteria-fermented vegetables like kimchi need to be covered in liquid – anything that pokes up above the waterline will mould. Fermented bean products like soy sauce or pastes like *doubanjiang* are the opposite. They start off with beans that mould in the open air, then switch to a careful regimen of closed and open-vat curing that precisely regulates the biome – and the taste – of the finished product.

More than just playing with new ingredients, the sauces and pastes of the Song marketplace perfected the art of layering natural processes to gradually build complex and sophisticated flavours. One preparation, named after Jinshan Temple in Hangzhou, combines fresh squash, aubergine and lotus root with Sichuan peppercorns, liquorice, fennel, perilla leaves and garlic with yellow soybeans. Looking past the exotic added flavours, note the precision in the instructions. The large-cut fresh vegetables leave air in the fermenting vat, which is sealed shut.

Jinshan Temple Salted Beans (Song)

Fresh squash (2 cun chunks), fresh aubergine (quarters) tangerine peel (washed clean), lotus root (rinsed, cut in half), fresh ginger (thick slices), Sichuan peppercorn (by sight), fennel (small amount), liquorice root (crushed), perilla leaves, garlic cloves (with peel).

Mix the above ingredients together evenly. Add a layer of yellow beans [to a fermenting jar], then a layer of the mix, and then a layer of salt. Repeat these layers until [the jar] is completely full. Close up the entrance and seal with mud.

Cure under the hot sun for half a month. Empty and mix the contents, return to the pot and seal it up to cure in the sun for 77 days. Do not add any water, since the salt will release water from the aubergine and melon. Use as much as you need as dictated by the amount of salt.[6]

I made this recipe using a clear glass vat and enjoyed a front-row seat as it cured over the following three months. As expected, the salt released the water from the vegetables, gradually submerging the mixture in liquid. Had we been making kimchi or most other bean pastes, this would have marked the change from aerobic to anaerobic fermentation. However, while other recipes from the time add a starter like red rice flour, this one seemingly left nothing to ferment. Rather, the mixture had simply pickled. After three months, I dutifully fished out the beans, ground them up into a paste and fried them with cabbage. The taste was pleasantly salty but without the recognizable umami of a fermented bean paste. Whether or not the result was accurate to the Song-era recipe, I could at least comfort myself with the knowledge that I was recreating the far older process of invention through trial and error.

With these new tastes came new dishes, based on an ever-developing suite of techniques. One cooking style that becomes increasingly common from this time is *baochao*, the method of high-heat quick stir-frying that people most frequently associate with Chinese cuisine. *Mrs Wu's Records from the Kitchen* gives examples of a two-part method, cooking first at a low temperature to fix the texture of the meat, followed by a second high-heat pass to infuse the flavour of aromatics. The name of the first dish specifies that it is made with fresh meat (presumably pork), as opposed to various forms of preserved meat:

Method to Prepare Fresh Meat (Song)

Cut a piece of good meat into slices, rub with soy sauce, braise to remove blood, and fry until the colour just starts to turn from red to white. Remove the meat and slice into thin strips, add thin strips of preserved melon, pickled radish, garlic, cardamom, Sichuan pepper, sharen and sesame oil and fry while mixing. When serving add vinegar as needed and mix in. The taste is lovely.[7]

Stove-Braised Chicken (Song)

Prepare [that is, clean and gut] one chicken, boil until it is eight-tenths done and chop into small pieces. Add a small amount of oil to a pot. Once the oil is hot, add the chicken pieces to quickly fry and cover with a plate or bowl. While the chicken is warm, add equal amounts of vinegar and wine and a small amount of salt and fry until even. When the liquid is gone, again add vinegar, wine and salt; do this over and over until the chicken is soft, remove and serve.[8]

New techniques satisfied a craving for novelty. A source from the later Song period (after Jurchen attacks had driven the capital to the south) recalls a trip among the Barbarian (non-Han) mountain people, who had the custom of dipping thinly sliced meat in broth, a quick technique that saved fuel and one that any Chinese diner would recognize as yet another version of today's hotpot. The author noted that Han Chinese now used this style to cook pork and sheep.[9]

Stylish recipes travelled from place to place, giving birth to a known complement of tastes and techniques. The following crab recipe comes from *Mrs Wu's Records from the Kitchen*, but the dish also appears elsewhere, with different names and only slight variations in ingredients:

Fresh Crab (Song)

Crack open and pulverize crab, either uncooked or boiled. Add sesame oil, cardamom, fennel, sharen, powdered Sichuan peppercorn, white pepper and ginger water and mix into a paste. Add onion, salt and vinegar, for a total of ten flavours and toss to combine. Can be eaten immediately.

Other sources call this dish 'clean hands crab', since you would need to wash your hands before and after eating it. Some versions simply mix crab and vinegar. Others add sour plum and tangerine. Regardless of how the dish was made, the point is that it became a national fad, the kind of thing you can only experience if you have public knowledge of cuisine.

So, what was on offer in the teahouses of Bianjing? Meng puts it all on display. Along with the dozen types of *geng* and vendors selling roast chicken, stewed duck, 'head-down' sheep, sliced crispy tendon, ginger shrimp, drunken crab, crispy water deer and deer jerky, we have:

Two-colour kidneys, cold starch noodles, 'chess pieces', mock pufferfish, white thrush, mandarin fish, mock yuan fish, cassia parcels, cassia soup, foetus with vinegar, sandfish with intestine, shark in casing, twice-cooked perilla fish, mock clams, noodles with fat, velvety meat, hubing, bones in soup, sheep cooked in milk, 'noisy hall' sheep, horn-cooked kidneys, steamed goose and duck arranged on a plate, lychee kidneys, 'return to the origin' kidneys, stewed breast, oven-cooked delicacies, duck strips arranged as a lotus flower, wine-roasted cow stomach, sheep-head strips cooked in a weak sauce, pot-cooked sheep, sheep-head strips, goose duck strips, chicken strips, plated rabbit, fried rabbit, onion rabbit, mock wild fox, mock water deer, steamed quail, fresh fried pork, fried clams, fried crab, plated crab and clean hands crab.

As we only have the names, the actual content of some of these dishes requires guesswork. Based on other dishes, we can assume that lychee kidneys were probably cut into the shape of lychees, rather than being prepared with fruit. The dish Meng calls 'chess pieces' refers to food cut into small rounds – the shape of the pieces in Chinese chess – and it probably looked like a smaller version of the shared autumn dish he describes further on:

Offerings Rice (Song)

During August, everyone prepares autumn offerings of cakes and wine. People take dishes of pork and sheep meat, kidneys, udder, stomach and lungs, along with duck cakes and melon, and cut to the shape of chess pieces, flavoured with an enticing sauce and arranged on top of rice. This dish is called 'offerings rice' and is shared with guests.[10]

The dish of 'drunken crab' may seem familiar from contemporary dishes like 'drunken chicken'. But the similarity is deceiving. The modern dish (or dishes, since there are many variations) either braises the bird in rice wine or marinates a cooked and pieced chicken overnight in flavoured wine. The Song dish was more probably a fully preserved crab – the word translated as 'drunk' here being a verb to describe the method of pickling in wine. The nineteenth-century *Flavouring the Pot* contained dozens of recipes for 'drunken crab', using combinations of salt, bean paste, soy sauce and spice, along with various kinds of wine and brewing lees. The pickled crabs could be eaten as is, dunked lightly in hot soup or stewed with eggs.

Wine-Pickled Crab (Qing)

Soak 10 jin of female crabs in water. Remove and place overnight in a covered basket. When the crabs have stopped spitting out white foam, place them in a pickling vat and wait for half a day. Mix 10 jin of water with 5 jin of salt and add to the vat. Add 1 liang of Sichuan peppercorns. After two or three days, dump out the brine, rinse the crabs and remove the legs. Return the crabs to the vat and seal it shut. They will be ready after seven days.

- or -

Using 1 jin of vinegar and 2 jin of wine, pickle the crabs in a ceramic vat. They will be ready after one week.

- or -

Mix sweet wine with strained bean paste:[11] first place seven parts wine and three parts paste into a vat, take the live crabs and use a chopstick to poke a hole in the underside of each one. Add a small amount of salt and seal. They will be ready after three to five days.

- or -

Stuff the underside of crabs with Sichuan peppercorns and salt. Use 2 jin of brewing lees, 3 jin of yellow wine, 1 jin of soy sauce. Seal into a vat and use after ten days.

But there's something else to notice – what's with all the 'mock' dishes? Other sources from this period mention mock sheep's eyes and mock kidneys. The previous chapter's Manchu-Han Feast includes a dish of mock bear paw. We might guess that rare ingredients like wild fox or pufferfish might have been replaced by a cheaper stand-in, but *kidneys*? A meat-heavy cuisine like the one in Song-dynasty Bianjing certainly had plenty of kidneys to go around. Rather, I suspect that the lure of mock dishes was probably just a way to attract the attention of fickle customers – another example of chasing novelty in a crowded marketplace.

Mongol Invasions

With a few starts and stops, all the trends we see starting in the Song dynasty – the development of the market, the influx of new foods and growing elite appreciation for cuisine – would continue through the next eight centuries.

As far as 'stops' go, the Mongol conquest of northern China was probably at the top of the list. The invasion brutalized cities and countryside alike. Some areas took centuries to recover the Song-era population.

As we have already discussed, the Mongols went on to rule China for 150 years, calling their government the Yuan and eventually establishing a capital in today's Beijing. But they never integrated with their Han subjects, nor did they fully trust them, instead staffing important positions in their military and government with outsiders, especially Muslims from Central Asia. These foreigners, known as 'coloured eyes', settled in large numbers across China. Like the Mongols, they also brought their food.

The great book of Yuan dynasty food – the *Principles of Eating and Drinking* – reflects this mix. Written by the Yuan court dietician Hu Sihui, the book presents a remarkable melding of culinary traditions, combining Chinese methods and ingredients with Mongol tastes and the Turkic influence of Central Asia. The book blends these traditions so well that scholars are still unsure whether Hu Sihui himself was Chinese, foreign or something in between. The great French sinologist Françoise Sabban describes the cuisine of the *Principles of Eating and Drinking* as 'Chinese in appearance, Mongol at heart, laced with exoticism'.[12]

Among much else, *Principles of Eating and Drinking* gives us recipes for whole roasted game birds, geese, rabbits, sheep hearts and sheep kidneys, as well as numerous raw dishes, especially sheep meat and organs. The Turkic influence appears in recipes for pilaffs made of sheep cooked with wheat or millet, as well as in the following recipe for stuffed aubergine, which appears first in *Principles of Eating and Drinking*. Minus the tomatoes (which had not yet reached China), the more elaborate version in the *Practical Collection of Vital Home Skills* closely resembles the classic Middle Eastern stuffed aubergine dish known as *Sheik al Mehshee*:

Aubergine Mantou (Yuan)

Finely chop sheep meat, sheep fat, sheep tail, onion and orange peel. Remove the stalk from a fresh aubergine, stuff with the meat filling and steam. Add garlic, lao and minced coriander before eating.[13]

Minced Aubergine with Meat and Oil (Yuan)

10 white aubergines, stems removed. Cut each aubergine open and scoop out the insides. Finely chop 3 aubergines and steam these along with the hollowed aubergines until cooked. Deep-fry the hollowed aubergine until golden yellow and remove from the oil. Smash the 3 chopped aubergines into a paste. Use 5 liang of good lamb, chopped roughly, 50 pine nuts, chopped fine, and 1 liang each of salt, bean paste and ginger. Mix onions and slices of tangerine peel in vinegar. Use 2 liang of oil to fry the meat and spices together until cooked. Mix these evenly into the aubergine paste, adjust the spices and return them to the hollowed-out aubergine. Serve with garlic and lao.[14]

Food as Medicine

More than anything else, the *Principles of Eating and Drinking* is a book of medicine combining knowledge from across a world that the Mongol conquests turned into an 'information superhighway' stretching from Beijing to Cairo.[15]

Chinese medical theory understands the human body as a system of energies, known broadly as *qi*. Different sorts of *qi* connect to the vital organs and flow freely along set paths within the healthy body. But not too freely. Problems arise when any one of these forces is too weak or too strong, or if the passage of *qi* is blocked or diverted. The role of the physician is to maintain or restore balance by stimulating the body with acupuncture or massage or to correct the sort of imbalance caused by lack of sleep, over-exertion or any number of external stimuli.

And of course, no stimulus is more important than diet. The science of medicalized diet is very old in China, obviously much older than the Yuan. Ideas of 'food as medicine' developed step-by-step with food itself – some Neolithic sites contain medicinal herbs, the early stages of an evolving corpus of medical knowledge that was eventually collected into the great classic, the *Yellow Emperor's Book of Internal Medicine*. That book summed up the relationship nicely: 'To a hungry man, food is nourishment, to a sick one it is medicine.'[16] We have already seen some references to medicalized diet in the person of the Zhou court dietician and in some of our previous banquets: the 'long life soup' at the Tang Tail-Burning Banquet was most probably a concoction of medical herbs.

The practice of medicalized diet is based on understanding the qualities of food itself. Some foods were known to have curative properties. Regarding persimmons, the eighth-century *Dietetic Pharmacopeia* advises the following: 'those long bothered by red or white diarrhoea [that is, with blood or mucous] or gastrointestinal cramps can take a vinegared persimmon, crush it and use a cloth to wring out the juice. Drink this on an empty stomach to fix the problem.'[17] On the other hand, an overdose of certain foods could also cause problems. The cooling properties of spinach posed no threat to northerners, with their hearty diet of meat and wheat. But for fish-eating southerners, too much spinach would 'rapidly chill the intestines and weaken the legs'.[18]

More than just helpful tips, medicalized diet was a complete theory of nature and, just like fine cuisine, the art of food-as-medicine really starts to come into its own during the Song and beyond. In addition to integrating techniques and theories from outside of China, the *Principles of Eating and Drinking* drew on millennia of dietary medicine, using a language of medical effects, benefits and dangers that overlaps with literal tastes to simultaneously capture the essential medical and culinary nature of different foods.

For example, mutton is described not as gamey or oily, but 'sweet in taste, greatly heating, not poisonous'. These three terms are medical code. The first two place foods within the categories of 'five tastes' and 'four natures'. 'Sweet' describes most meat and grains and refers to nourishing properties. Other foods are referred to as acrid, sour, bitter or salty. 'Greatly heating' is one end of a spectrum that progresses from hot to moist, cool or cold. 'Not poisonous' simply means that the food is harmless, even in large amounts.[19] The book then goes on to explain mutton's specific medical benefits: 'Helps to warm wind, promotes sweating, alleviates fatigue and cold, strengthens *qi*.'

The *Principles of Eating and Drinking* portrays the cook as both physician and artist. It is not enough simply to prescribe food as medicine – the ingredients, spices and preparation must also appeal to the appetite:

Sheep Organ Geng (Yuan)

Cures weak kidneys and declining function, injuries to bone marrow.

Sheep liver, stomach, kidneys, heart and lungs (1 each, wash in warm water), butter (1 liang), white pepper (1 liang), orange peel (2 liang, white removed), biba (pepper casings – 1 liang), fermented beans (1 ge), good ginger (2 liang), cardamom (2 liang), onion (2).

First, simmer the liver on a low fire until cooked. Strain off the cooking water. Place the liver and all of the medical ingredients inside the stomach, sew up the entrance and place inside a cloth pouch. Boil until fully cooked, add the 'five flavours' [that is, fix the seasoning].[20]

Other dishes in the same collection introduce dishes to cure incontinence (brassica *geng*), weakness of the spleen (carp *geng*), wind, weakness and pain in the feet and kidneys (deer hoof soup) and of course that old favourite, weakness in the male reproductive organs (sheep kidney *geng*).

It would be hard to overstate just how profoundly the assumptions of medicalized diet continue to affect every aspect of Chinese cuisine and food culture. The *Principles of Eating and Drinking* is just one drop in a river of tradition that started before antiquity and continues today. For millennia, people in China have followed common-sense rules for varying diet by season. Some of these rules are woven into cultural traditions, something we see in Meng Yuanlao's description of holiday foods in Bianjing.[21] Even now, you can go to any village and find people instinctively coordinating their diets to each of the agricultural year's 24 two-week cycles. More than a simple reminder of what foods are coming into season, these customs represent the distilled knowledge of what the body needs to fight off the seasonal maladies: chills, infections, dryness or heat. Even if they don't delve deep into medical theory, most people in China will have a common-sense understanding of the foods that suit hot or cold weather, and which foods are beneficial or dangerous to men or women, the very young or the very old. That common sense is the accumulated knowledge of centuries.

Compare the fourteenth-century recipe above to another sheep *geng* – this one from a book of medical recipes published in 1985.[22] The recipe is simple: boil one or two sheep shin bones in clean water, add between twenty and eighty red dates and a 'moderate amount' of glutinous rice. No salt, no spices – this soup is to be taken like medicine, three times over one day. The book describes each of the key ingredients in familiar terms. Red dates are 'sweet in taste, moist and enter via the spleen and stomach pathways'. Sheep's shins 'govern weakness of the spleen', 'give health to the waist and feet' and 'strengthen teeth and bones'. Glutinous rice 'benefits qi, and fortifies the spleen and lungs'.

Separated by more than 650 years, these two recipes are more than just variations on the same basic theme of sheep soup (the second one is more like a flavoured porridge, closer to the current usage of *geng*). The modern recipe echoes the structure of the *Principles of Eating and Drinking* because the two books draw from the same well of knowledge. The hundreds of recipes in the 1985 book – or any other book of Chinese medicalized diet – all follow this exact pattern, breaking down foods into a standard vocabulary of basic natures and therapeutic functions.

Beyond even this, both recipes – and Chinese medicalized cuisine more generally – share the same philosophy of food: a two-part approach to diagnostic dining that starts with identifying what ails the patient/diner and then scouring both the kitchen and the library to come up with the most therapeutic list of ingredients. Then (and only then) are you ready to cook.

Local Cuisines Take the Stage

China's 2,000 years of empire peaked with its last two dynasties: the Ming (1368–1644) and the Qing (1644–1911). Despite having similar-sounding names, the two were very different. Following the demise of the Mongol Yuan, the Ming represented the return of Han Chinese rule. The Qing was another conquest from the outside, not by the Mongols but from the Manchus to the northeast.

These two dynasties – more than five centuries in all – represent China's evolving imperial system at its apex. Transformations we have already seen set in motion – China's growing wealth, power, influence and trade – all endured and continued to accelerate. So did cultural development: areas like art, literature and opera all evolved to new heights of elegance.

The development of the commercial economy made merchant families extremely wealthy, fuelling an arms race for culture and prestige. For all their power, merchants were not an elite class. They were not officially 'despised' like entertainers or prostitutes, but in some people's eyes were not a whole lot better. Chinese officialdom had a love-hate relationship with commerce. The Ming had supercharged the imperial economy by monetizing taxes and relied on merchant houses for such complex logistics operations as supplying grain to soldiers along China's far-flung borders. But the dynasty also reinforced a rigid Confucian social hierarchy that placed the refined work of scholars at the top and the parasitic profit-grubbing of merchants at the bottom. This Confucian disdain wasn't something that you could laugh off. Merchants spent fortunes trying to buy their way into the ranks of the scholarly elite, both because they sincerely accepted the cultural rhetoric of learning, refinement and morality and because culture opened doors. Merchants needed social status to conduct business. Even those who had more than enough money for themselves and their descendants strived for social position, spending fortunes building temples and orphanages and working their way into the refined circles of painters and poets.[23]

The quest for culture invariably led to the table. Wealthy families employed armies of cooks and vied to impress friends and clients with their generosity and sophistication. Foreign traders visiting the home of the wealthy Cantonese merchant Pan Wenyan in 1769 were fascinated by the lavish Chinese banquet, but positively floored by what they had the previous day – a full spread of European dishes, all expertly prepared by cooks brought in from Western employ in Southeast Asia. And of course, shock and awe was precisely the intended effect. This was hospitality, but it was also a power move. Just as in entertaining a business client today, a conspicuous display of cultured wealth is intended to leave the visitor both grateful and at least a little intimidated.

With all this money sloshing around, food culture became more lavish and more competitive. Moreover, since this was also an arena of literary achievement, there was no shortage of people to write it all down. Books of prose and poetry record the exquisite elite entertainment in the wealthy cities of Jiangnan: the leisurely dining along the Suzhou canals, the business banquets in fast-paced Hangzhou or Nanjing.[24] Books like 1764's *Pleasure Boats of Yangzhou* celebrate the culinary splendour of Qing China's richest commercial cities, recording local specialities – frogs fried with shredded pancakes, pork hock in vinegar and wine, chicken and duck in white and red oil, deep-fried shrimp, plate-grilled duck, chicken and duck innards. Writers from Jiangnan describe regional delicacies like cured Jinhua ham or simmered eel from the rivers near Hangzhou's scenic West Lake:

Braised Jinhua Ham (Qing)

The ham from Jinhua is the most renowned. When cooked, the taste becomes even better. Take a large square piece from the centre and soak it overnight in water that has been used to wash rice. In this way, you will remove the saltiness. Then add some good papaya wine and sanfu laoyou [a strong Jiangnan soy sauce] and simmer slowly over a low fire. It is ready to eat when the meat has become soft, and the soup is rich and fragrant.

Red-Simmered Eel (Qing)

Simmer eel in wine and water until tender; use tianmian-jiang in place of dark soy sauce.[25] Add to a pot and cook out the liquid. Add fennel and star anise and remove from the pot.

There are three mistakes when preparing this dish. The first is that the skin comes out wrinkled and not crisp; the second is that the meat breaks apart in the bowl and can't be picked up with chopsticks; the third is that salt and fermented beans are added too early, making the meat tough.[26]

Let's look at that last paragraph in the recipe for simmered eel. You will notice that recipes in this book are formatted a certain way, different from ordinary quotations. So, which is this? For the food writing of scholarly elites like *Pleasure Boats'* Li Dou (or Yuan Mei, who would copy the same advice in his *Garden of Contentment*) it's hard to decide. These writers are obviously not talking directly to the cook, but rather are demonstrating the discerning eye of a connoisseur, one who intends to impress his friends by identifying the flaws in the dish. But since we can be sure that the kitchen will hear about it, I still consider it part of the recipe, just in a more roundabout form.

Of course, China wasn't just Jiangnan. A new wealth of food writing reveals the diversity of China's regional cuisines, and the pride that people took in their particular culinary culture. Local guides and memoirs record each individual cornucopia. One early nineteenth-century source from coastal Shandong boasts forty different types of seafood. Other Shandong writers like early Qing agronomist Ding Yizeng dwell with obvious pride on the enviable wealth of produce available in his home town, listing ninety sorts of fruits and vegetables, livestock and seafood and food craft products like sauces and oils.[27] Farther inland, the cuisine of mountainous western Shandong (the part where Confucius had lived) was known for its produce: beef, onions, millet and sesame, and above all for its heavy use of salty and sour flavouring pastes. I called Shandong home for two years, and if I were to pick one dish that embodies that province, it would be coastal seaweed pickled in spiced brown vinegar. Or maybe carp from the Yellow River, fried crisp and topped with sweetened vinegar sauce. Or maybe just a plate of dumplings served with a piece of raw garlic and a dish of – you guessed it – brown vinegar. The late nineteenth- or early twentieth-century *Thoughts on a Vegetarian Diet* noticed something similar:

Shandong Cabbage (Late Qing)

Cut cabbage into square pieces and fry in sesame oil until fragrant. Add soy sauce and old vinegar, cover and cook until soft. Do not add any water, the two tastes should be strong. It is good served hot or cold. Restaurants in Jinan (the capital) are proficient at making this famous old dish.

Besides regional produce, another key difference that separated regions was not food, but fuel. According to one source, 'villages use wood stoves, cities burn coal.' Since coal burns hotter than wood, the emergence of coal explains why certain parts of China could develop industries like advanced metal smelting. It also explains why they could create recipes using high-temperature stir-frying and complicated roasting techniques like the one for crispy-skinned duck.[28]

Street vendor cooking over a coal stove, 1910. A wood-burning stove would have been far too heavy to carry around in this way.

Sichuan had always been known to prefer strong tastes – even the ancient texts note that people in Sichuan really liked their ginger. But even in Sichuan, chillies were not an instant success. Long after the spicy peppers were introduced to China, chillies are still nowhere to be found in the *Garden of Enlightenment*, a book of Sichuan recipes from the late eighteenth century, even in recipes that have 'hot' in the name:

Sweet and Hot Cabbage (Qing)

Take a cabbage that includes both heart and leaves. Cut it into pieces and place in a winnowing basket. Dip the pieces briefly in rapidly boiling water, remove and lay out to dry. Mix good rice vinegar and white sugar, add thin-sliced ginger, Sichuan peppercorns, mustard and sesame oil as needed.

Mix with the cabbage and place into a vat. The flavour will be lovely after three or four days.

Inland Sichuan also had a taste for seafood, which was brought in dried from the coast. The *Garden of Enlightenment* also gives instructions for reconstituting dried delicacies like shark fin and abalone (repeated soaking in fresh changes of water, just like *bacalao*). Alongside local river fish, dried seafood became a star of Sichuan cuisine, and featured in elaborate seafood banquets. A 1909 guide to food in Chengdu lists 45 different seafood dishes, including dishes of shark fin braised in soy sauce, served in soup and cooked with crab roe, as well as numerous preparations of sea cucumber, fish stomach, abalone, dried scallops, dried razor clams, squirrelfish, squid, fish skin and shrimp.[29]

In terms of actual dishes, much of what we know today as Sichuan cuisine is actually a recent import based on the refined techniques of Jiangnan and Guangdong.[30] The exchange was carried out through migration, ordinary farmers moving from the crowded east to the more open west, as well as the geographically mobile class of merchants and officials. It also travelled through the new culture of food literature.

In his massive *History of Sichuan Cuisine*, historian Lan Yong traced some of the iconic dishes through earlier generations of cookbooks, written all across China. The dish of Twice-Cooked Pork, often called the 'king of Sichuan cuisine', is a simple classic. As the name suggests, it is made by cooking pork twice, first by boiling a whole block of pork (hind leg or belly) to just under-done, then cutting the cooled meat into thin slices to stir-fry with aromatics: bean paste, green garlic shoots, Sichuan peppercorns, dried chillies and salty *tianmianjiang*. The taste of this classic dish changes the farther one travels from Sichuan (in Japan, Twice-Cooked Pork is often made with bacon and is more sweet than spicy), but for the most part, the ingredients and the technique leave little room for variation.

As closely as the dish is identified with Sichuan cuisine today, the modern version of twice-cooked pork does not appear in Sichuan menus or historical sources until the 1920s. Where it *does* appear – not with the same name but a similar technique – is in *Mr Song's Book of Longevity*, a book of recipes from early sixteenth-century Jiangnan:

Salt-Fried Pork (Ming)

First cook the pork until it is done. Slice it very thin, return it to the pan and fry until it changes colour. Add a small amount of water and cook until done. Scoop out any excess liquid and fry slowly. Even up any pieces that are not cooked. Add Sichuan peppercorns, salt and appropriate items [vegetables] and cook again.[31]

Even more striking, we only need to look back a few years to see that today's iconic classic used to look quite different. The

Fisherman drying his catch in a Shandong coastal village, 1937. Air drying
seafood preserves the flesh and concentrates its taste.

version in the 1956 *Family Cookbook* starts by dusting the pork in
sugar and steaming it inside an earthenware bowl, before frying
the sliced meat with garlic shoots and green beans. The 263-
page *Sichuan Cuisine* compiled in 1977 by the Sichuan Fruit and
Vegetable Company only includes versions for dry-cured ham or
sausage, which are first steamed to soften the meat, not to cook it.

But perhaps no path was as tortuous as that travelled by
Gongbao jiding, the dish familiar to many as *Kung pao* chicken. In
its most basic form, the dish we know today consists of chicken
(*ji*) cut into small cubes (*ding*), fried with numbing Sichuan
peppercorn and topped with crispy peanuts. That's the dish at

its core and as we will hear in a later chapter, there are many, many variations on that basic platform. The common story about *Gongbao jiding* is that the dish was invented by nineteenth-century Qing official Ding Baozhen, who was originally from the spice-loving southern province of Guizhou and subsequently stationed first in northern Shandong and then in the southwestern province of Sichuan, his retinue of cooks picking up new techniques at each post. In some versions of the story, the cooks created the dish to please their master's cosmopolitan palate; others claim that Ding got into the kitchen and invented the dish himself. In any case, the '*Gongbao*' in the name of the dish only makes sense if you know that it is probably an adaptation of one of Ding Baozhen's official titles.

Lan Yong is sceptical that this is the origin of what he calls 'perhaps the most richly mythologized dish in the entire history of Sichuan cuisine'. The opposite of Twice-Cooked Pork, *Gongbao jiding* has deep roots in Sichuan, pre-dating the Ding Baozhen story by centuries. A dish called 'Sichuan Chicken Cubes' appears in a Yuan-era collection called the *Practical Collection of Vital Home Skills*:

Sichuan Chicken Cubes (Yuan)

Clean 1 chicken and remove the organs, fry the meat in 3 liang of sesame oil, add thin-sliced onion and ½ a liang of salt and cook until seven-tenths done. Add a spoon of bean paste and ground white pepper, Sichuan pepper, fennel and a bowl of water to the pot. Add the chicken to the water to finish cooking and finish the dish by adding a bit of fine wine.[32]

This same recipe is repeated almost word for word in a number of Ming-dynasty cookbooks. Another very similar dish for fried chicken cubes (this one is not specifically identified with Sichuan) tracks through cookbooks of the Qing. So, when did this centuries-old recipe for chicken cubes become our dish of *Gongbao jiding*? Lan Yong thinks this one came from the early twentieth century, which is also when peanuts are first mentioned, and when the dish started to appear in English and Japanese-language cookbooks.

Other cities and regions all had their characteristic dishes and ways of eating. Guangdong was known for fresh ingredients and for seafood in particular; the northern plains for saltier, heartier cuisine. Beijing was home to the palace and the entire imperial bureaucracy, but it was hardly a centre of culture, at least not in the eyes of the wealthy south. Much of what we would come to know as Beijing cuisine was transplanted from Shandong.

China's food culture itself was nothing new. But new wealth and a flood of new food writing made regional cuisines much more visible than ever before. This is just one of many ways that China's food itself increasingly took on a life as a cultural commodity.

Wine and Song

Wine has a special place in food culture and cultured (as in civilized, not fermented) food. Like medicine, wine culture is so deep, so fundamental to every topic we have covered so far, that every part of this book – wealth and hospitality, local cuisine, medical theory – could easily be 'paired' with a related discussion of wine.

Wine is an indispensable part of eating. The phrase commonly used to praise a lavish banquet or a rich local food culture – 'good food and fine wine' – gives the two parity of importance. Wine is an indispensable part of human relations. Ancient ritual offered wine to show obedience to heaven and man. This custom remained and deepened over time.

It was the aura of romantic inebriation that brought wine into elite culture. Just like the Western image of a passionate artist

Self-portrait of late Ming artist Chen Hongshou, c. 1627. The image of a poet
in drunken repose is a familiar theme in Chinese painting.

cradling a half-finished bottle of red, we have the Chinese ideal of
the poetic recluse, alone on a mountaintop, the breeze ruffling his
long robes, hair loose and dishevelled, a freshly penned poem at
one side and a gourd freshly emptied of wine at the other. As different as they are, both images revolve around the idea that wine
frees the soul and the creative imagination.

The ancients had condemned drinking as a vice, but over time,
alcohol's cultural standing began to improve. Wine picked up an
identity of Daoist transcendence and artistic nonconformity.

So, what is it that separates an inebriated free spirit from a regular old drunk? A significant part of it was this sort of cultural model or what today's science of marketing might call 'brand ambassadors'. Like any aesthetic ideal, China's wine culture was heavily influenced by the fame of individuals, people who embodied the unique pairing of literary talent and the liberating effects of drink. Not surprisingly, many of these free spirits were poets.

For fifth-century poet Tao Qian, wine was one of the simple comforts of home and friendship, but also a way to forget the cares of life:

Return to Country Life, Poem Number 5

I strain the new wine,
And treat my neighbours to a chicken.
The sun sets, the house grows dark;
With thorny firewood as bright candles.

Ninth Day of Ninth Month in the Jiyou Year [409]

Changes come one after the other
Isn't this life tiresome?
. . .
How can I relate my feelings?
Just let me enjoy my cloudy wine.

Zhang Yue, a Tang poet whom we will encounter again later, expressed the euphoria that many readers will recognize as a very particular stage in the grand drama of a drunken evening:

Written While Drunk

When I'm drunk, my delight knows no limits –
Even better than when I'm sober.
My movements all become dance,
And every word is a poem!

But of all of China's romantic drinkers, none was more famous than the Tang dynasty free spirit, Li Bai; this comes from 'Sharing a Drink beneath the Moon':

> If you find happiness in wine
> Don't share it with the sober.

The most celebrated poet of China's golden age of poetry, Li Bai's poems are deeply emotional, reflecting on joy and loss, reunion with old friends and the poignant feeling of seeing people and places for the last time. Wine provides the setting for these meetings of hello and goodbye, and sets free pent-up emotions that are too profound or too painful to face:

Waking from Drunkenness on a Spring Day

> Life in the world is just a big dream;
> I will not spoil it with any labour or care.
> So I stayed drunk all day,
> Lying helpless at the porch in front of my door.
>
> When I awoke, I blinked at the garden lawn;
> A lonely bird was singing amid the flowers.
> I asked myself, what time it could be
> The Spring wind was telling the orioles.
>
> Moved by its song I soon began to sigh,
> And, as wine was there, I filled my own cup.
> Wildly singing I waited for the moon to rise;
> When my song was over, all my senses had gone.[33]

The Garden of Contentment

In the same way that wine culture was about far more than intoxication, earning the reputation of a culinary sophisticate required far more than just the financial wherewithal to stuff your guests with abalone and swallow's nest. Food touched upon all of the areas of culture prized by China's bookish elite – religion, medicine, classical texts, agronomy and poetry, all filtered through the sieve of taste and refinement. This is what the great sinologist K. C. Chang meant when he said that the Chinese gentleman was known for 'his knowledge and skills pertaining to food and drink'.[34] The connoisseur knew which teahouse had the best opera performance, which out-of-the-way dining hole was known for unmatched skill in a particular dish and which obscure writers and artists would make good table companions. And of course, one had to know the food itself – what was in season, what food came from where and how to match a rare wine with a poem. A connoisseur had to eat with culture and style.

The rising status of cuisine fed into a new wave of food publishing. This was a good time for Chinese publishing generally, with new printing centres popping up to serve a market hungry for popular topics like fiction, drama and religious texts.[35] Food was part of this wave, with dozens of new titles coming into circulation. The late-Ming title *Mr Song's Book of Longevity* outlines over a thousand types of food – both edible and medicinal – and 1,340 different preparations. *Yi Ya's Recorded Thoughts* is a snapshot of Jiangnan food markets, introducing 150 different types of local products. The more general category of poetic writings also features food as a facet of local life and colour. In the pages of his memoir, the Tang poet Zhang Yue (the one who dances when he drinks) outlines 58 local specialities from 14 different places. The mid-Qing *Flavouring the Pot* concisely recounts over three hundred recipes, many of which were repurposed from older collections.[36]

Of these new books, none was better known than the 1792 *Recipes from the Garden of Contentment*, the work of China's rogue and roguish gourmet Yuan Mei. A scholar and poet from the southern city of Hangzhou, Yuan Mei's book is a paean to local produce, the arts of cuisine and the pleasures of the table.

Yuan begins with exposition, short passages on what the cook must know: the true nature of food, flavour, colour, seasons and utensils. These are followed by a list of cardinal sins: cooks who destroy food with artifice or showmanship, ones who are careless, who slavishly follow fashion, resort to using heated dishes, over-cook meat or dump everything into one pot, producing 'soups that resemble silted water from an agitated barrel; grey broths like the leftovers in a dye vat'. Yuan Mei's ire is not only for the cooks. He reserves special irritation for drunken guests:

> Only one who is alert can tell the difference between right and wrong. Likewise, only one who is mindful can discern the differences between good and bad flavours. Yi Yin once observed: 'The profound nuances of flavour cannot be rightly expressed in words.' If a drunkard cannot even speak, how can there be any hope that he can express, much less discern the flavours of anything?

> I occasionally see people playing drinking games during banquets, their minds clouded and absent from too much alcohol. In such an inebriated state, those great dishes they were eating might as well have been sawdust. The heads of those preoccupied with drinking are somewhere else entirely, with their faculties for judging food thrown out the door. If one really must indulge in drink, first have a proper meal where the dishes can be tasted, then only afterwards bring out the alcohol. In this way, you get the best of both worlds.[37]

Yuan then goes on to describe no fewer than 326 separate dishes, although in a way that suits the table more than it does the kitchen. Just like many modern cookbooks, this is a book *about* food, one that is 'produced at a desk rather than by the fire'.[38] Technique is often presented in fairly basic terms. Instead, where we see the author most clearly is in the titbits of information that he attaches to different recipes: the best way to enjoy a particular dish, where he has eaten it in the past or who is known to prepare it especially well. Some of these descriptions are just a simple note, others go on at length:

Taro Flour Balls (Qing)

Grind taro into a paste and dry in the sun, combine with rice flour and form into balls. The Daoists at Chaotian Gong make taro flour balls filled with wild chicken. They are delicious.

Method for Making Crispy Cakes (Qing)

Take 1 bowl of solidified pork oil and 1 bowl of clear water, mix these together and pour out onto raw flour like you are making ganbing [rolled pastry]; work the dough until it is soft. Separately, mix steamed flour into pork oil until the mixture is even and soft; it should not be stiff. Shape the raw flour mixture into walnut-sized balls and the cooked flour mixture into slightly smaller ones and then stuff these inside the raw flour balls. Roll to 7 cun long and 3 cun wide. Fold these into the shape of bowls and fill with melon pulp.

Braised Bamboo Shoots with Ham (Qing)

Slice winter bamboo shoots and ham into squares and braise them together. Soak the ham twice to remove the salt and braise with rock sugar until tender.

According to Xi Wushan, if you have already cooked the ham and wish to save it for another day, you must keep it in the cooking water. If it is kept without its cooking water, it will dry out; if kept in clear water, it will lose its flavour.

And those frogs? Yuan Mei only outlines the basics. With the possible addition of chillies, this recipe is very similar to how frogs would be prepared today:

How to Cook Water Chickens (Qing)

Use only the legs and discard the rest of the body. First, scald the legs with oil [ladle hot oil over the top], then add the highest quality soy sauce,[39] sweet wine, and braise with ginger and squash. Or cut into pieces and fry. The taste is similar to chicken.

Regardless of whether he could function within the kitchen, Yuan Mei most certainly did know his way around a library. Just like other cookbooks of the time, *Recipes from the Garden of Contentment* draws freely on other texts, and not just the work of other elite writers like *Pleasure Boats'* Li Dou. The recipe for taro flour balls was copied word for word from *Flavouring the Pot.* So was the detailed recipe of boiled sheep's head:

Boiled Sheep's Head (Qing)

Clean the sheep's head of fur, and burn off anything that cannot be cleaned. Wash the head clean, cut it open, cook until tender and remove any fur from inside the mouth. Cut the eyeballs into thirds, remove the black membrane, chop fine and cook in a soup of a fattened old hen, add mushrooms, 4 liang of sweet wine and a cup of soy sauce. To make it spicy, add 12 small peppercorns and 12 sections of onion; if using garlic, add 1 cup of good rice vinegar.

Yuan Mei's recipe is identical, down to the number of pepper-corns, the only addition being that of diced bamboo alongside the mushrooms.

So, does that make Yuan Mei a plagiarist? If he was then he certainly wasn't alone. *All* the food books from this period drew on each other; these authors were just copying down recipes that were already being spread in countless kitchens across China. What all this writing – and all this copying – did was to allow cuisine, just like other areas of Chinese culture, to spread and develop a national character.

The Banquet: *Dream of Red Mansions*

China's late imperial cuisine reached its peak alongside other arts and occasionally crossed over into them. Food is especially prom-inent in the characteristic literary form of the time – the novel. Describing the dishes at a feast or the culinary quirks of a side character does more than just dress out a scene, it also leaves clues about mood, status, personality and motivation.

The late-Ming novel *Heroes of the Water Margin* is the story of 108 antiheroes who, one by one, flee corrupt society to seek refuge on a remote mountain. Along the way, there is plenty of fighting and feasting, with food taking a symbolic role to advance the plot and explain each of the characters.[40] The most common theme is drinking and many of the episodes either begin or end with inhuman amounts of alcohol. The heroes especially love their beef, which symbolizes both their strength and their out-sider status, since cattle slaughter was restricted by law. In one famous scene, former soldier Wu Song finishes an evening of drinking by staggering outside and beating a tiger to death with his bare hands. Quoting his tavern order to 'slice me off two *jin* of beef!' is still a way of announcing to the world that your evening is going to get wild.

Moving from martial arts to erotic romance, food also plays an outsized role in the *Plum in the Golden Lotus Vase*. This Ming novel revolves around the romantic exploits of a dissipated youth who spends time, money and physical effort on a string of sexual liaisons. It's thus no surprise that we hear constantly about foods that rebuild strength. Not just the main character, but all of the courtesans, prostitutes and consorts that he meets along the way – one of these gives the main female character a gift of fresh cheese to 'moisten the inner organs, ease constipation and aid the twelve meridians'. The main character is advised to eat stewed pigeon, a dish that any reader of the time would have recognized as a way to nourish the blood.

The food in *Plum in the Golden Lotus Vase* also conveys just how lush these dissolute lives are. Tucked into the story are over two hundred separate dishes: roasted pig's head, stewed trotters, marinated goose gizzards and webs, steamed sun-dried chicken, deep-fried roasted bones, fried kidneys, smoked meat, fried noodles with tendon, sour bamboo soup, crystal (deep-fried with egg whites) trotters and goose . . . All in all, the book mentions 21 different techniques just for cooking meat. But the meat the book's characters especially love is duck, which we see marinated in lees, stewed, braised, cured in spices, smoked, roasted, baked and cooked over a spit.[41] A sustaining dish of duck from the early eighteenth-century *Secrets of the Table* puts us right inside the novel:

Duck Geng (Early Qing)

Boil a duck to seven-tenths done. Remove from the water and dice [lit. cut to the size of dice]. Return to the cooking water and add spices, cooking wine, soy sauce, bamboo, or any type of mushroom or fungus. Pine nuts or shelled white [blanched?] walnuts would also be suitable.

The novel that is synonymous with food even today is the eighteenth-century *Dream of Red Mansions*, which describes the rise and fall of an aristocratic family, with two branches living in adjacent compounds. Although the precise setting is never clearly stated, the meticulous description of life leaves little doubt that this is meant to take place in the high years of the Qing dynasty. As the novel's many plots twist and turn, we peer into the over-lapping worlds of scholars and servants, men and women, rich and poor, the fine details of their interactions reflected in care-fully chosen words, gifts and gestures. Much more than just a nice story, the *Dream of Red Mansions* is a storehouse of insight into the complex society of the Qing at its zenith.

Part of the novel's realism is in its detail: the clothes, homes and furnishings of a mildly wealthy rural household, along with the customs, greetings and small rituals that make up daily life, including the food that frames the plot and the characters. Meals are the site of conflict and reconciliation, plans are hatched over plates of snacks and betrayal is often served with a cup of tea.

Dream of Red Mansions mentions dozens of dishes by name: soup made with sour bamboo and chicken skin, lotus leaf *geng*, soup with wild duckling, soup with ham and fresh bamboo, soup with shrimp balls and chicken skin, roast wild chicken, wild chicken feet, fried wild chicken, fried duck bones, fried quail, marinated quail, marinated goose feet, smoked dried duck, duck marinated in wine and steamed, quail eggs, stewed chicken eggs, pork shoulder stewed with ham, lamb steamed in milk, roasted deer, chicken bone marrow with bamboo, steamed *baozi* with tofu skin, salt-fried bean sprouts, steamed taro. We also see congee made with red rice, sticky rice, field rice and river rice and flavoured with duck, dates, smoked meat, salted vegetables or swallow's nest. The eggs below are from *Secrets of the Table* and would have been a nice, simple treat. The *Dream*'s characters would also have been keenly aware of the distinct medicinal properties of the spices in the broth:

Eggs Cooked in Sauce (Early Qing)

Boil chicken and duck eggs until six-tenths done, and then use a chopstick to lightly crack the shells. Add tianmianjiang to the cooking water, along with cinnamon, Sichuan peppercorn, fennel seeds and onion whites. Cook for an hour and then add 1 cup of shaojiu.

After cooking the chicken and duck eggs, along with Jinhua ham, scoop them out of the pot. Crack egg shells again and return to the pot to cook for another 1 or 2 hours. The taste is exquisite.

If the shells are removed completely, the taste is even better.

Compared to the dishes in *Plum in the Golden Lotus Vase*, you'll notice more wild game, sheep and deer. While both books reflect a generally southern taste, *Dream of Red Mansions* also shows the influence of the Qing's Manchu rulers. There is dairy, too, including the combination of meat and milk seen in previous chapters. One moment of drama breaks out when Nursemaid Li, who once had breastfed the family's favoured son, was denied a bowl of yoghurt:

Nursemaid Li demanded, 'Don't you talk to me about drinking this bowl of cow's milk, I deserve something more valuable than this. Does the young master forget how he grew so big and strong? He drank my milk that came from my blood and now he is going to be angry that I drank this bowl of cow's milk'? And in a huff, she finished off the bowl.[42]

Medical concerns also feature prominently. Older family members talk constantly about their ailments and how to fix them. At one point the Dowager eats a dish of foetal lamb steamed in milk, instructing her younger relatives that this dish is specifically to preserve the strength of the elderly and that they are not to touch it. Another character recovering from illness is served a dish of taro cake with sticky dates, which, like the stewed pigeon, rebuilds the body's strength after over-exertion. The fermented dish of sour bamboo with chicken-skin soup is given as a hangover cure.

Dishes change by season: warming foods in winter and cooling ones to dissipate the heat of a summer afternoon. Besides making medical sense, this attention to seasonality is also a nod to the Confucian precept to eat according to nature's own schedule. One minor character is shown bragging about his lavish birthday presents, which include an out-of-season lotus root and watermelon, hinting at a self-serving recklessness that we eventually see erupt in a murderous temper.

Where did the novel's cuisine come from? A bit of detective work can trace individual dishes to contemporary recipe collections like *Flavouring the Pot*.[43] Take, for example, the following passage, where the main character is preparing for an audience with the Dowager:

> Baoyu nodded and changed his clothes, then sipped a little of the lotus seed and date broth that a maid had brought on a small plate, then took a piece of crystallized ginger from the plate that Xueyue brought him.[44]

While most readers are following the narrative, wondering what Baoyu will say to the Dowager, we might instead choose to ask, 'What about that piece of crystallized ginger'? Actually, even calling it crystallized ginger is an unavoidable bit of licence from the translator. The original text actually means *prepared* ginger and a bit of effort to find the recipe in a slightly earlier collection from roughly the same place tells us exactly how:

Prepared Purple Ginger (Qing)

4 jin of ginger, remove the peel and rinse, pat dry and place in a porcelain bowl. Add 1 jin of sugar and 2 jin of soy sauce. Chop 2 liang each of cinnamon, star anise, orange peel and perilla into small pieces and mix thoroughly. Leave this to dry from the beginning to the end of the hot season, covering the bowl with a red thread mesh to keep out insects. At the end of the season, it is ready to store. This ginger is really powerful, it can cure all sorts of ailments.[45]

So, we now know that this piece of crystallized ginger was in fact more salty than sweet, heavily spiced and dyed brownish purple from the soy sauce and perilla leaves. Ginger also comes with a kick, so this last act of taking a piece on his way through the door might have been a subtle hint that Baoyu was more nervous than he was letting on, similar in narrative function to seeing a character grab a cigarette before walking into the big meeting. Or maybe Baoyu just wanted to freshen his breath. In any case, this small detail hardly changes the plot, but it does bring us just that tiny bit closer to the character and his time.

One dish is so synonymous with the book that it is easily mistaken as a pure invention of the author. More than just a passing mention, this dish is given as a complete recipe, which pops up in the middle of a conversation – as recipes so often do:

Salted Fish Aubergine (Eggplant, Qing)

Laughing, the Dowager said, 'Bring our guest some salted fish aubergine.'

Lady Feng obediently grabbed a piece of salted fish aubergine in her chopsticks and placed it in Granny Liu's mouth and smiling said, 'You eat aubergine every day, try ours and tell us how you like the taste.'

Granny Liu laughed, 'Stop kidding me, if aubergine could taste like this, forget grain, we would grow nothing but aubergine.'

Everyone had a laugh. 'Really, it is aubergine, no kidding.'

Taken aback, Granny Liu responded 'This really is aubergine? Well, I wasn't paying enough attention. Let me try another piece carefully.'

Lady Feng placed another piece in Granny Liu's mouth. And after chewing it for some time, Granny Liu smiled, 'It has some aubergine taste, but it doesn't seem like aubergine. Tell me how you prepared it, so I can make it for myself at home.'

Lady Feng replied, 'It's not hard. You take freshly picked aubergine and remove the peel. Take only the good meat, cut it into cubes and deep-fry them in chicken fat. Then take dried chicken, shitake mushrooms, spring bamboo, flavoured dried tofu and different-coloured melon seeds, cut them into cubes and braise them in chicken broth until the liquid is all gone. Mix with vegetable oil and a spoon of sesame oil and store them in a tightly sealed porcelain jar. When you want to eat them, just toss them with some fried chicken feet and there you are!'

Despite a conspicuous absence of fish, this dish has come to be known as 'Salted Fish Aubergine'. Hobbyists with a passion for historical cuisine have focused on it as one of the characteristic dishes of the novel, and made their own versions, resulting in a fairly wide variety of interpretations, some of which have precious little to do with the dish described by Lady Feng. Some video channels recreate it simply as a dish of fried aubergine, cooked while wearing period costume, or in the romantic surroundings of an outdoor kitchen.

I tried the recipe exactly as described, using rendered pork oil instead of chicken fat. As expected, the fried aubergine absorbed an obscene amount of oil, which may be precisely why Granny Liu initially mistook the vegetable for a meat dish. Or it may be a case of the book neglecting to mention the common steps of steaming or drying the cut aubergine before it is fried. Certainly, if the dish is meant to be stored, most of the water would need to be cooked out and the easiest way to do that would be to sun-dry the cubed aubergine first before frying it. In any case, something does seem to be missing from the description.

To add to the confusion, some editions of the book present a *second* version of this same iconic dish. This one is significantly more elaborate:

Salted Fish Aubergine (Second Version)

You take new aubergine from April or May, remove the peel and the stem, leaving only the good flesh. Cut this into strips as fine as hair and dry it in the sun. Cook one fat hen into soup and steam the dried aubergine over the soup so the flavour enters the aubergine, then again dry it completely. Repeat this nine times, each time drying out the aubergine until crisp. Store it in a porcelain jar and seal it up tight. When it is time to eat, take out a small plate and mix it with fried chicken feet.

Hearing this, Granny Liu shook her head and replied, 'By the Buddha, you used ten chickens to make this? No wonder it tastes so good.'

I quote these two recipes at length because they significantly change the meaning of the encounter. Granny Liu was, after all, a poor relative. It is one thing to serve her a well-prepared dish of aubergine fried in animal fat, artfully braised with chicken and vegetables, but another thing altogether to present her with a single dish of aubergine that requires not only ten chickens but days of labour. The first one is showing good taste, the second one is taking a ridiculously luxurious dish and casually passing it off as the simplest of trifles. Even if the gift was well intentioned, the episode (which ends with Granny Liu suffering from some particularly unpleasant gastric distress) shows that these two halves of the family live in very different worlds.

But whichever version, the dish is no mystery – nor was it invented by the novel. We have already seen other dishes of crispy fried aubergine. The Yuan dynasty dish of 'meat and oil aubergine' is one. An even earlier dish for 'quail aubergine' describes steps similar to the second version:

Quail Aubergine (Song)

Chop a fresh aubergine into fine threads, dip in boiling water and toss with salt, bean paste, Sichuan pepper, dill, fennel, Chinese liquorice, orange peel, almond and red bean paste until even. After sun drying and steaming the pieces, store them. When it is time to eat, soften them in boiling water and fry them in sesame oil.

This recipe comes from the twelfth-century *Mrs Wu's Records from the Kitchen* and, like most of the wisdom in that book, it seeks to solve a practical dilemma of the garden – in this case, how to preserve a sudden abundance of fresh vegetables. This method does indeed reduce a table full of aubergines into a surprisingly small pile of thin, dried strips that can be saved in a covered jar.

Just like pork that has been cured into bacon, the dried aubergine then becomes its own culinary product. The recipe in *Mrs Wu's Records from the Kitchen* advocates softening the thin strips with a simple dip in boiling water, to retain the dish's taste and texture.

I prepared this version and had a great deal more success with the dish than with the one adapted from the novel. Rather than boiling water, I briefly braised the thin strips in a dish of stewed pork. (This was at the insistence of a neighbouring grandmother who passed by as I was moving my bamboo drying trays into better sun.) The reconstituted aubergine retained its chewiness and intensity, but it was clear that too much cooking in water (for example steaming over ten pots of chicken broth) would have broken it down completely. In any case, the name 'Salted Fish Aubergine' isn't referring to the flavour, it is the technique of spicing and drying the aubergine for long-term storage – just as one would with salted fish.

So, let's set a table. Because the book's characters are constantly eating, we have plenty of settings to choose from – sprawling family banquets and intimate garden parties, held inside or outside the family home, on occasions happy and sad. But I am partial to the banquet introduced at the beginning of this chapter, the small New Year party held by the family's elderly Dowager Shi.[46]

Over the course of the evening, we see a parade of dishes come and go. The food stays physically in the background but remains

Quail aubergine. These spiced and dried strips can last for months.

The dowager's garden parties were times to relax.

in the forefront of conversation: a constant stream of comments expressing concern that the servants are all well fed, that it's not the New Year without dumplings or that duck congee is too oily for the Dowager's stomach. The only time we actually see the food is when the dishes are being taken away.

So, what would this party have served? We can make a few guesses based on dishes that appear elsewhere in the novel. Taro, winter bamboo, quail and deer are all typical winter foods: cold by season and warming by nature. And from the many cookbooks of the time, we can choose plenty of ways to imagine how they might have been prepared.

As China's final dynasties grew more powerful and wealthy, its cuisine grew ever more elaborate. *Red Mansions* may be fiction, but it's fiction that hits close to real life, reflecting the tastes, customs, mores and values of a culinary tradition that had reached a peak of sophistication. The novel continues to captivate readers, not just fans of fiction, but those hoping to capture the taste – if only in romanticized form – of China's imperial-era cuisine.

4

Fancy Foods and Foreign Fads
China Eats the World

Shanghai has always been a city of workers. Not far from
the city's iconic spots - the imposing banks along the Bund,
the lithe art deco architecture of the French concession
or the stately courtyards of the Chinese elites - were
neighbourhoods of humbler terraced houses and tangles
of crowded tenements. Along the city's edge, the truly poor
took up residence in makeshift shelters of reed mats.

This was Shanghai in 1921. New Year's Day,
to be precise.

Turning off Nanjing Road, the city's famed commercial
street, we duck into a side alley to escape the chill and
climb up a flight of stairs to the Sweet Fruit and Cookies
Café, serving European and American high cuisine. We
settle the bill - one yuan per person - before taking our
seats. For this price, we can look forward to a set lunch
chosen from no fewer than fifteen items.

Besides being good value, this lunch is also something
of an adventure.

We've already had a glance at the menu and some
of the dishes seem familiar enough - soup with ham,

chicken and mushrooms, chilled beef, pork ribs cooked with
pineapple, boiled ham, roast chicken and five-coloured
vegetables. But other dishes are more exotic. Fish with
pea and shrimp sauce or stuffed pheasant served on a
bed of spinach with a smoked meat sauce – seem like very
different ways to eat otherwise familiar foods. Some
of the dishes, like this *'mianzhipi'*, are an absolute mystery.
And what in the world is 'Empress pudding'? We'll soon
find out.

With the optimism of a new year, we settle into our seats,
confident that regardless of how the meal turns out, at least
we can look forward to a coffee at the end.

Culinary Celestials

The earliest Europeans to visit China were, in a word,
awestruck.

Arriving in the 1200s, the first trickle of intrepid visitors
– Friar Odoric, William of Rubruck and of course Marco Polo –
knew little or nothing of China before setting out on their travels.
This was the era of Mongol rule, so, travelling east, each went first
to pay their respects at the courts of Mongol princes. They were
none too impressed by what they saw. They admired the Mongols
for their martial prowess and rough honesty, but also considered
them to be wild and barbaric.

Those who ventured farther and found their way to the
wealthy commercial cities of China's coast were astounded by
the sheer wealth of the place. Friar Odoric noted that silk was so
common that even commoners could wear it. Marco Polo, who
spent the longest time and travelled the most widely inside China,
described cities of wealth and size that would rival the great port
of Constantinople. It's little wonder that he wasn't believed.

Among the scenes of plenty, Marco Polo describes the bustling food markets of Hangzhou:

> In each of the squares is held a market three days in the week, frequented by 40,000 or 50,000 persons, who bring thither for sale every possible necessary of life, so that there is always an ample supply of every kind of meat and game, as of roebuck, red-deer, fallow-deer, hares, rabbits, partridges, pheasants, francolins, quails, fowls, capons and of ducks and geese an infinite quantity; for so many are bred on the lake that for a Venice groat of silver you can have a couple of geese and two pairs of ducks. Then there are the shambles where the larger animals are slaughtered, such as calves, beeves, kids and lambs, the flesh of which is eaten by the rich and the great dignitaries.
>
> Those markets make a daily display of every kind of vegetables and fruits; and among the latter there are in particular certain pears of enormous size, weighing as much as ten pounds apiece and the pulp of which is white and fragrant like a confection; besides peaches in their season both yellow and white, of every delicate flavour.[1]

Elsewhere, Marco Polo observed the abundance of grain, livestock, fish and spices: cinnamon, cloves, ginger, spikenard, galingale, rhubarb and a fruit resembling saffron (possibly turmeric), as well as 'other spices which never reach our countries, so we need say nothing about them'. Marco Polo visited the salt wells of Sichuan and recounted the 'enormous quantities' of sugar (another relative rarity in Europe) made in Fuzhou. He praised the quality of the rice wine almost everywhere he visited. At a time when Europeans considered pepper a luxury, he recorded that cities like Hangzhou were importing unbelievable amounts.[2]

Other early visitors marvelled at the foods they had never imagined. A Spanish missionary who lived in the southeastern province of Fujian in the mid-seventeenth century waxed lyrical about the wonder that is tofu:

The delicacy that is widely used, common, inexpensive and abundant in all China and which is eaten by everyone in that empire, from the emperor to the most ordinary Chinese person – the emperor and lords as a treat and the ordinary people for sustenance and necessity – is called tofu, which is bean paté. I did not see how they make it; they make milk from the beans, curdle it like cheese as large as a millstone, five or six fingers thick. The whole mass is as white as fresh snow. It has everything you can wish for. It can be eaten raw, but is normally cooked and prepared with vegetables, fish and other things. On its own it is bland, but cooked in the aforementioned way it is good and is excellent fried in cow butter. They also dry and smoke it, mixing in caraway seeds, which is even better. It is incredible what vast quantities of it are purchased and eaten in China and hard to conceive that there is such a large quantity of beans. A Chinese person who has tofu, vegetables and rice does not need anything else to work.[3]

One thing that Marco Polo did *not* do was bring back the recipe for noodles – the story being that the technique was supposedly taught to his sailors by a beautiful village girl. That bit of orientalism was invented for an American pasta marketing campaign during the 1920s. (Although it is true that Arab traders probably did introduce spaghetti, which is different from the pasta of the ancient Mediterranean.)

A few centuries after Marco Polo's overland trek, European merchants began arriving by sea, and for a time they continued to uphold this prevailing image of China as a prosperous country that ate well. In 1769, a homesick young English cadet described the two spectacular dinners he enjoyed at the home of wealthy Cantonese merchant Pan Wenyan:

> These fêtes were given on the 1st and 2nd October, the first of them being a dinner, dressed and served à la mode Anglaise, the Chinamen on that occasion using and awkwardly enough, knives and forks and in every respect conforming to the European fashion. The best wines of all sorts were amply supplied . . .
>
> The second day, on the contrary everything was Chinese, all the European guests eating or endeavouring to eat, with chopsticks, no knives or forks being at table. The entertainment was splendid, the victuals supremely good, the Chinese loving high dishes and keeping the best of cooks.[4]

This first phase of the culinary encounter between China and Europe flowered during the early years of the Canton trade. Western merchants and missionaries – often fairly elite personages – set up shop in Guangzhou, the only city that was open to most of them, and tried as best they could to make themselves comfortable there. This meant bringing in the comforts of home, but for this adventurous group, 'home' could be a fairly fluid idea. Many brought along cooks, families and tastes that already reflected a lifetime of travel.

One example of this sort of mixing is the unique cuisine of the former Portuguese colony at Macao, recently named a UNESCO City of Gastronomy. A database of recipes collected from Macanese home and restaurant cooks covers a wide range of styles: some dishes of unmistakable European or Chinese origin and others that were clearly adapted from Portuguese settlements in Goa, Malacca, Angola and Brazil.[5] Macanese cuisine developed much of its unique taste from ingredient substitution – turmeric for saffron, coconut milk for dairy, smoky *chouriço* for Chinese sausage or dried ham, tamarind or sour plums in place of lemon and a two-way exchange of rice wine and grape wine. Macanese cuisine also incorporated such entirely new tastes as Malay chilli *sambal* or pungent *balichão* (*belacan*) shrimp paste. Over time, these blendings produced Caldeirada de Carne, a meaty stew that combines chicken, beef, ham and Chinese sausage in one pot, as well as dishes like chicken stir-fried with turmeric, rich curries and steamed egg and milk desserts.

Sick Man at the Table

Just one century after our young merchant was struck by the cosmopolitan hospitality of Pan Wenyan, the prevailing Western images of China had changed from those of wealth and sophistication to those of poverty, depravity and filth.

Just one century, but what a century it had been. In that short time, the tide of trade had turned against China, due in large part to the British introduction of opium. Money began flowing out of China and when the country tried to stop it, the response was not one but two disastrous wars with Great Britain. But the problems didn't stop there. Over the eighteenth century, China's population *tripled*. That sort of massive population growth outpaced the ability even of the new wonder crops to feed. And sooner or later, hungry people tend to get violent. One internal rebellion during the nineteenth century killed more people than the *entire* mortality of both sides of the First World War – and that was just one rebellion out of a century of violence. As the Qing government became mired in corruption and dysfunction, foreign observers were increasingly likely to see China not as the Celestial Kingdom, but as the 'sick man' of Asia.[6]

More and more foreigners were living in China, but the great majority lived in sections of cities like Tianjin or Shanghai that were under direct foreign administration, the nineteenth century's answer to a gated community. By the dawn of the twentieth century, the foreign presence was looking a lot like slow-motion colonization. You can still see the foreign influence of this period in its architecture: French churches in Shanghai, Russian onion domes in Harbin, thick-walled German houses in Qingdao and red brick British administrative buildings in Tianjin.

Foreign residents in China were also more connected to home. A world with steamships is much smaller than one plied by sailing ships, and by the close of the nineteenth century, foreigners living in treaty ports could access directly the latest news, fashions and food from London, Paris or San Francisco.

All this made cultural interaction very lopsided. As Westerners came to view China through the lens of the strange and exotic, they adopted a very different view of Chinese cuisine. It was during this time that such absurdities as restaurants padding their meat stores with neighbourhood cats began to appear as stock images in popular pulp adventure novels.

The global expansion of Western power coincided with another big revolution – industrialization. Along with the new reign of the steamship, all manner of innovative technologies were revolutionizing how food was made, processed, stored and transported. Each advance made the world that much smaller and new foods that much cheaper, and by the turn of the twentieth century, these changes were coming in faster than ever. Naturally, this increasingly global food system followed the contours of imperialism and centred on where the money was, notably in such great trade cities as Liverpool and London. But it wasn't only for the rich. On the eve of the First World War, a working-class table in London might routinely serve the produce of the world: exotics like tea, coffee and cocoa, as well as more ordinary foods

– beef from Argentina, butter from New Zealand or apples from Canada – because importing these foods from across the globe was cheaper than producing them at home. With some dismay, an American economist writing in 1924 described just how quickly and deeply his countrymen had become accustomed to and even bored by the wealth of globalization:

> Today one sits down to breakfast, spreads out a napkin of Irish linen, opens the meal with a banana from Central America, follows with a cereal of Minnesota sweetened with the product of Cuban cane and ends with a Montana lamb chop and cup of Brazilian coffee. Our daily life is a trip around the world, yet the wonder of it gives us not a single thrill.[7]

Foreign Foods

For China's food, this meant two things. The first effect of globalization was that Chinese diets started to include more and more foreign foods. Now, if you have been paying attention, you will know China is no stranger to foreign foods. The vast majority of China's fruits, vegetables, grains, spices and cooking techniques originally came from somewhere else. What made this influx of new foods unlike the new vegetables of the Han or the Tang, the high-yield rice of the Song or the New World miracle crops of the early Qing was that those earlier exchanges were all food systems that were transplanted to China – that is, new crops being grown on Chinese soil. This was different. It was the dawn of China's integration with global production chains. From this moment on, more and more people in China would be eating food that was produced somewhere else.

Think about the humble tin of condensed milk. We might think of condensed milk as a dessert, a sweet topping for fruit or ice cream. But when it was invented in 1850, canned milk was revolutionary. Canning extended the life of a fresh product from under one day to months or years. The result was that milk suddenly became available where it never had been before – it was provisioned to soldiers of the Union Army, followed cowboys into the American West and miners into the Australian gold fields.

And eventually, it came to Asia. In 1876, a village chieftain in inland Malaya surprised a visiting British official with English biscuits and a cup of *teh tarik*, strong dark tea sweetened with condensed milk. In 1880, the Chinese city of Canton was importing 34,000 tins of the stuff per year. By the 1930s, it was commonplace in middle-class Chinese households, at least in places like Shanghai.[8]

What drove Chinese people to embrace this new food? Association with Westerners was one factor. While China was in a political tailspin, the British Empire was confidently striding the globe. Governments across the region faced the choice of either digging in or trying to adapt to the new reality, starting by understanding whatever it was that made the Westerners so powerful.

Japan was the first to jump ship, deciding that it was time to 'leave Asia' and embark on a programme of reforms to emulate Western science, military practices, dress and diet. In terms of food, that meant abandoning centuries of a largely vegetarian diet and encouraging ordinary people to eat meat, especially beef. The young Meiji emperor kicked off the new custom by eating beef to celebrate the new year in 1872.[9]

Beef became the centre and symbol of a new culture war, the fault line in the tug of war between past and future. As one character in the satirical story *Sitting around the Stew Pot* described to a fellow diner:

Excuse me, but beef is certainly a most delicious thing, isn't it? Once you get accustomed to its taste, you can never go back to deer or wild boar again. I wonder why we in Japan haven't eaten such a clean thing before? ... We really should be grateful that even people like ourselves can now eat beef, thanks to the fact that Japan is steadily becoming a truly civilized country. Of course, there are some unenlightened boors who cling to their barbaric superstitions and say that eating meat defiles you so much that you can't pray any more before Buddha and the gods. Such nonsense shows they simply don't understand natural philosophy. Savages like that should be made to read Fukuzawa's article on eating beef.[10]

He was, of course, referring to inveterate Westernizer Fukuzawa Yukichi. In an article entitled 'On Meat-Eating', Fukuzawa defended the practice to those who were not yet won over to this new culinary modernism:

Since ancient times, our nation of Japan has engaged in agriculture and people have taken the five grains as their staple food, with meat being eaten only rarely, giving rise to a nutritional imbalance in people's bodies, which naturally produced many ill and weakened persons. But now, with the development of methods for farming cattle and sheep, we should expect to supplement this nutritional deficiency by using the meat and drinking the milk that will be produced. And yet, there remain many people who blindly dislike this, saying that meat eating is filthy, in accordance with the customs our nation has followed for many long centuries. This is a specious argument born out of ignorant blindness that demonstrates a lack of knowledge about the natural disposition of human beings and a failure to discern the principles of the human body.
...

Today in our country, the lack of meat eating is producing malnutrition and not a few persons suffer from diminished vitality. In short, it is a national loss. And if one already knows about this loss and moreover has available measures that would compensate for it, what could possibly be the reason for not implementing those measures? If there was a household that said that having a large number of sick persons is our family tradition and which therefore declined to use medicine, could we call them wise?

And for milk:

In fact, we should call it the one medicine that works for all diseases. In the various countries of the West, it is not merely used for medicinal purposes – milk, of course, is part of their daily diet and beyond that they use such products as cheese and butter in the same way that we use katsuo dried bonito flakes in our country. In such places as Switzerland, a mountain country with very little fish, people living in mountainous regions are able to maintain a nutritious diet using only meat.

That being so, if the people of our nation too from this day forth were to open their eyes and devote their minds to learning the ways of using milk, we would achieve cures for incurable diseases, a long lifespan with no aging, bodily health and spiritual animation and for the first time we will not feel ashamed to be called Japanese.[11]

Despite resistance, especially from Buddhist monks (who had their own reasons to dislike the new regime), beef took off in a big way. Not just for its health value, but as the foundation of new braised beef dishes like *gyūnabe* (similar to the better-known *sukiyaki*). For Meiji Japan's circle of political and social reformers, eating like the West was the way to join the one club that mattered. For others, it was fashionable, modern and, for the relative few who could afford to eat beef regularly, tasty.

Likewise, China's foreign enclaves introduced plenty of new food fads. Fashionable consumers were won over to new tastes like imported red wine, Scotch whisky, coffee and cheese. Some of these new tastes were an easier sell than others. Beer (which we will be hearing more about later) was an immediate hit. Dairy wasn't new, but the convenient and clean bottled milk produced by Western dairies was. Ice cream first appeared in the 1920s and became such a huge hit that authorities in cities like Shanghai faced the constant challenge of finding and shutting down unsanitary local producers.

Culinarily, China put up stiff resistance. The political reformer Sun Yat-sen famously reflected a prevailing sentiment that, for all its scientific and military might, the West was culinarily backward: 'China lags behind in all areas of modern civilization,' he said, 'but in the realm of cuisine we have no peer.'[12] Twenty years later, a writer named Qin Meng disgorged his own more elaborate version of the same sentiment, complaining among much else that the distraction of being forced to endure the horrors of Western cuisine was impeding the work of China's diplomats abroad.

It is a fact that Chinese cannot stomach Western food. I personally cannot stand it. European and American cooking is generally clean and sanitary, but its tastes are simple and it is often raw and primitive. This is something that Westerners themselves will admit to.

The problem with Western food isn't the ingredients, it's the cooking. When Westerners eat chicken, it's either fried or stewed. But in the hands of a Chinese master, there are eighty ways to prepare a chicken, including the organs and blood. Simple Western methods don't have any idea of this!

According to my own research, Western civilization values science and the physical world. They can discover atomic power, but secrets like cooking a chicken with a piece of broken plate inside to make it tender – these are completely beyond their understanding. In Britain's Buckingham Palace, the most formal meal consists of eleven dishes, with a dish of roast quail at the centre. In China, even a 'budget banquet' is better than this![13]

How right was he? To answer the question, we can start by trying to understand the sort of Western food that Qin Meng might have encountered in a city like Shanghai. Most Chinese cooks wouldn't have travelled to Europe for advanced culinary training but instead learned by observation or apprenticeship in a working kitchen or from cookbooks like 1925's *Secrets of Western Cooking*. Since Qin mentions fried chicken, let's start there:

Fried Chicken (1925)

Equipment

1. Frying pot and stove
2. Kitchen knife and scraping knife
3. Bowls and plates

Materials

1. 1 tender chicken (feathers and organs removed; take off the head and wings. Remove the large bones and chop the carcass into four pieces and smash with the back of the knife. Salt and pepper on both sides)
2. 2 spoons of flour
3. 2 spoons of breadcrumbs

4. 2 egg yolks (mixed)
5. Salt and pepper powder (small amount as needed)
6. Worcestershire sauce (small amount as needed)
7. Pork fat, 4 liang

Method

Take the prepared chicken pieces and place them in a bowl. Add Worcestershire sauce as needed and let sit for 30 minutes. In a bowl, mix the flour, egg yolks and breadcrumbs. Add the pork fat to a pan and heat until it is bubbling. Add the chicken and cook until it is golden tea-coloured. Place the cooked chicken on a plate lined with Western [imported] paper to absorb excess oil. Switch to another plate and serve.

How unusual would this fried chicken really have been for a Chinese diner? Not very. We can compare it to a Chinese recipe in *Flavouring the Pot*:

Dry-Fried Chicken (Qing)

Cut chicken into 5 fen cubes, deep-fry and mix in salt and Sichuan pepper; wrap these in pork caul and deep-fry [a second time].

It is hardly outside the realm of imagination that two cultures would independently come up with the idea of deep-frying chicken. But the two versions seen here are somewhat different. The familiar Western version consists of whole pieces of chicken, lightly breaded and deep-fried. The *Flavouring the Pot* technique of mincing and frying the meat before wrapping it into nests with pork caul to fry a second time is more complex and more in line with dishes that we have seen before, like the salt-fish aubergine that uses intensely flavoured dried or preserved meat and vegetables. There are also plenty of dishes that take deep-fried chicken pieces and cook them in aromatics. In other words, the Western version would hardly have scandalized a Chinese diner.

Other dishes in the *Secrets of Western Cooking* – cold salads, butter cakes, German bread (which in the collection is actually a bread pudding) or sago pudding – would have been more novel. At least as they are presented in the *Secrets of Western Cooking*, many of the dishes are bland in the extreme. Meat is either roasted or stewed, generally with little flavouring beyond red wine and butter. The recipe for 'macaroni soup' consists simply of cooked macaroni served in water, similar to the way that unflavoured noodles might be served at the end of a Chinese meal.

How did Chinese and Western culinary spheres interact? Even after the fall of China's imperial system, the country's cuisine continued along an upward trajectory. China's new Republic was an era of great restaurants and a time that many still associate with the refined high living of splendid gourmands. This culinary glamour extended to iconic Western restaurants in the international port cities. The Kiessling Restaurant in Tianjin, the Peace Hotel in Shanghai and Taiping guan in Canton were all places to see and be seen. But while the higher end of Western restaurants no doubt served up something more exciting than macaroni in water, the appeal of foreign food was never just about the taste. It was fundamentally a function of how Chinese elites saw the West and themselves. For the generation of reformers who understood China's problems as coming from a backward culture, Western dining, including profoundly alien customs like drinking ice water, eating meat cooked rare or inviting women to the table, all made the journey from abhorrence to admiration.[14]

Writing in 1914, Peking University professor Isaac Taylor Headland recalled the valiant effort that his Chinese colleagues put forth in learning to accept Western food:

There are three kinds of food common to us that the Chinese, when they first come in contact with the foreigner, do not like. These are butter, coffee and cheese.

I have had guests who would force themselves to eat these things when I knew that the very odour of them was offensive. I remember one evening I invited Professor Lu – a very large, corpulent professor – of the Peking University to dine with us. It was the first time he had dined in a foreign home.

My table boy had been with us for years and I had never known him to be guilty of a smile while waiting at the table. During the dinner, when he passed the butter to Professor Lu, he was about to take half that was on the dish. The boy gulped and suggested in a half-under-tone that we never used so much. Professor Lu, perhaps to justify his mistake or perhaps to approve himself to his hostess, explained, also in a half-undertone: 'I am very fond of butter.'[15]

Chinese food was also taking new root outside of China, but globally this wasn't a single story. Each place it landed, Chinese cuisine adapted to local tastes and ingredients and social setting, pioneering new dishes and distinct social profiles. Most readers will recognize dishes like chop suey and the day-glo red sweet and sour pork that was the love of my Midwestern youth as Americanized imposters – 'inauthentic' in the sense that you would not find them on menus in China. But more recently people have come to the defence of American-Chinese cuisine as a tradition deserving of respect in its own right. I tend to agree, especially considering the many other hybrid Chinese cuisines that the people who decide such things justly hold up as things of beauty – the spice-rich Peranakan cuisine created by Fujianese communities in Penang and Malacca, Japanese *gyōza* or the unique 'chifa' cuisine in Chile.

Cover of 300 *Chinese Recipes for the Home* (1933), a book of Chinese recipes which introduced mostly Cantonese cuisine and dining customs to Japanese readers. Dishes were either steamed, deep-fried or braised. The technique of stir-frying in a round-bottomed wok is notably absent.

As with Western restaurants in Shanghai, the attraction of Chinese cuisine wasn't just about the food itself. Despite the cloud of racism that loomed over Asian migration, many Americans made a regular habit of what they thought was Chinese food, because it was cheap, convenient or exotic. Chop suey was all the rage in the 1920s, and the Pacific theatre of the Second World War cemented the place of China in American consciousness. Buwei Yang published *How to Cook and Eat in Chinese* in 1945. Nor was this process uniquely American. Just before Japan launched its brutal invasion of China, a Japanese women's group published its collection of *300 Chinese Recipes for the Home*, adapting Cantonese and Shanghai dishes to a Japanese kitchen:

Steamed Egg and Chicken (1933)

This is a dish of ground meat and egg that is rolled and steamed. The pieces can be arranged individually on a plate or can be included in a box assortment (*kamabokodai*).

Ingredients (for 5): 100 monme [375 g] ground chicken (can substitute ground pork), 5 eggs, 1 onion, sake, small amounts of ginger, soy sauce, salt, sugar, pork lard and starch.

1. Grind the chicken meat twice and chop the ginger and onion extremely fine. Crack and mix each egg, add one spoonful of sake, mix for three minutes and add a little salt. Cook each egg in a tamagoyaki pan.

2. Grind the chicken meat with a mortar and pestle, add one and a half spoons of starch, two spoons soy sauce, two spoons sugar, the onions and ginger and a small spoon of MSG and mix for three minutes.

3. Spread the prepared egg sheets with starch mixed in water, add an even layer of the meat and roll by hand to make two or three layers and wrap each one in a bamboo net. Steam for 20 minutes on medium heat.

When completely cooled, remove the bamboo net and cut into small bite-sized pieces of 2–3 bu [6–9 mm] thickness.[16]

This recipe also contains an early reference to MSG, which shouldn't be surprising since the stuff was first produced in Japan. MSG would become more common in China as the country began industrial production, but really only took off in the 1980s.

What about the wider trickle-down effect of Western food in China itself? How did the tastes and styles of Western cuisine circulate out of the elite establishments and into the menus of more everyday restaurants, both Western and Chinese?

For this, we return to our course lunch at the Sweet Fruit and Cookies Café in Shanghai. One of many competing menus advertised in local newspapers, this set meal rang in 1921 with a lavish spread of 'Euro-American cuisine':

Sweet Fruit and Cookies Café, New Year's Menu (1921)

1. Ham, chicken shreds and mushroom soup
2. Fried stingray rolls, green pea and shrimp sauce
3. Stuffed pheasant fillet on a bed of spinach with smoked meat broth
4. Pork ribs cooked with pineapple, mashed potatoes
5. Fried shrimp with fresh lettuce and a dipping sauce
6. Boiled ham
7. Roast capon
8. Five-colour vegetarian dishes
9. Fried potato strips [French fries]
10. Chilled smoked beef tongue
11. Celery salad
12. Mince pie
13. Empress pudding
14. Fresh fruit
15. Coffee or tea[17]

For a diner of the time, this menu would have straddled the border between ordinary and exotic. Ham, thin-sliced chicken and mushrooms made obvious sense as a soup. But other dishes would have no doubt confused the uninitiated. Words like coffee and salad were transliterated by sound. The meaning of 'mince

Advertisement for the set lunch and dinner menus at the Sweet Fruit and Cookies Café, Shanghai, in *Minguo ri bao* (Republican Daily News), 1 January 1921.

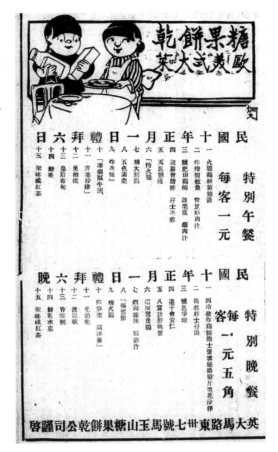

pie' makes no sense from the characters alone. Literal translation renders their meaning as something like 'exempt from treatment', and sounding out the northern pronunciation of *mianzhipi* is equally unhelpful. It was only after finding the dish on a Hong Kong food blog that I checked the Cantonese pronunciation and heard a sound that I would recognize as 'mince pie'. And that Empress pudding? It strikes me as mildly ironic that of all the dishes, the one with the most recognizable name remains the greatest mystery. Anglophone cooks of the time gave that name to a number of deserts – sponges with custard and jam, rice

The new fashion of Western dining was a maze of unfamiliar names and tastes.

pudding baked in a pastry crust or steamed with currants. But if it took me some effort to figure out this menu, just imagine how bewildering it would have been to a Chinese reader a hundred years earlier.

By looking at the other menus on offer here and in other cities, it becomes clear that by the time of our New Year's banquet, items like ice cream, coffee and butter were all becoming a very familiar part of Chinese menus. Besides congee, fried rice and dim sum, the 8 *jiao* (0.8 yuan) daily lunch at the Tianyi Cantonese restaurant in Suzhou included a typically southern spread of soup with chicken shreds and ham, deep-fried katsura fish, five-flavour young pigeon, beef in tomato sauce and shrimp egg fried rice – all finished with milk pudding, milk and coffee.[18] Or the deluxe (1.2 yuan) menu from the Central Garden restaurant in Nanjing, which in 1934 included chicken cream soup, ice cream and coffee.[19]

And while set-menu restaurants like Sweet Fruit and Cookies primarily served a Chinese clientele, the presence of tens of thousands of Europeans, Russians, Americans and Japanese living in Shanghai meant that there were also plenty of places catering specifically to foreigners. The Shanghai Library still has a collection of these menus, mostly in English, for restaurants that served simple tiffin, as well as American-style diner fare of eggs, coffee, hamburgers and sandwiches. Just as today's global cities and tourist destinations retain their own ex-pat enclaves, it was possible for many of China's resident foreigners to live an entirely separate existence, including eating the foods of home.

Industrialization

The second change was that technology began to transform China's own food chains. One reason why cities like Shanghai could suddenly go crazy for ice cream was that ice cream was available. For that to happen, you need milk and a freezer, the latter

Exterior of the Tsukunoya Japanese restaurant in 1930s Shanghai. Then, as now, Shanghai was home to China's largest expatriate communities.

consisting either of natural ice carried south by motorized ship or rail or electronic refrigeration. One area that I have explored in my own research is meat. For most of its history, China produced meat in a fairly traditional manner – that is to say, farmers or dealers brought livestock to market, where the animals were slaughtered and the meat sold on the spot.[20] There are a lot of reasons why this arrangement is not ideal – it is dirty and inefficient, especially for crowded cities. Shanghai had such terrible problems with sanitation that they banned dealers from bringing in meat from the outside – which meant that the animals had to be slaughtered in the middle of a teeming metropolis.

In this sense, a Chinese city like Shanghai in the mid-1800s was not so very different from London or New York at roughly the same time, at least in the sense that they all faced the same sorts of challenges. What changed all this was the railways. In the United States, lines connected Western cattle ranges to stockyards in Kansas City and Chicago and from there to markets on the eastern seaboard and beyond. The railways completely changed the landscape – and the business model – of how meat was produced. Transportation consolidated the industry, albeit in a way that didn't suit critics like Upton Sinclair, but everything else being equal, the concentration of resources brings efficiency and lowers production costs.[21] Something very similar happened in China when two new railways connected the vast Mongolian grasslands and the soybean fields of Manchuria to the city of Harbin. The northern city became a major slaughtering and processing centre – 'China's Chicago' as one observer called it – and began shipping chilled and frozen meat to markets in China and abroad. Modern transportation infrastructure created similar marriages of supply and demand all across China.[22]

And that's just one innovation and one industry. Besides advances in transportation, technology also meant canning and freezing, new ports and new irrigation systems, electric lights and mechanized processing. Later, it would include the mixed blessing of chemical fertilizers and pesticides.

It wasn't all good news – far from it. China faced major famines in the 1880s and 1920s, each of which condemned millions to agonizing deaths by starvation. Although both these famines were caused by natural disasters, there was also the problem that older systems to keep emergency grain reserves had fallen into disrepair. Any progress was pulled violently off track by the Japanese invasion of Manchuria in 1931 and of northern China in 1937. The fighting decimated everything – land, the people and food infrastructure. Chinese generals tried to slow the Japanese advance by flooding the Yellow River and unleashing a sea of mud that destroyed millions of farms. When the Japanese finally did leave, they took a lot with them, from railway ties to dairy cattle.

'Revolution Is Not a Dinner Party'

Four years after the Japanese defeat, the Communists raised their flag over the city of Beijing and declared the People's Republic of China. There are three things we need to know about this. The first is that the country they inherited was a real mess. Between rebellions, local warlords, the Japanese invasion and the Communists' own decades-long war against the previous government, China had not seen peace for nearly a century. The second is that the ideology of the Communist Party was based on the guided transformation of production, a project that demanded increasingly radical reforms of how people worked and lived. The third is that the rise of the Communist government made China – at least for a time – an ally of the Soviet Union.

How did these three factors influence food? The first two are fairly obvious. Reforming production meant putting a decimated country back on its feet, but it also meant refusing aid from former allies like the United States and devoting scarce resources to fighting the Korean War. The switch to a planned economy meant dismantling millions of businesses, making the State the only buyer – and the only source – for basic goods like cloth, grain or cooking oil. More than that, the idea of collectivization was connected to a larger ideal of completely rebuilding society. Decades before they ever came to power, the leaders of China's Communist Party had come to reject half-measures. When Mao Zedong wrote early on that the revolution was 'not a dinner party' he was quick to follow with what it was: 'Revolution is an insurrection, an act of violence by which one class overthrows another.'[23] In their own words, China's Communists were aiming to destroy the very foundations of the old society.

In its place, they would build a new society, one in which all life becomes communal. In the 1950s, small farms were forced into vast communes and harvests were owned and stored collectively. This was an absolute disaster. Some people were so amped up by propagandistic promises of eternal bumper crops that they feasted like gluttons in the communal dining halls, even as much of the harvest was rotting in storage. Some didn't have even that choice and instead had their grain forcibly expropriated to export to the Soviet Union. And since this social revolution was a political project, nobody dared own up to its failure. Nobody knows how many died during this 'Great Leap Forward'. Conservative estimates place the number at 20 million.[24]

During what many simply remember as the 'difficult years', people ate what they could, often producing lifelong love-hate associations with these famine foods. Some who spent years subsisting on a staple like corn or sweet potatoes are to this day scarcely able to tolerate even the smell. Others manage to retain warm memories of the foods of their youth, even if that youth was blighted by famine. One Beijing taxi driver told me about a cherished food of his childhood, a noodle soup made from something called *yupi*. I initially thought *yupi* meant 'fish skin' and responded that it would indeed make a very nice noodle soup. The frustrated driver then swerved across three lanes of traffic, coming to stop in front of a roadside elm tree. Pointing emphatically, he shouted: '*That*, we used to eat *that*!' It turns out that the *yupi* he was talking about was not fish skin, but *elm bark*. Exactly the same sound but a significantly more surprising meaning.

Wildly intrigued, I managed to locate not only a recipe for elm bark noodles but a vendor of 'food grade' elm bark flour. After a few short days of anticipation, my main ingredient arrived and I was ready to make my elm bark noodles, which according to the recipe I found online consisted of a 1:1 ratio of wheat and bark flour, mixed with water as needed. Within seconds, I knew that something was very wrong. The mixture clearly was not water soluble, meaning that no matter how hard I mixed, the water simply pooled on top, rather than mixing in. With a great deal of effort, I managed to form the sludgy mass into something like noodles, but this did not significantly improve the experience. The noodles had a plastic taste and texture and their journey through my gut was quick and entirely unenjoyable. This is not surprising, since bark is after all mostly *cellulose*. It is possible that a less barky ratio might produce a different experience, but I haven't yet had the guts to revisit this one.

For a while, China's rush of socialist optimism enthusiastically embraced the Soviet Union. Knowing how bitterly the two countries would eventually fall out, it is easy to forget that initially, the Soviet Union was not just China's new big brother, it was also the alternative to the capitalist culture of the newly minted enemies in the USA and Britain. For most of the 1950s, China was in love with all things Russian. Chinese newspapers embraced Moscow's fashions and praised the courteous and glamorous service of the city's department stores. Shanghai households clandestinely rid themselves of Western products and sought out Russian-branded goods.[25]

This politically promoted Sovietophilia was reflected in food, at least at the level of aspiration. Chinese newspapers praised Soviet food production, reporting extensively on how the institution of socialist farming produced bumper crop after bumper crop. They especially liked to talk about the glories of Soviet dairy production, which was rather akin to how earlier generations had once idealized the beef-eating British.

Even if Russian cuisine didn't reach deep into Beijing society, the city's Moscow Restaurant (affectionately abbreviated to *lao Mo*, or 'ol' Mo's') became a local landmark. Established in 1954 as part of an exhibition that attracted 42,000 visitors each day to come and gawk at the Soviet Union's economic and cultural achievements, the restaurant stayed on and even expanded to include a theatre and bakery. Despite the steady parade of Communist Bloc dignitaries that dined there and the imposing grandeur of its 'Soviet modern' interior, *lao Mo* was a restaurant for the people. *Beijing Daily* gushed about the snow-white tablecloths, spotless glasses, precisely arranged place settings and fresh flowers that adorned each table – never neglecting to mention that patrons were ordinary workers. In one report, the person dabbing his mouth with a fine linen napkin was in fact a carpenter from the Wuchang Shipbuilding Factory. He clearly enjoyed the experience, telling the paper that 'I have been in Beijing for a few weeks and I have never eaten as much or as happily as I did today.' Cost wasn't an issue. At a time when an educated worker might earn between 25 and 60 yuan per month, a complete meal including soup, dishes and even a beer cost under 2 yuan. Workers from across the country got ration coupons specifically to dine at *lao Mo*.[26]

For the thousands of Chinese diners who visited over the course of the first decade, *lao Mo* was a glimpse into the bright future of a new workers' world, a once-in-a-lifetime experience of socialist solidarity. But more than that, it was a first taste of *lieba, hongcai tang* and *hongchang* (Russian bread, borscht and red smoked sausage).

All this goodwill – culinary and otherwise – quickly turned sour after the two countries split. Moscow under Nikita Khrushchev repudiated Stalin's legacy and China chose to go the way of violent social revolution. As famine and the winds of revolutionary austerity reached the table, Western foods again transformed into symbols of political revisionism. 'Eating milk and white bread' became a propagandistic euphemism for the cheap luxuries afforded to traitors. Many older Chinese will still remember somewhat fondly the phrase 'socialism is a pot of beef and potatoes' – without necessarily knowing that it was a version of a quote by Khrushchev, the era's arch-villain – or remembering that the sentiment was viciously condemned by the Chinese press.

Lao Mo itself remained open throughout the tumultuous 1960s, although the hordes of Red Guards who occupied the Soviet Exhibition Hall during the Cultural Revolution demanded that the cooks switch from Russian to Chinese 'people's' cuisine. When the restaurant revived its old menu during the early 1980s, it became a nostalgic beacon for Beijingers craving a return to normalcy. In 1987, *lao Mo* released a Chinese-language cookbook of *600 Russian Dishes*. Evoking the restaurant's famously expansive menu, the recipes give us a glimpse of the cuisine that our Wuchang shipbuilder had found so profoundly satisfying: sour vegetable pickles, cream sauces, poached fish, beetroot soup, breaded cutlets and Kievan chicken.[27]

Clearly, these recipes come straight from the restaurant's own kitchen. The first step in making the beetroot soup is to cook 3 kilograms (6½ lb) of cabbage, beetroot, potatoes and onions in 4 litres (approx. 1 gallon) of beef stock. The Kievan chicken is a finicky process of shaping a partially deboned chicken breast around a puck of frozen butter, before multiple passes of breading and frying, and then serving it surrounded by pastry cups of green peas, on a special plate used for fried bread and with a paper flower covering the exposed chicken bone. Even a skilled cook could never have imagined making these dishes at home. Ingredients like cabbage and beetroot were available in abundance, but the butter used in the Kievan chicken was something that existed only in the Friendship Store set up specifically for foreign diplomats. You might as well suggest finishing the dish with a sprinkle of powdered moon rocks.

So why even include them? Because cookbooks are like travel magazines – they feed the imagination. And after decades of war, famine, revolution and socialist austerity, Chinese people were starting to dream of something new.

China's global moment

So, what did coffee, fried chicken, roast beef and beetroot soup really mean to China? We have already seen China absorb wave after wave of foreign foods: from Central Asia and the Indian Ocean, from Mongols and Manchus and from the New World. In many ways, the arrival of Western food was just another trend, one that brought new ingredients and techniques that became part of Chinese cuisine.

But what made this moment different is that Western cuisine arrived just as China was truly globalizing, impelled by the undeniable force of industrial transformation and the winds of political realignment. It also coincided with radical changes to how people were living. People were on the move. Some were crowding to megacities like Shanghai, others were being shoehorned into rural collectives. China was being fundamentally reshaped and these changes would inevitably and unidirectionally transform the substance of food.

5

'Life's a Banquet'
Food Culture in the Go-Go '90s

Our next meal is one that we watch on screen. The setting
is in Taiwan, in a small house just off a noisy street.

A sequence of fast cuts shows a gourmet feast taking shape
inside a cramped kitchen. As the camera keeps close to the
work surface, each dish one by one comes to life. We first
see a pair of hands reaching into a cistern of water to grab
a large white fish, which is quickly dispatched by means of
a chopstick shoved down its throat and then cut into thick
pink fillets. We then see the owner of the hands, an older
man struggling to wrestle a live chicken through the door.
Seconds later, he is shown stuffing the plucked and gutted
bird into a tureen, which is filled with broth and topped
with slices of cured ham and a cloth for steaming. In rapid
glimpses, we see a goose being bought in the market, then
its headless body being blown full of air and covered in a
thick brown sauce ladled out of a vat and roasted over an
open flame. Other dishes speed by in close-up – delicate
shrimp cooking in broth, a clay pot full of pork belly
sprinkled with rock sugar, a pair of hands deftly making
a steamer of delicate dumplings, squid and chilli peppers
tossed quickly in a wok.

But anyone waiting to see the finished dishes will be in for a disappointment. For all the care the camera took to show the dishes being made, the actual dinner offers little more than a quick pan over a luxurious table. The most careful viewer might just barely make out a few of the dishes: the fish has been deep-fried and served with a red sauce and slices of roasted goose are barely visible on a plate in the background. In the foreground, we catch a quick glimpse of the tureen containing the steamed chicken and a lonely dish of steamed pork.

The only sign of the squid and chilli dish is when we see the untouched plate emptied into a lunchbox.

Year Zero

Historians divide time into epochs. It's our way of making sense of the past. We're not the only ones who do so. A number of political regimes (and at least one former Beatle) have used this same sort of rhetoric to break with the past and stake out the future, setting the clock back to 'Year Zero' – that is, the moment that everything changed forever.

In retrospect, a good candidate for China's Year Zero would have been 1978, which is the year that the Communist government introduced the market reforms that would replace two decades of revolutionary extremism and initiated the market reforms that remain in place today. Known as 'Reform and Opening', these new policies would change the daily lives of billions, in China and eventually across the globe.

To start, let's consider the state of China in 1976, the year that Mao Zedong's massive state funeral parade rumbled past Tiananmen Square. The state economy, to put it generously, was on life support. Factories were empty because the workers were all out 'making revolution'. Agriculture wasn't doing much better. China was still overwhelmingly a nation of farmers, but since the state procurement price for basic staples – especially grain – was so low, few were inclined to provide for anything beyond their own needs. Compounded by the fact that everything was owned collectively, these factors created an economy of bare minimums – minimum effort to fulfil state quotas and predictably little on the shelves. Most people lived off the coupons that rationed every daily commodity: vegetables, cooking oil, sugar, cloth. Anything that could be considered a luxury – such as meat or canned goods – was exported to earn precious foreign currency or saved for the tables of a small circle of elites.

The economic reforms that followed wave by wave in the 1970s and '80s completely transformed this landscape. The state slowly began to embrace private ownership and market competition. It dissolved collective ownership and let people keep more of what they made, which encouraged them to make more. Political changes brought new technologies to a country that had left its industries stuck in the 1950s. It is easy to forget just how closed China was. Forget the Internet or mobile phones, even owning a foreign-language book had for decades been more than enough to get your house ransacked and expose yourself to a savage beating – or worse. Knowledge of the outside world had been warped by years of propaganda. When Richard Nixon made his groundbreaking visit to China in 1972, rumours abounded that the U.S. president was so fabulously wealthy that he would wear a new suit of clothes each day and simply throw the old one away.

For China's food producers, a category that included most people, the new policies were like a bolt of lightning. Farmers still had to fill official grain quotas, but they also had the freedom to work for themselves, growing vegetables or fruit, raising pigs and chickens or starting little backyard industries baking cakes or making tofu. Some of these small industries would eventually grow into very big businesses – China's largest chicken producer started during this time with one man and a yard full of chickens.

Joining all these new food producers came a trickle, and then a wave, of foreign brands setting up shop in China. Fortune favoured the earliest arrivals. Nestlé built a factory in the far north (this was incredibly big news for a cash-poor country like China) to make powdered milk and its creamer Coffee Mate. Nestlé made a product, but it also made an impression. When I first lived in China during the early 1990s, it seemed that every household had a boxed set consisting of one bottle each of Nescafé and Coffee Mate – pristinely preserved in its original packaging – sitting in a place of honour on a tabletop or bookshelf. One friend living in humid Sichuan told me how her parents had bought such a set, which developed a cake of blue mould soon after it was opened. Not knowing how to drink coffee and unable to simply throw away such an expensive item, they sat and drank the mouldy coffee, wondering how in the world the Westerners could possibly enjoy such a wretched taste. Coca-Cola had an easier road to acceptance, as did other early arrivals: M&Ms, Dove chocolate bars, Vitasoy, Oreo cookies and Pringles crisps. And for every foreign brand, there were dozens of Chinese imitators – running the gamut from very close resemblances to blatantly false labelling. Some were terrible, but others were good as or better than the original.

The last piece of the puzzle was the Chinese consumer. For years, the planned economy had prioritized bringing in foreign exchange, meaning that anything of value was sold abroad. But by the 1990s, the balance had started to shift to the domestic market. Seemingly overnight, a retail landscape sprang into existence. Little shops selling daily necessities, street markets full of vegetables and vendors hawking street food. It seemed that any place where people gathered, you would see the country's two most persistent entrepreneurs – a photographer who would take your picture wearing a homemade historical costume and a vendor selling bottled water. I remember once taking a fairly exhausting hike through some mountains in Shandong and after hours of not seeing another soul, I reached the top, where I was greeted by an old woman with a Styrofoam cooler of bottled water. How she had got there I had no idea, but we were both extremely happy to see each other.

By the 1990s, China's food market was booming, fed by and feeding hundreds of millions of new consumers. What did they want? Convenience was key. Most home kitchens were rudimentary at best, consisting of a shared, unventilated cooking space and no refrigerator. People living in school or factory dormitories didn't have even that. But they did have giant communal water boilers, which afforded the small luxury of using the endless supply of hot water to make instant ramen, warm up a tin of canned beef or stir into a cup of sweetened milk powder. Travelling at busy times like the New Year holiday might mean a twenty-hour train trip (believe me, I know), and you were well advised to stock up beforehand, not just for your own needs, but to trade and socialize with the other passengers. A smart traveller came well prepared with a plastic bag full of shelf-stable provisions – salty snacks, packaged biscuits and instant coffee (Nestlé hit the jackpot with the single-serving sachets of '3 in 1' that combined coffee, creamer and sugar into one irresistible powder).

Street food vendors – the foot soldiers of convenience – reached every street corner, selling every manner of quick delicacy – steamed buns, pulled noodles, deep-fried hot dogs on a stick and of course lamb and beef kebabs dusted with cumin and chilli powder and cooked over a charcoal fire. Not all the news on the street food front was good, however. There was a constant drumbeat of scandal about the origin of the meat that went into the dumplings. But there was money to be made and many of these small vendors held the attitude that any cash saved on materials meant that little bit more to take home when it was time to pull up stakes and head back to the village.

After years of revolutionary austerity, people also wanted novelty, fun, glamour and culture. The restaurant sector was quick to capitalize on this new market for elegance. Before closing its doors in 1952, Beijing's Taifenglou restaurant had been a feature of the city's elite circle for decades. Sensing the opportunities of the new era, the restaurant prepared a reopening that would recapture the glamour of its heyday. The previous manager oversaw the recreation of the old dishes, personally researching two hundred menu items and convening an outside committee of 'gourmets' to vouch for the authenticity of the tastes, as well as for the old standards of service.[1]

But for every classic restaurant that aimed to recapture lost glory, there were new ventures opening, first by the tens then hundreds, all fighting to carve out a place in an increasingly packed market. Competition drove wave after wave of new food fashions. For a while, Beijing roast duck remained the de rigueur definition of fancy dining because that was what was served to visiting diplomats. Then came steak and after that boiled crayfish. If I had to pick one dish that best represented the early 1990s, it would be orange drink crispy lotus root. For a brief window, it seemed like every home cook was enthralled with this dish, made using those two iconic luxuries of the era: Tang instant orange juice powder and a refrigerator:

Orange Drink Lotus Root (1990s)

Peel and cut 1 lotus root into 3-mm slices, parboil for 1 minute and immediately cool in cold water. Mix 1 spoon of orange drink powder and 1 spoon of honey, toss in the cooled lotus slices and chill for 6 hours.

Other culinary fads grew out of the reimagining – and remar-keting – of local tradition. In the late 1970s, some clever individual came up with the idea of consolidating China's many regional tastes into 'four great cuisines' – Lu (Shandong), Huaiyang (Jiangsu), Chuan (Sichuan) and Yue (Guangdong). That idea did so well that four cuisines soon became eight. The image stuck, as did the idea that each classic style had a few 'must-try' dishes.

In other words, China was reinventing its culinary herit-age for a new market of consumers, both at home and abroad. Individual cities and provinces each strived to develop their own gastronomic status. Part of this push included mass vocational training for cooks – Sichuan Province got an early start with this in the 1980s – sponsored by the provincial tourism department. Early brochures show the training – long lines of trainee cooks, all standing at mock-up stoves, deftly tossing woks in unison. The good news is that once the tourists started to pour in, Sichuan had tens of thousands of trained cooks ready to man the barricades. The not-quite-as-good news is that these cooks all learned a suite of standard techniques and tastes. It turns out that mass training isn't terribly conducive to maintaining diversity. The message that this new generation of cooks learned was the same that I heard when I attended a similar trade school in Sichuan some decades later – that professional cooking is all about replicability. Most customers, especially tourists, come for a few star dishes and those dishes will provide most of your revenue. Banish all thoughts of creating the great new taste. Like a washed-up rock band forced to constantly replay their old hits, your job in the kitchen is to make those star dishes over and over, in exactly the same way, because that's the taste the customer is expecting. And if you can cut some costs along the way, all the better.

It wasn't just the restaurant cooks. Mass production created a new national market for items like condiments. Millions of house-holds replaced grandma's homemade bean paste with a standard product manufactured and advertised on an industrial scale. This is when spicy Pi (rhymes with 'tee-hee') County bean paste, memorably praised in an early ad campaign as the 'soul of Sichuan cuisine', made its great transformation from a style of condiment to a branded commodity that before long was available in stores nationwide.

You'll no doubt have noticed a certain Ouroboros-like quality to these different processes. Mass marketing of places, products and cuisines creates tastes and desires; mass training of cooks and mass production of condiments satisfies these desires; and a mass culture of food reinforces what consumers are taught to expect. And just like that, we have the seeds of a national consumer culture, alongside a reinvigorated notion of national cuisine. Like a snake eating its own tail, the loop gets smaller and smaller as time goes on.

Which means that we are not far from fast food.

The emergence of Western fast food actually marked the point where these two trends converged: the place where the excitement of foreign brands met consumer desire for convenience and novelty. Simply calling it 'fast food' far undersells the transformation unleashed by the Golden Arches and its many deep-fried competitors. Food has always been fast. Nothing is faster than picking an apple off a tree, but traditional street foods like *baozi* – steamed buns with a meat filling – are a close second and they are (or at least were) available on every street corner.

The first major player on the scene was Kentucky Fried Chicken, which opened its first Chinese store near Tiananmen in 1987 and still remains the leader, in significant part because it has always been willing to adapt its global offerings to local tastes. But it was McDonald's that got most of the media attention. Coming hot on the heels of the historic opening of the first McDonald's in Moscow, China got its first Big Mac attack in 1990 – not in Beijing, but in the economic boomtown of Shenzhen, just across the border from Hong Kong. Beijing soon followed – I visited the Wangfujing store soon after it opened, not because I especially craved what was on the menu, but because as an English teacher living in a provincial city, a trip to the Beijing McDonald's was high on the list of things to do for the sake of sheer quirkiness. The feeling was indeed surreal, at least for me. Everyone else was busy enjoying the clean surroundings, the air conditioning and the free coffee refills. For most, the food itself was fairly incidental to the experience, a phenomenon that a generation of anthropologists spent the subsequent decade slicing into increasingly thin pieces. By the late 1990s, the chain had spread to most major cities. Millions of only children, the famous generation of 'little emperors', came to regard a trip to McDonald's as a special treat. Those children are now grown up and many bring to the chain a deep feeling of nostalgia.[2]

Eating at Home

The rise of fast food is indicative of the depth and speed of the new era's cultural change, the national desire to ditch the grim fatigues of permanent revolution for a new doctrine of enjoyable consumerism. Eating out meant new cuisines and new experiences. At home too, food was again becoming interesting and even fun.

Cuisine had not been lost entirely during the era of revolution. Far from it. The early years of China's revolution produced in many a sincere pride in patriotic austerity. Published just as China was preparing for full-scale collectivization (the preface even mentions that the recipes could be scaled for the home or a canteen kitchen), the 1956 *Family Cookbook* could be called optimistic, as it included among its 63 recipes more meat and fish than most families would normally have consumed. But it also reflected the simple tastes and gave a clever nod to ingredient substitution that matched socialist China's new aesthetic of patched-up workers' overalls. Note the four-ingredient simplicity of this classic pork dish:

Rice-Flour Steamed Pork (1956)

Ingredients

½ jin pork with skin
1 liang dry-rice flour
1 liang soy sauce
2 qian salt

Method

1. First use a red-hot iron to scorch the skin of the pork (it is best to use three-layer pork belly) until it is golden. Place the meat in a bowl of water and use a knife to cut away any charred parts, leaving only the white. Cut the meat into slices 2 cun long and 1 fen thick. Marinate the slices for 2 minutes in soy sauce. Heat 1 liang of rice in a pan until browned and use a stone to crush into powder (or use already-milled rice flour); spread the flour on the slices of pork and arrange inside a bowl to resemble stairs.

2. Steam the prepared bowl of rice flour pork over high heat for 1 hour 10 minutes. After 1 hour, dissolve the salt into 4 liang of water and sprinkle over the dish and steam for an additional 10 minutes. It is now ready to eat.

This unique dessert uses two items that certain parts of the country would have had in abundance – sugar and fresh tomatoes:

Tomato and Egg Cake (1956)

Ingredients

½ jin chicken eggs
11 liang tomatoes
5 liang cooked (note: steamed and allowed to cool) flour
½ jin sugar

Method

1. Separate the eggs, place the whites in a noodle bowl and beat with chopsticks until they form white peaks (until a chopstick placed in the eggs remains upright), pour the egg yolks into a small hole in the egg whites, then add the sugar in the same way. Mix until small bubbles start to form. Steam the tomatoes for 5 minutes and squeeze the flesh into a bowl (discard the seeds and peel). Sift the flour and stir with tomatoes into the egg mixture.

2. Arrange four long pieces of wood into a grid on top of a steamer, with a piece of thin cloth between them. Place the egg mixture inside and steam over high fire for 25 minutes.

3. After the egg cake is steamed, use two people to lift the four corners of the wood rack, carefully moving it from the steamer to a wooden board. Then place a second board on top and turn everything over so the cake and steaming cloth come out together. Cut into four pieces and then into 36 pieces.

We also have to remember that the communes, the same ones that ended up being partly responsible for the horrific famine of the late 1950s, were intended to improve material well-being. By combining labour and resources, the communes would make productive tasks like farming more efficient, ushering in a wave of wealth, leisure and harvest after rich harvest.

In the ideal, communal canteens were supposed to liberate women from the drudgery of cooking (thus freeing them up for the much more exciting task of working in the fields) and ensure healthy, delicious food for the entire community. Cookbooks like 1959's *Cooking for Commune Canteens* started by quoting the directive that outlined the ideals behind their founding:

> Canteens must be established well. Members must have their fill of food that is good, prepared in clean surroundings and appropriate to local and ethnic customs. Canteens should have a dining hall, a vegetable garden and workshops for tofu, starch and bean paste. They should raise pigs, sheep, chickens, ducks and fish. The food should have variety and taste. There should be

'Run the canteen well, see production swell,' 1958. Communal dining promised to liberate women, but the move was often from one kitchen to another.

consultation with nutritionists for food that has all of the nutrition and calories necessary. The elderly, children, sick, pregnant and breastfeeding mothers should have all the extra care they need and members should be allowed to cook at home. Canteens should be run democratically, with leaders chosen from politically reliable people and ideally elected.[3]

While it is easy to see the endless stream of films and posters as nothing more than crass propaganda, it is also clear that the cookbooks, consisting of technically simple recipes that nevertheless call for unsparing amounts of fish, pork and fresh vegetables, were written in order to be used:

Milkfish Roasted Pork with Water Bamboo [to serve 20] (1959)

Ingredients

6 jin milkfish, 1½ jin pork leg, 5 jin water bamboo (jiaobai), 4 liang wine, 12 liang soy sauce, 3 liang oil, 1 liang sugar, 2 liang onion, ½ liang ginger.

Preparation

1. Scale and remove the bones from the milkfish. Remove the head and rinse clean. Cut each fish into six pieces and rinse again in boiling water. Remove the peel from the pork and cut the meat into thick slices. Boil the water bamboo until cooked and slice thin.

2. Add 2 liang of oil to the wok. Add the ginger first, then the milkfish. Stir briefly and add 8 liang of soy sauce, the wine and 1 jin of water. Cook over a low fire for half an hour.

3. Separately, heat 1 liang of oil in a wok. Add the pork slices and stir briefly. Add 4 liang of soy sauce and the sugar. Cook for 5 minutes and add to the pot with the fish, along with the water bamboo. Heat over a high fire for 3 minutes to finish.

White Sliced Pork over Lettuce Hearts [to serve 20] (1959)

Ingredients

2 jin pork shoulder, 6 jin lettuce hearts, 4 liang soy sauce, 1 liang sesame oil, 2 liang salt.

Preparation

1. Cut the lettuce hearts into pieces and place in a bowl with the salt. After 10 minutes, drain the water and arrange on a plate.

2. Boil the pork. After the meat has stopped releasing blood, cook it for another 5 minutes, remove from the pan and allow to cool. Cut into 60 thin slices and place over the lettuce hearts. Cook the soy sauce and sesame oil to finish. [Unclear whether to pour over the top or to serve on side.]

Even after the famine had subsided, the next few years struggled to balance the virtue of revolutionary austerity against the idea of the socialist good life. My 1973 edition of *The People's Cookbook for the Masses* (first printed in 1966) begins with a quote from Chairman Mao explaining that the Communist Party is focused on solving the real problems faced by the masses: clothing, food, housing, fuel, rice, oil and salt, healthcare and marriage. After the break with the Soviet Union, China's revolutionaries had pilloried Khrushchev for his non-doctrinaire consumerist Communism. Personal safety demanded that the author first find

Early socialist-era cookbooks. From far left: *Jinan Cookbook*, *The People's Cookbook for the Masses*, *Sichuan Cookbook* and *Family Cookbook*. The two cookbooks for public canteens are in the foreground.

solid ground by locating a quote affirming that the Chairman does indeed want you to eat well.

Once inside, *The People's Cookbook for the Masses* outlines 270 recipes, each contributed by a place and sometimes by a particular work unit, such as the kitchen of a state-run restaurant or a municipal food services company. Most recipes are relatively simple. Few have more than a handful of ingredients, giving a good indication of what was available at the time. Vegetable oil is used only for deep-frying; stir-frying uses pork fat. Some recipes for chicken begin with the instruction to kill the bird. There are few prepared sauces and relatively scant use of fermented beans – yellow bean paste, bean paste or soy sauce. Chillies barely appear, even in the small number of dishes that originated in Sichuan.

The *People's Cookbook for the Masses* lives up to its title. This is all very ordinary food, even down to the names of the dishes. Gone are metaphors and euphemisms. Dishes are generally identified in a completely utilitarian manner. Submitted by the Suzhou Culinary Training Unit, the dish called 'Green Peppers Fried with Pork Strips' does indeed consist of green peppers and pork cut into thin strips, and relatively little else:

Green Peppers Fried with Pork Strips (1973)

Pork leg, 3 liang
Green peppers, 4 liang
Pork oil, 8 qian
Soy sauce, 6 qian
Sugar, 2 qian
Wine, 3 qian
Salt, 3 fen

1. Cut the pork into thin strips and place in a bowl until needed. Wash the peppers, remove the stems and seeds and cut into strips.

2. Add 4 qian of pork oil to the wok. Cook at high heat until eight-tenths done, fry the pork until cooked. Add the soy sauce, sugar and wine and cook until bubbling. Return to the bowl.

3. Heat another wok and add 4 qian pork oil. Add the pepper strips and toss briefly. Add the salt and fry until cooked. If needed, add a small amount of water or broth. Add the pork strips to the same pan and cook until the liquid bubbles. When cooking, take care not to let the peppers turn brown [from overcooking].

Now compare this book to the same title three decades later, the *New Edition People's Cookbook*. Actually, numerous updated versions of the classic had been published throughout the 1990s and beyond. My 1999 version is not much longer than the original, but the content is significantly different. Ingredients and equipment are more diverse. The reappearance of dishes with names like the Sichuan dish of 'Cherry Blossom Pork' suggests that a certain amount of culinary romanticism had again caught hold. No longer tied to individual cities or establishments, some of these newer versions now sort dishes not by ingredient but by the new classification of China's 'four great cuisines'.

Changing Tastes

With all these cookbooks from across the twentieth century, we are finally in a position to start comparing different versions of the same dish. Let's go back to one of the great icons of Sichuan cuisine: *Gongbao* (aka *Kung pao*) chicken:

1. *Family Cookbook*, 1956

Gongbao jiding (1956)

Ingredients

½ jin chicken (1 bird)
2 liang pork fat
2 qian dried red chillies
2 liang pickled red and white radish
1 liang soy sauce
1 liang spring garlic
1 liang cucumber
1 liang peanuts
1 spoon of fermented tofu liquid
Starch

Instructions

1. Remove the feathers and internal organs from the chicken, twist off the neck and separate the two legs and breast. After the entire bird has been broken into six parts, twist off the head, remove the breast and leg bones, and cut the remaining meat into small cubes. Use a knife to cut the rib bones fine and cut the neck into small cubes. Cut the cucumber and pickled red and white radish into cubes. Slice the garlic at a bias. Slice the dried chillies into long strips.

2. Heat ½ jin of pork fat (1 liang will be used up in the frying) over a high fire and then lower the heat. Mix the chicken pieces with soy sauce and starch by hand until evenly coated, add to the oil and again return to high heat. Once the chicken is the colour of egg yolks, scoop it out. Keep 1 liang of pork fat in the wok and add in the cucumber, pickled radish, peanuts and chiles. Stir a few times and return the chicken, and add soy sauce mixed with starch.

3. Before serving, add the garlic and fermented tofu liquid.

2. *Chongqing Famous Recipes*, hand-written 1960

Gongbao rouding (1960)

Ingredients

3 liang pork tenderloin
1 egg
A few slices of garlic
Small amount as needed: onion, salt, soy sauce, red chilli oil, vinegar, ginger, white sugar, Shaoxing wine, bean powder mixed into water

2 liang pork fat
A few dried red chillies

Method

Remove the silver skin and cut the meat into cubes. Mix with the bean powder, wine and salt. Add the soy sauce, vinegar, sugar, bean powder, ginger, onions and garlic as needed to a bowl and stir into a paste. Fry the red chilli oil and add the dried chillies until reddish brown (literally to the colour of a cockroach), add the diced pork and stir quickly to break up the meat. Add more chilli oil and the bowl of liquid, quickly stir-fry and remove from the pan.

3. *People's Cookbook*, 1973

Does not appear. None of the book's other chicken or pork recipes strike me as anything close to the dish.

4. *Sichuan Cuisine*, 1977

Does not appear. The recipe for Sichuan peppercorn chicken cubes is similar in flavour but notably does not feature peanuts.

5. *New Edition People's Cookbook*, 1999

Gongbao jiding (1999)

Main Ingredient

200 g chicken breast

Supporting Ingredient

50 g peanuts

Flavours

10 g soy sauce, 3 g cooking wine, 4 g vinegar, 2 g salt,
1.5 g MSG, 10 g sugar, 25 g dry chillies, 10 g Sichuan
peppercorns, 3 g starch, 1 egg, 5 g onion, 3 g ginger, 2 g garlic,
50 g oil

Preparation Method

1. Cut the chicken into 1.5-cm diagonal cubes, add 2 g soy
sauce, 1 g cooking wine, 0.5 g salt, 0.5 g MSG, 1 g starch, 1 egg
and mix until everything is an even paste.

2. Slice onion, ginger and garlic and add to a bowl, mix in
the [remaining] soy sauce, cooking wine, vinegar, salt, MSG,
sugar and starch to form a liquid.

3. Boil the peanuts in water to remove the peel, add to oil
at 5–6 level heat and fry until cooked. Make sure to keep the
white colour and do not let them brown.

4. In a hot wok, add the Sichuan peppercorns and chillies
and fry until the peppercorns are black and the chillies are
dark red, add the chicken and stir-fry until cooked, then
add the mixed liquid, quickly stir-fry until the liquid coats
the chicken. Add the pre-fried peanuts, stir a few times
and plate.

Where do we even begin? First, let's compare the books
themselves. Books 1, 3 and 5 cover all of Chinese cuisine and each
was circulated to a national readership. Books 2 and 4 are books
of Sichuan cuisine, both produced in Sichuan. Of these, number
2 is most clearly the work of a local cook. It is hand-written, with
many mistaken characters and frequent use of Sichuan local

language (for example, instructions to fry chillies 'to the colour of a cockroach' uses the local term '*touyoupo*' – madame oil thief – rather than the standard *zhanglang*).

The three recipes show a wide range of techniques, ingredients and tastes. Comparing first to last, we exchange a fresh-killed chicken for deboned chicken breast, deep-frying for stir-frying and pork fat for vegetable oil. The pork dish from 1960 does not include peanuts, the chicken dish from the late 1990s is loaded with them. One recipe uses pickled vegetables, others use no vegetables at all. One stirs in a spoon of pungent tofu fermenting liquid, yet another cooks the dish in red chilli oil. The most recent measures its ingredients to a fraction of a gram, while the hand-written recipe of the Chongqing cook simply notes to use ingredients 'as needed'.

If nothing else, this little exercise should put to bed once and for all the utility of culinary archaeology, at least if conducted in the interests of authenticity. We may be able to find the *oldest* of something, but age alone shouldn't make it authoritative. Each of these books represents a moment in time and each one should be considered genuine in that regard.

Yet it hardly needs to be said that the results of each of these recipes would be wildly different. The first is a dish of bone-in chicken, fried crisp in pork fat, then fried again with a small handful of chillies and the crunch of salted vegetables. The last one is sweet and twice as spicy, with numbing Sichuan peppercorns, in addition to the dried chillies. Stir-fried in vegetable oil, the dish's boneless chicken breast would add relatively little taste or texture. The two books from the 1970s omit this supposedly essential dish entirely and the one from 1956 subtly changes its name, replacing the word for 'palace' 宫 in the first syllable with the homophone character for 'public' 公.

A New Place for Food

These evolving tastes and recipes were just the tip of the iceberg; what was really changing was the entire place of food in mass culture. The magazine *China Food* shows the range of popular issues that were now becoming entangled in the growing world of mass-market food publishing. I managed to get my hands on a stack of these magazines from 1988, a time when China's confident new consumer culture was just starting to hit its stride. A good portion of each issue is devoted to nutrition and health – food advice for the aged or for rejuvenating sagging skin, diets for people with liver problems, diabetes and high blood pressure. For couples, one article forcefully advocates a 'harmonious husband and wife diet', dishes heavy with walnuts, chestnuts and sesame, which are supposed to raise sperm count and boost flagging sexual desire – though the included recipe for fried candied chestnuts, deep-fried in oil, then pan-fried in sugar and melted pork fat, seems like a fairly stodgy start to a romantic evening.[4]

There are cultural discussions about and around food: what the French writer Honoré de Balzac wrote about coffee, interviews with cooks in foreign embassies and food in film and literature. A section of questions submitted by readers answers curiosities like why frozen fruit loses its taste and gives advice, especially about nutrition. And of course, the magazine featured a parade of new, branded products, including full-page colour ads for Changyu wine, Harbin beer, powdered soybean milk and tinned Danish butter biscuits.

Actual recipes take up only a small portion of the total publication and these run the range from straightforward household dishes to those, like the intricately sliced 'golden hair' lionfish, that were probably best left to the professionals. There was a special love for the pressure cooker, which was a brand-new addition to Chinese home kitchens. In the magazine, pressure cookers

'Supply high-quality products, wholeheartedly serve the people,' 1978. This production poster visually reads like a catalogue of desirable items. A kettle, steamer and pressure cooker take up the foreground, with colourful plates and thermoses on the shelves behind.

提供优质产品 全心全意为人民服务
TIGONG YOUZHI CHANPIN QUANXINQUANYI WEIRENMIN FUWU

were shown being used for everything from steaming dumplings to baking bread and of course stewing meat. At least one of these recipes strikes me as questionable. A 1988 recipe for pressure cooking meat adds just a few tablespoons of liquid and very likely resulted in many burned pans – and hopefully nothing worse.

Just as today, many people simply enjoyed reading the recipes rather than actually making them, an early expression of the culinary voyeurism that today gets dismissed as 'food porn', but really just means that there are ways to enjoy food besides eating it. Even if it existed only in your imagination, food was becoming fun.

Cocktails were a big fad. In the culinary imagination of the late '80s, cocktails often consisted of garish multicoloured liqueurs and fruit juice carefully poured in layers in a tall glass and served in a fashionable setting like the lobby of an international hotel.

According to friends who frequented the Beijing underground club scene in the 1980s, some local inventions were harsh but otherwise not unpleasant:

Rum and Honey Cocktail (1980s)

Ingredients

½ bottle of rum, 1½ teaspoons of honey, 1 small spoon of lemon juice

Mix with ice. Garnish with orange peel and cherry blossoms.

Despite never having tried it, I have a vicarious nostalgia for the coffee cocktail, which sounds very much like something I might have cooked up at the late stage of some noteworthy evening. If cinema is to be believed, this drink is best enjoyed while wearing an oversized suit jacket with the sleeves rolled up:

Mixed Coffee Drink (1980s)

Ingredients

½ glass prepared (instant) coffee, ½ glass baijiu, ¼ glass brandy, ½ glass rum, ½ glass cream, 3 eggs, ¼ spoon ground almonds

1. Beat the egg yolks until foamy, add sugar [not mentioned in ingredients] and continue to mix, while slowly adding in the baijiu. Then add the rum and ground almonds, mix and refrigerate.

2. Beat the egg whites, then add the pre-prepared egg yolk mixture and the other ingredients and lightly mix. When it is evenly mixed, serve in a cocktail glass. Serves five people.

Baijiu, which translates literally to 'white wine', is a spiced *shaojiu*, usually ranging between 70 and 100 proof. *Baijiu* is an acquired taste, and after nearly three decades of trying, I am no closer to acquiring it. The very idea of a *baijiu* cocktail strikes me as the stuff of nightmares, but this last drink takes the extra step into the realm of waking hallucination:

Ingredients

1 shot glass baijiu, ½ small cup instant coffee (prepared), 1 spoon lemon juice, 1 shot glass absinthe

Technique

Pour all ingredients into a cocktail glass, add a small amount of ice and mix. Serves one person.

Beer

But most people drank beer.

Beer brewed with wheat and hops was a relatively new addition to China's storied drinking culture and was initially a very foreign taste. China's earliest brewery was founded in 1900 in the Russian city of Harbin, followed soon after by an Anglo-German brewery in the city that would soon be synonymous with beer – Qingdao (aka Tsingtao). Chinese brewers followed: Beijing's Five Star Beer in 1925 and Five Sheep Beer in Guangzhou in 1934, but just as with red grape wine, beer was initially associated with foreigners. This group included Japan, which took over Qingdao and its brewery in 1914 and became one of the city's major export markets.

Among Chinese consumers, beer only really became a mass drink during the 1980s. China's brewing industry continued to develop after 1949 but was constrained by the scarcity of grain and the lack of a domestic market. Both problems solved themselves during the 1980s, just as economic reforms were encouraging millions of new small industries that added value to local agriculture by turning corn into oil, pigs into ham, beans into tofu – or grain into beer. From 1980 to 1988, China's beer output grew ten times, from 690,000 to 6.5 million tons. Most of this beer was made in small, local breweries – by the end of the decade, nearly every county had one. Beer produced locally was consumed the same way, a cheap product that rarely made it much farther than the nearby street market.

Brands like Qingdao – which in 1993 became the first Chinese company to list on the Hong Kong stock market – had bigger plans, laying the foundation for global expansion. Qingdao also found a vast domestic market, especially in the 1990s when millions of Chinese households suddenly had the income to buy a refrigerator and upmarket products to put in it. By the end of the century, hundreds of local breweries had been put out of business or consolidated under a few big consortia: Qingdao, Snowflake, Yanjing or local branches of global brands Budweiser or Carlsberg.[5]

Banquets

The ultimate symbol of China's early reform period was the banquet. Look through any Chinese newspaper from the 1980s and you will see the country's leaders doing one of a few things: giving a speech, walking through a factory or entertaining foreign dignitaries at a banquet. Any restaurant lucky enough to have hosted an event in this last category made endless use of the publicity.

The era's new love affair with banquets was a striking reversal of official hostility towards fancy dining. Back when the Chinese Communist Party was still a struggling insurgency up in the mountains, cadres were forbidden from accepting hospitality from local elites for fear that it would look like – or lead to – corruption. Like so much of Communist performative puritanism, this policy supposedly emerged *sui generis* from the earthy wisdom of the peasants. According to Mao Zedong's own account of the early peasant movement in Hunan (the same account that clarified the all-important distinction between dinner parties and violent revolution), local peasant committees established these restraints themselves. One committee decided that hospitality should not extend beyond dishes of chicken, fish and pork. Another limited banquets to no more than eight dishes, another to five and yet another banned feasts altogether. When one family held a feast to celebrate their son's wedding, the peasants 'swarmed into the house and broke up the party'.[6]

In contrast, the high-level banquets of the Reform era were by their nature showy affairs and they could quickly get very expensive. In a country that was just eking its way out of poverty, these displays easily crossed the line from exaggerated hospitality to the truly vulgar. With guests pressured to toss down bottles of prestige alcohol like Maotai, xo brandy or imported Scotch whisky, the bill could quickly come to thousands of yuan, all before any food was served. And since massive food waste was a sign of abundance and generosity, much of the food that did reach the table was destined to stay there – ultimately to end up in the bin.

In popular discourse, official banquets were a source of universal opprobrium, synonymous with corruption. This is because a banquet is first and foremost a social occasion. That's fine for family and friends, but when you accept lavish generosity from outside that circle, there's a very good chance that someone is expecting something in return. And like any gift, the higher the price tag, the higher the stakes.

Foreign observers put forward explanations that the banquet was both the essence of Chinese culture and a way of cementing a protective network in the absence of legal safeguards. At least one writer was sure that China's entire banquet subculture would disappear once the country entered the WTO, thus forcing its business practices to become less personal and more rational.[7]

Regardless of who did the inviting, attending a formal banquet was an acquired skill – a very particular exercise in decorum. There were (and still are) dozens of books explaining banquet rules to bemused foreigners: where and when to sit (wait until you are seated and adamantly refuse the seat of honour opposite the door); how to properly toast (wait until the hosts have all offered their toasts and ask a friend to signal you when it's your turn); how and when to reach for food that is served in the middle of the table (when in doubt, wait to be invited).

If we strip away the self-interested pursuit of exchanging entertainment for favours, the spirit of banquet rules still applied to the hospitality of smaller, friendlier gatherings. Drinking culture, especially in the north where I spent the early 1990s, was a gauntlet of generosity. One could scarcely refuse a drink that was offered and becoming extremely drunk was a sign of real friendship. In its advanced stages, the ritual of competitive toasting (in which you show respect by touching your glass *lower* than the person across from you) frequently ended with at least one of the two parties tumbling out of his chair. (Yes, the gendered language is intentional. This is almost exclusively a male way of drinking, at least in public.) And whenever possible, you wanted to grab the bill. Literally so. I once saw the customary tussle over the bill at a streetside stall end in a dislocated shoulder.

I won't draw too deep from my own well of drunken banquet stories, except to relate the time when I walked out of one thoroughly intoxicated lunch to use the toilet and for some reason thought it would be fun instead to wander out of the restaurant and hop on a public bus. My hosts were some fairly important people – enough so to have cars and personal drivers – and seeing the bus pull away, they all scrambled to give frantic chase, while

I remained blissfully passed out in the back. Amid the next day's fog of hungover shame, I came to learn that the same group had called repeatedly to make sure that I was all right – and to ask if I was free to join them for dinner that evening.

Images in Film

Back to our film banquet. With all this actual eating going on, why spend our time looking at a film?

Like much of the food culture of the time, fancy dining during the early 1990s was largely aspirational. The doors of world culture had only started to open, but the economic reality had not yet caught up. Like the recipes in the magazine *China Food*, the era's banquet culture was an experience that most people could only enjoy vicariously.

Some of the era's food entertainment was comically over the top. Hong Kong films made an art form of exaggeration. Crime dramas showed the baddies endlessly toking cigars and sucking down gallons of French cognac – that's how you knew they were bad. Comedies like the 1996 film *God of Cookery* brought slapstick martial arts to the kitchen. Complete with campy performances, flying knives and kung fu chopsticks, the film's humour comes from its excess. Another Hong Kong film, known in English as *The Chinese Feast*, had built its story around a fictionalized version of the Complete Manchu-Han Feast.

But undoubtedly the film that captured the spirit of the time was Taiwanese director Ang Lee's much quieter classic, 1994's *Eat Drink Man Woman*. The story of an ageing chef struggling to hold on to the affection of his three strong-willed adult daughters, all the film's action takes place against a backdrop of food, either being cooked or being eaten.

More than just scenery, food is a main character. The chapter introduction shows the stark difference between the care the main character takes in preparing the food and the disinterest the diners have in eating or even acknowledging it. Now, I'm no film critic, but that juxtaposition seems to be a fairly clear metaphor for the changing priorities within a family that is reaching for a way to communicate across generations. Just the sort of message that would have deeply resonated with viewers fresh out of China's tumultuous 1980s.

That same sort of mismatch carries through the rest of the film. In one of the more memorable scenes, the old chef follows his young granddaughter to school to deliver a boxed lunch that turns out to be a grand feast of braised pork ribs, shrimp and bitter melon. Her classmates are amazed, but the girl herself is mortified by all the attention. In another, a potential match for the widowed chef is shown chain smoking and leaving her cigarette butts in a half-empty plate of food. But there is also continuity. The eldest daughter is seen preparing food for her new husband, copying not only her father's passion but his techniques, including the chopstick-to-the-gullet technique for killing the fish. The camera initially treats the daughter like the father, focusing strictly on the cooking surface, but later follows her to the table as her husband receives each dish with obvious appreciation.

What did all this mean to Chinese viewers in the go-go '90s? They certainly would have found it familiar. Although this is a Taiwan film, it has none of the exaggerated fantasy of Hong Kong movies. Nothing about the setting or the cuisine is presented as exotic.

Eat Drink Man Woman (opening meal)

Dongpo pork: Pork belly slowly stewed with soy sauce and rock sugar.

Shark fin-stuffed chicken: Chicken (preferably an old hen) stuffed with shark fin, abalone, ham and dried scallops, sewn shut and steamed whole. In the film, the dish is shown served in liquid and topped with sliced ham.

Cold jellyfish: Salad of jellyfish that is blanched and sliced and tossed with vinegar and thinly sliced cucumber.

Fried two crisps: Cuttlefish and duck gizzards stir-fried with fresh chillies.

Dried scallop brassica hearts: Fried brassica with dried scallops.

Rock sugar treasure: Knuckle of pork cooked in rock sugar and braised in a brown sauce.

Chrysanthemum pot: Hotpot flavoured with chrysanthemum. Served in the film with sliced raw fish and green vegetables.

Deep-fried squirrelfish: This dish demands advanced knife skill from the chef. Scenes of the preparation showcase the precise angle and depth of each cut and the technique of pouring hot oil over the fish to open up the cuts.

Fried chimes: Tofu skin, rolled with filling and fried crisp. The name refers to the sound of the crunchy skin.

Roasted duck: The preparation of the duck is not shown. The step of blowing the duck carcass full of air suggests that the duck is to be roasted, although it could also have been stewed. The finished dish is shown sliced on a plate.

Pinched soup dumplings: Thin-skinned pork dumplings are pinched shut to keep the liquid inside. Shown served in soup.

Most of the ingredients that make up the gorgeous dishes are all extremely common – chicken and pork, a fish from the market, very ordinary sauces and vegetables. But then again, so is the fruit in a Vermeer still-life. What sets these ordinary ingredients apart is that they are made with exquisite skill and care – such as when we see a brief glimpse of the daughter making a dish of Zu'an tofu by slicing and moulding thin sheets of tofu around a filling to be steamed.[8] Economically, the family is not at all wealthy. The home and kitchen are humble. It is the skill and devotion of the chef and his eldest daughter that transform the ordinary into something extraordinary and extraordinarily meaningful.

The comfort and beauty to be found in *Eat Drink Man Woman* serves to remind us that for all the promise of China's economic

Changes came fast in the new economy. For some, at least, the family dinner was a safe space to dream of an exciting new future.

reforms, this was also a time of frightening change. Politically and economically, there were very real concerns that the whole thing could collapse. For millions of families living on the mainland, the prospect of living without the 'iron rice bowl' of the inefficient but at least predictable life under collectivization created a new sense of insecurity. Quite different from the striped cocktails and giant shoulder pads of 1980s Hong Kong cinema, there was something very attractive about three generations of this very ordinary family coming together around food, especially in a way that showcased the continuation of closely held traditions that had been badly eroded on the mainland. Against the dizzying new world of wealth promised by the new economic reforms, it reminded viewers both of home and comfort and of a refined culinary tradition that was barely a dream during the years of revolutionary austerity.

6

Franchise Fever
The Price of Efficiency

For our next banquet, we don't even need to leave home. In fact, leaving home is something we do less and less often these days.

Without even looking up from our phones (another thing we do less and less often), we can order our dinner, track its delivery and, once all the dishes have been freed from their tiny plastic prisons, snap a picture to post on social media.

And tonight's dinner will definitely be worth a picture. Delivery is old hat. We already get food delivered almost every day. Judging from the mounds of takeaway boxes filling up our rubbish, so do all our neighbours. But tonight's dinner is hotpot, and the order comes complete with a miniature version of the same set-up that we would be using in a restaurant – a plug-in chafing dish, three plastic containers of frozen beef shaved neatly into two rows of identical curls, as well as carefully wrapped servings of cabbage, corn, green sprigs of tonghao and frozen tofu. One plastic bag contains a dozen individually wrapped containers of spices and sauces, yet another has six cans of sweet orange soda.

A nice little surprise, we see that the restaurant has
included, at no extra charge, a handful of bright yellow
snack cakes, each plastic package printed to look like
a Minion from the film *Despicable Me*.

After about ten minutes of unwrapping, we discover that
we have more food than table. But it undoubtedly makes
for a very nice picture, especially with all the Minions lined
up to wave at the camera.

Like It's 1999

To fully appreciate the massive changes of the past two decades, let's start with a snapshot of China in 1999, as the country stood on the eve of joining the World Trade Organization.

In a big city like Tianjin – one of China's largest and where I had been living for two years – the changes of the *previous* decade were already hard to miss. Everywhere you looked, old housing was being knocked down to make way for new high-rises, bicycles had largely given way to cars and everyone had or wanted a Nokia mobile phone. The Internet was just making its presence known – mostly in dimly lit Internet bars, where students spent hours in sugar-fuelled video game duels.

Like every Chinese city, Tianjin was abuzz with commerce – much of it in the informal street markets where vendors hawked cheap items like off-brand T-shirts or pirate DVDs. Supermarkets were still a novelty, but every major city had a few. Megastores like the French chain Carrefour introduced millions to the idea of plastic-wrapped produce. They also had bread that was baked on-site, hot roasted chicken and even rarities like cheese. But look more closely and you could see that the reality still hadn't quite caught up. Even in the big chains, much of the retail space was filled with exactly the same stuff that the vendors were peddling outside.

Dining out had moved upmarket. After their initial splash, KFC and McDonald's had become fairly commonplace – eight or nine of each in the city centre – the growing crowd of such lookalikes as the restaurant chain Red Sorghum and Ronghua Fried Chicken making it feel like there were even more. Pizza Hut had just arrived but was a bit pricey and many people were still not sure how they felt about the idea of eating cheese. The most talked-about new arrival was Starbucks, although the idea of spending 40 yuan – roughly the price of two McDonald's set meals – on a single coffee still seemed almost obscene. Restaurants were everywhere, mostly representing a few basic cuisines – after the general northern-style, Sichuan and Guangdong were the most common, along with the occasional outlier: Korean barbecue, Japanese *tonkatsu*.

Much of the food scene was still on a very small scale – street-side sellers of steamed cakes, buns and dumplings. The fare from these street vendors was quick, easy and intensely local. Every place has its favourite noodle dish: pulled beef noodles in the northwest, spicy *dandan* noodles in Sichuan, 'crossing the bridge' rice noodles in Yunnan, noodle dumpling soup in the southeast, garlicky sesame paste noodles in Shandong and salty *zhajiang* noodles in Beijing. Nothing says Shanghai like a bowl of noodles topped with salted mustard greens or my favourite – onion oil.

Onion-Oil Noodles

Precook and set aside one serving of noodles.

Slice a handful of green onions (slightly wilted is best) into 2.5-cm sections, setting aside the whites. Making sure that the onions are completely dry, fry the green tops in ¼ cup oil at very low heat until they turn crisp and slightly brown. Remove the onions from the oil and add ½ teaspoon of white sugar, 2 tablespoons of soy sauce and the cooked noodles.

Heat the oil and mix to coat the noodles evenly. Serve with the dried onion and crispy peanuts.

My favourite cure for cold winter mornings was and is *jian-bing guozi* – a thin pancake made of mixed-grain flour spread out over an iron griddle, then topped with a raw egg that cooks as it is smoothed flat, followed by chilli paste and green onion, then folded around sticks of fried dough (or a sheet of crispy fried dough if you are in Beijing). Salty, greasy and steaming hot off the flat iron plate, the mere thought of one of these beauties was enough to get me out of bed for a 5 a.m. train departure, even in the dark of a Tianjin winter.

Like most vendors, my guy had a cart that showed up in the morning and disappeared by noon. For consumers, this kind of agility also created uncertainty, especially regarding hygiene.

Jianbing guozi in a village market near Beijing. With aggressive urban planning, these sorts of roadside vendors are quickly disappearing from many cities.

Simply put, you never knew what was in those steamed buns you were buying. Stories abounded and no doubt many of these were true. One memorable TV exposé revealed *baozi* that were stuffed with flavoured cardboard.

A Brave New World (Trade Organization)

China joined the World Trade Organization late in 2001, hurling the country into a whirlwind of global trade and investment. The change supercharged all of the trends of the 1990s.

With the firehose of Chinese exports now pouring into the global market, China suddenly had a lot of wealth, which was reflected in rising incomes. In the twenty years between 1978 and 1999, per-person income in the cities grew by about 330 per cent, just over three times. In the twenty years *after* joining the WTO, household disposable income grew by nearly seven times – roughly twice as fast. Suddenly that Starbucks latte didn't feel so far out of reach – or even that special.

In the other direction, China also started to buy more of the world's imports, especially food. Food grains like rice and wheat remained a politically protected category – China's government did not want to become hostage to world markets for a basic necessity – but other produce was fair game.[1] Just look at the difference between corn, which was classified as a food grain and soybeans, which were not. Corn imports stayed low, but soybeans suddenly became a major import item. So major in fact that China became the world's largest importer of soybeans, far surpassing the European Union. As China's buying power grew, the country's appetite for soybeans transformed global markets. Soybeans became a major U.S. export to China and Chinese state-linked food producers started buying up land overseas, as well as major seed and processing companies like Syngenta, Nidera and Wilmar. In a relatively short time, China's appetite for soybeans has dramatically transformed the ecology of places like Brazil.[2]

But what in the world was China doing with all these soybeans? Two answers: oil and pigs. Soybeans became the main source of cooking oil and the main feed for the hundreds of millions of hogs being raised in concentrated feedlots across the country. This in turn explains one of the most significant changes to the Chinese diet – the rapid increase in meat consumption. Not just pork, but chicken, beef and dairy, including both direct food imports and domestic livestock raised on imported feed – all very fundamentally global.

In fact, food from all over the world was now flooding into China's market. Milk from New Zealand, plastic-wrapped tiramisu from Russia, wine from Chile, barley from Australia, garlic from Korea. That doesn't even account for illegal trade, like the hundreds of thousands of cattle smuggled into China each year from South Asia. Any one of these commodities had its own story and the opportunities of the China market meant that story often included political strong-arming. Even when relations were smooth, the sheer size of the China market transformed almost every country that they opened up to. New Zealand had long been a dairy exporter, but the essentially bottomless market for milk and infant formula in China created a domestic boom that drove cattle-grazing prices to unseen highs.[3] New Zealand reaped the benefits of consistent support for free trade with China. This could work the other way as well – after criticizing China for its handling of COVID-19, Australia found that its wine exports had been taken off the shelf.

The other big story was finance. Foreign companies had already been able to set up operations in China, either as independent entities or as joint ventures with Chinese companies. But, on the whole, the foreign presence inside China was still relatively small. Joining the WTO exposed Chinese producers to real international competition, but it also brought them opportunities for new investment and expertise. Foreign investors were hungry to get in on the ground floor. In many industries, the influx of new money meant the consolidation of small local producers into mega-businesses. Remember the hundreds of local breweries established in the 1980s? This is when they got hoovered up and rebranded. The same thing happened with dairy. During the late 1990s, Nestlé went around the country buying any successful dairy it could find – the Chinese business press called the company an 'acquisitions madman'. But it wasn't just foreign companies who stood to benefit. The same processes built China's own agribusiness conglomerates: today's dairy giant Mengniu first grew exponentially after a 2002 infusion of foreign capital from Morgan Stanley.[4] Over time, Chinese investors have balanced the influence of overseas capital (notably with the influx of state and state-linked investment following the global financial crisis of 2008), but one change was permanent. The scope, operation and aspirations of China's food industries have all become fundamentally global.

Shopping

Even if many of these background transformations were invisible to consumers on the ground, their combined effects have radically transformed China's entire food landscape. Looking at the two major areas – shopping and dining – we see the same trends: big companies overtaking smaller competitors, creating a food experience that was cheaper, more convenient and more streamlined, but also less personal and less local.

Take shopping. In the late 1990s, the foreign megamarket was still something of a novelty. Most big cities had one or two, but they were few and operating beneath potential. In the years after WTO, foreign pioneers like Carrefour, Isetan and Ito-Yokado were joined by new competitors like Walmart, Sam's Club and Costco, as well as a growing number of Chinese challengers. Stocking the shelves was no longer a problem, nor was drawing customers to expensive retail spaces. (Convincing them to buy in bulk was another matter.)

Beyond demand, China's 'supermarket revolution' had another driving force – urban planning.[5] Especially after the 2003 outbreak of SARS, which was spread to humans by infected poultry, Chinese cities began actively moving to dislodge informal food markets of all sorts. Informal street markets had another drawback – they didn't pay tax. 'Wet markets' remained, but were increasingly corralled into purpose-built consolidated centres with tiled counters, regular disinfection and government supervision.[6] Behind the scenes, retailers relied increasingly on trunk wholesale distributors like the ones in the Xinfadi market, which supplies 90 per cent of Beijing's produce. The era of the farmer pulling up to a street market with a truck full of melons was coming to a close. Just like much of the U.S., it was becoming easier for Chinese urban consumers to buy out-of-season fruit from thousands of miles away than it was to get fresh produce from the farm just outside of town.

Restaurants

The catering sector, specifically restaurants, underwent a similar transformation. Starting with the biggest cities, single-outlet restaurants, the kind that had been the standard just a few years earlier, began to disappear. What replaced them? Chains and franchises. Not just Western fast food, but makers of noodles, hotpot, fried chicken, *baozi* and even upscale dining. The reason is a mix of factors, all coming down to the cold reality that multiple-store chains were simply a better way of doing business.

Start with the new mall that replaced your old shopping street. For the restaurant, moving into a mall means paying higher rent.

Restaurant signs hanging in a provincial capital mall. Many franchise kitchens have no open flame and thus tend to serve food that is steamed or braised.

This not only squeezes the owner's profit margin, it also means they want all of their floor space to be earning money, not wasted on something as trivial as a kitchen.

Enter the franchise. Efficient, cheap and instant – and operationally not so different from fast-food outlets – large franchise chains prepare a good deal of their food off-site. Sauces are pre-mixed, vegetables are washed and chopped, the meat sliced, marinated, cooked and sealed in a vacuum bag, which is how it all arrives at the kitchen door, the kitchen often consisting of a few microwaves, a wall of steamers and perhaps a pot for cooking noodles. Not all franchised eating places are this pared down, obviously, but even the higher-end franchises are able to capitalize on efficiencies of scale, doing as much as possible off-site to save time, kitchen floor area and the cost of skilled labour, while also producing food that is highly standard in quantity, appearance and taste.

The ability to make a standard product time after time brings us to another great innovation of franchises – consolidated branding and advertising. With rising costs and growing competition, the importance of maintaining a brand grew exponentially, not just for luring customers, but for attracting investors and potential franchisees. A single restaurant might live or die by daily sales, but for many chains, the *real* goal is to take their company to IPO – initial public offering – status. For these big-scale plans, the future depends on a record of constant growth – not how much is coming out of the kitchen, but how many new kitchens are being opened.

Now, this all may sound a little perverse, but to anyone who lived through the dot-com bubble of the late 1990s, it should also sound familiar. Much of what animated China's food industries after 2010 was speculation, a lot of money chasing any and all opportunities, with everyone hoping to get in on the ground floor of the next big thing.

Sometimes that next big thing turned out to be a short-lived fad. Founded in 1864, the restaurant Quanjude was one of Beijing's traditional purveyors of northern-style roast duck. Although not unscathed by the violence of the Cultural Revolution, it was one of a few restaurants to operate continuously through the revolutionary period, when a Beijing duck banquet was often the de rigueur photo-op for visiting delegations. By the 1980s, the restaurant had returned to its former glory and was setting up new branches in Beijing and nationwide. This sort of expansion made a lot of sense as roast duck scales up well – the slow and complicated wood roasting is all done off-site, with restaurant space reserved for crisping the skin and preparing the side dishes. As the restaurant continued to grow, Chinese newspapers confidently predicted that Beijing roast duck would take the world by storm. The problem was that Quanjude's owners became overly ambitious and planned massive global expansion as the company prepared for a 2007 listing on the Shenzhen stock market. It turned out that these grand plans greatly overestimated both the global appetite for Beijing duck and the ability of the chain to maintain quality while tripling its number of stores. The result was predictable. Reviews punished the restaurant and sales fell along with the stock price. As of this writing, Beijing duck has yet to become (as boosters at the time promised) the 'new McDonald's'.

Just like any other industry, the very *idea* of technology had a magic pull for investors in food. Founded in 2017, Luckin Coffee promised to be the next Starbucks. Their reasoning? Besides having already expanded to nearly 3,000 outlets in China, Luckin Coffee had a phone app and such low delivery fees that home customers found it easier to order a coffee than make one. The store price of signature drinks was relatively high, but unlimited Internet-based coupons made consumers feel like they were getting a premium product at a bargain. Luckin also advertised with a heavy dose of nationalism, using endorsements from local celebrities and playing up their ambitions to become a Chinese global brand. For a while, it seemed to work. Boosted by rumours of their supposedly flawless algorithm which, just like that of the office-space company WeWork, made them a 'technology company' first, Luckin held their IPO in 2019, attracting massive investments from sovereign wealth funds in Qatar and Singapore. But it soon became clear that the app was just an app, that the company was haemorrhaging money (selling your product at a loss will tend to do that) and that the company's growth figures were in fact based on massive accounting fraud. The stock was forced to stop trading and Luckin was kicked off the NYSE. They have since experienced a resurgence in China, in 2022 surpassing Starbucks with 6,500 outlets, but they are still no closer to making a profit.

Chinese investment money was also going overseas. For years, China had single-mindedly focused on bringing in foreign exchange, but by the 2010s, a significant amount of money was starting to flow in the other direction. During that heady decade, China invested over a trillion dollars in assets overseas, concentrated especially in strategic areas like energy, mining and technology. Food was a small part of this big picture, representing just under 10 per cent of the total invested, but it attracted attention because the idea of China buying food producers brought up images of a hungry China literally 'starving the world', and because the style of investment (facilitated by cheap government loans) was to swagger in and buy the biggest name company on the block. Some of the early purchases, like when a much smaller Chinese company bought u.s. pork producer Smithfield, tried to soothe these concerns by paying far above the company's valuation. Others, like Shanghai-based dairy Guangming's multibillion-yuan purchase of an Israeli dairy cooperative, were spectacular failures, suggesting that some Chinese buyers were simply burning through cash before the music stopped.[7]

Alternatives

So, to sum up, China's joining the wTO took existing food trends and added rocket fuel. Within a few short years, the country's food landscape had changed so quickly that a visitor transported from the 1990s wouldn't have recognized the place. Shops, markets and entire streets of restaurants were gone. In many places, local favourites had been completely replaced by global brands, national chains and standardized tastes.

The price of efficiency was that food had become depersonalized. At one time, you might have walked out of your door and had two choices for *shaobing*; you might dislike one of your two choices: one might be too salty (either the *shaobing* or the person who made them), maybe the owner short-changed you once, or you might not like the idea that he rolls his dough with a cigarette hanging out of in his mouth. Regardless of how you made your choice, these small shops and the products they sold were part of a human network, your own world of people, habits and tastes. The arrival of big retail chains, selling factory-made foods, took the process out of sight and out of control, which is all fine as long as you have trust in the people and processes that brings food, cut, washed and wrapped in shiny plastic, to your local hypermart.

That is, until you don't.

Late in 2007, rumours began to circulate on Chinese social media that a well-known brand of powdered infant formula was making children sick. Before long, it was confirmed that the product had already affected hundreds of thousands of infants, including eight who would later die of kidney failure. The reason was that the formula had been laced with melamine, an industrial plastic that mimics protein in certain laboratory tests. In other words, someone was watering down the raw milk and then adding a poisonous chemical to cover the fact. And it turned out that someone was *everyone* – farmers, collection stations, middlemen . . . people at every stage of the chain were skimming a little extra profit and making the final product just a tiny bit more deadly. This wasn't the first time that corrupt practices had poisoned China's milk supply. Just a few years earlier, a plant in Anhui had been caught stripping protein from its milk powder, which is why the protein tests had been implemented in the first place.[8]

Reaction was intense and immediate. For one thing, nobody wanted to buy food from China. Not just milk; foreign markets for Chinese fruit and seafood exports disappeared overnight. China's parents felt much the same. Although the poisoning was officially blamed on Beijing's Sanlu Dairy, the common sentiment was that the outbreak reflected practices that were rampant throughout the industry. Pricey foreign-made milk products flew

Selling *shaobing* in 1930s Beijing.

off the shelves and when that supply was exhausted, a vast black market developed to ship tins of infant formula to China from overseas. Years after the outbreak, there were still people making a living shuttling back and forth across the Hong Kong border, carrying two suitcases full of tins of formula powder into China on each trip. Stores as far away as Australia rationed how much a customer could buy at one time. China's government responded with sweeping food safety laws, but trust in the system was irreparably damaged.

In retrospect, the milk-poisoning scandal was just a trigger for forces that had already been brewing. China's consumers, especially the newly wealthy ones, had for years been growing more restless, seeking not just assurance of safety, but a return to authenticity in their food. For some, this meant rejecting GMOs or certain types of plastic packaging. Others sought out food that was certified organic or green, even if they didn't understand the difference between the two or fully trust the government bodies that provided these labels.

A more fundamental sort of reaction sought to restore a personal connection with agriculture. In 2008, with the Sanlu scandal at its peak, a group of PhD students from Beijing's elite Renmin University started the 'Little Donkey' farm in the hilly area just north of the city. Their inspiration was the Community Supported Agriculture (CSA) movement that was already deeply rooted in Europe, the United States and Japan. Little Donkey didn't just grow organic food, it was also a social and educational movement that gave urbanites the chance to reconnect with agriculture. Not long after, the same founders set up the Shared Harvest Farm, a larger venture about an hour away from the city.[9] In addition to being a working farm, Shared Harvest also runs year-round educational projects that bring in grade-school students to learn about composting, get their hands dirty planting flowers and see actual livestock running around. That last category includes the author, one of a handful of urbanites who flee the city on weekends to grow vegetables on small patches of land that we rent from the farm.

Little Donkey and Shared Harvest are hardly unique. Both are part of a Chinese CSA network that includes hundreds of farms and millions of consumers nationwide. Even before the COVID-19 lockdowns turned people to food delivery, millions of Chinese households were already using CSA platforms to buy vegetables, fruit, meat and a growing number of handcrafted food products.

A second, somewhat related trend looks back to recapture and revive China's food heritage. Starting just before China joined the WTO, a number of government departments began a movement to officially recognize and certify heritage businesses, both to raise public pride in China's commercial tradition and to keep foreign businesses from swooping in and buying up the recognition value of a well-known brand for cheap. You can see the results of this initiative today in the 'famous old brand' certification displayed proudly in shopfronts, advertisements and packages.[10] Other types of heritage certification aim to highlight unique local products and protect the human networks that preserve and continue handcraft traditions. Similar to the certification of *terroir* in products like Champagne or Parmigiano Reggiano cheese, heritage certification of products like Jinhua ham or the dark vinegar made in Zhenjiang ties a product to a place and, more often than not, to a particular community of craftspeople.

The formalization of place-based heritage inevitably leads to conflict. Projects like the UNESCO registry of Intangible Cultural Heritage is just one of the arenas that countries use to settle the question of who owns iconic foods – is hummus Arab or Israeli? Does borscht belong to Russia or Ukraine? Is kimchi Korean or Chinese? Sometimes a mutual solution can be found. The medicinal cooling drink known as *liangcha* is officially registered as the Intangible Cultural Heritage of China, Hong Kong and Macao, because the three decided beforehand to submit their application jointly.

But even with such goodwill, the lines around food heritage are rarely clear. The humble egg tart is an icon of Macao. A charred-top crème brûlée inside a flaky pastry crust, Macanese egg tarts are reminiscent of the equally iconic Portuguese *pastéis de nata*, sold by the thousands at the original bakery in the Belém district of Lisbon. But not so fast. Egg tarts are also a favourite of Hong Kong's *cha chaan teng* tea cafés, where they are made with a shortcrust instead of flaky pastry and the top not charred, in the style of a classic British egg-custard tart. Along with three dozen other foods and food techniques, egg tarts were inscribed as the Intangible Cultural Heritage of Hong Kong during the first round of registration in 2014. So is this a case of distinct lines of cultural transmission reaching to the two former colonies – British-style egg tarts to Hong Kong and Portuguese ones to Macao? Wrong again. Cantonese *dim sum* also has its own classic steamed-egg dishes like *dundan*, although these dishes are savoury, not sweet, and do not have the iconic crust. And just to make the story even messier, the shop selling those iconic tarts in Macao was actually started in the 1970s by British businessman Andrew Stow, who saw an opportunity to give locals a taste of home. His former wife sold the recipe to KFC, who now sell millions of them a day, all over Asia.[11]

Government certification could rocket a local product from obscurity to global fame. Starting in the mid-1990s, the government of Sichuan's Pi County went all in on promoting the locally produced bean paste, along the way getting a quote from a Chengdu artist to the effect that the bean paste from Pi County was the 'soul of Sichuan cuisine'. To be clear, Pi County Sichuan bean paste is indeed great stuff. A spoonful of bean paste fried up with aromatics like garlic and ginger makes up the foundation of many Sichuan dishes and the chilli-laced bean paste from Pi County is justly well known, taking pride of place in hundreds of millions of kitchens, including my own. But the 'soul of Sichuan cuisine'? Until recently, most rural Sichuan families would have fermented their own bean paste in a jar that sat in the courtyard, opened once a day to let in the sun. The taste of the bean paste improved with age and the precise recipe of your family's paste was your family's secret. No matter. With this one famous quote, advertising for Pi County bean paste confirmed the authenticity of a standard taste that is now inseparable from Sichuan cuisine, all based on nostalgia for a past that never really existed. After all, marketing is just the art of telling stories. Like consumers everywhere, Chinese consumers want to hear stories about authenticity.

The early years of China's economic growth had been rife with the vices of the nouveau riche, the sort of crass showing off and brand chasing that led people to drop thousands of yuan (generally of someone else's money) on a bottle of *baijiu* that might just get vomited up later in the evening. If that sort of conspicuous consumption was a feature of the 1990s, the early 2000s were the era of the all-you-can-eat-buffet. On the one hand, the buffet was economical, even something that you could turn into a game. When Pizza Hut brought its pay-one-price salad bar to its then small number of outlets in China, they probably expected that people would want to crowd as much food as possible on their plates. What they didn't expect is that this enthusiasm would become a science of making 'salad towers' that could grow over a foot tall. Reaching these heights required planning: in one

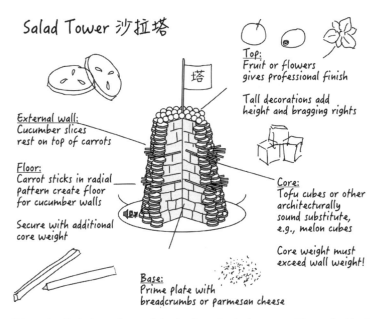

Salad Tower 沙拉塔

Top:
Fruit or flowers gives professional finish

Tall decorations add height and bragging rights

External wall:
Cucumber slices rest on top of carrots

Floor:
Carrot sticks in radial pattern create floor for cucumber walls

Secure with additional core weight

Core:
Tofu cubes or other architecturally sound substitute, e.g., melon cubes

Core weight must exceed wall weight!

Base:
Prime plate with breadcrumbs or parmesan cheese

塔

Schematic of 'salad tower', as explained to the author by former practitioner of said arts.

often-shared schema, a priming layer of breadcrumbs provides friction at the base of the bowl, allowing the careful builder to construct a circular retaining wall of stacked cucumber slices around the rim. As the wall grows higher, the inside space is supported by a weight-bearing core of tofu cubes or potato salad, sometimes interspersed with additional subfloors of carrot sticks. Ideally the structure would remain intact long enough to bring it back to the table and take a picture. The Pizza Hut salad tower became a short-lived fad, more for fun than for value, but disappeared when the chain abruptly pulled the salad bars from its restaurants in China.

To my mind, nothing sums up that decade better than the rise and fall of the Golden Money Panther chain of restaurants, where for the single-entry price of 268 yuan you could eat your fill of every food imaginable, from sashimi to foie gras, along with unlimited beer. For a time, the restaurant was wildly popular, spreading from Shanghai and Beijing into lower-tier cities and, somewhat inexplicably, even opening a hotel. But the decline was just as fast. The restaurant had over-expanded, started using cheaper vendors and soon stopped paying its suppliers altogether. By 2018 the chain was bankrupt, its cavernous gilded dining spaces lying abandoned like a ballroom on the doomed *Titanic*.

So, what happened? Besides a flawed business model, Golden Money Panther had fallen behind the times. In my one experience with the chain, the food was simply not very good. The steaks tasted processed, the sashimi had a faint whiff of ammonia and the pretty deserts were clearly mass-produced. Online reviews agreed that the restaurant offered a lavish appearance, but that the food itself was all of second-tier quality. Some of this decline may have been the death throes of a financially strapped business, but I suspect that the real change was less the food than the diner. As Chinese consumers grew wealthier, they also grew more discerning and less interested in gorging on cut-price foie gras.

By the second decade of the 2000s, there were unmistakable signs of a generational change. Younger people still wanted their Mercedes and their Prada bag, but they didn't worship these brands with quite the same abandon as their parents' generation. Some even started to mutter about the habits of the 'ugly rich', people with more money than taste and probably a few unattractive secrets about how they got that money in the first place. That generational change happened slowly and still is by no means complete, but at its root is a growing search for meaning and authenticity.

Some are taking this a large step further. With the sudden emergence of online marketing networks, this profound craving for connection has produced a wave of social media stars who sell the *experience* of authenticity. The first group is best embodied by the mega-influencer Li Ziqi, whose wordless videos have attracted hundreds of millions of views on YouTube and even more on Chinese sites like bilibili. Each of her videos focuses on the preparation of a single dish, often beginning with Li hiking up a mountain to gather fresh ingredients like bamboo shoots or forest mushrooms, which she then prepares and cooks using rustic implements in an outdoor kitchen and silently enjoys either alone or in the company of an elderly villager. Never mind that the setting is obviously staged, that recipes themselves are criticized for being impractical or that Li has an immense social media team behind the promotion of her unadorned lifestyle. What Li is selling is not instruction but emotion, the feeling of fresh mist rising off the ferns, the sound of water dripping from a bamboo pipe into a vat of clear water. She hardly invented the aesthetic. Much of it resembles the lovingly romantic visuals of food presented in the hugely successful TV series *A Bite of China*. But within this social media landscape, Li has staked out a unique territory. If the abusive screaming of rage-filled restaurant chefs occupies one end of the culinary-entertainment spectrum, Li represents the exact opposite pole. And like every successful social media star, there are thousands more like her enjoying more limited fame.

Another sort of technology-infused connection comes from online commerce. This of course crosses over with social media influencers as product sales are one of their main sources of income. But the effect of online commerce on small and handicraft food makers is much, much larger than just watching videos.

Take for example the dried cheese known as *rushan*. This traditional product from Yunnan in the far southwest is made by heating fresh milk and adding a lactic acid coagulant to separate out the protein. A skilled worker then forms the milk solids into a lump of fresh cheese, stretches the cheese to build elasticity, wraps it around bamboo poles to resemble a fan (the name *rushan* means 'milk fans') and then hangs the poles out to dry in the fresh highland sun. The finished sheets of *rushan* are hard as a rock, but steaming, deep-frying or grilling over a charcoal fire will soften them up nicely.

Until relatively recently, the only way you could get *rushan* was to travel to Yunnan. People who visited Yunnan tourist meccas like Dali or Lijiang were expected to return with a bag full of local products – *rushan*, rose petal sweets, dried spiced beef. The tourist industry obliged, with local shops selling all of these products in a variety of gift-ready sizes. This entire economy of local products is now obsolete, for exactly the same reason that a visitor to Beijing is no longer expected to return home with a bag full of McDonald's hamburgers – items that were once scarce are now readily available. Online platforms like JD.com and Taobao.com are now poised to deliver handmade *rushan* right to your door. This may be bad news for the tourist shops, but for producers, online commerce has expanded the fame and the market for local products beyond all imagination. Five years ago, my friend's *rushan* workshop in Dali was going through around 400 litres (roughly 100 gallons) of fresh milk per day. Selling directly to consumers all over China, she now does ten times that much. This same story is replicated for every conceivable handcrafted food product. Visit my own small kitchen in Beijing and you will find smoked pork belly, yak brisket, salted duck eggs and preserved bamboo, either gifts from friends or purchased online from producers all across China, not to mention a variety of niche produce, wines, oils, vinegars and sauces that I bought just because they sounded interesting.

The World in a (Styrofoam) Box

There is another side to all of this convenience. Beyond the obvious problem of all that packing waste (and there is a lot) is what the delivery model has done to restaurant dining. Yes, it's time to talk about delivery apps.

In a few short years, the 'app economy' has visibly transformed China's larger cities: hire bikes are suddenly everywhere and taxis have been completely replaced by ride-hailing. It's a pretty grand understatement to say that mobile phone apps have saturated people's consciousness and transformed everything down to the smallest detail of daily life.

Not least of all eating. The two major delivery platforms, Eleme ('are you hungry?') and Meituan both started around 2010. Each had the backing of one of the big tech companies, which means that each one was plugged into an existing ecosystem of payments, ratings and online commerce, not to mention a loyal user base. The sector immediately exploded, aided by the country's rollout of a 5G mobile phone service and not long after that, by the COVID-19 lockdown.

What made delivery – known as *waimai* – so enormously popular? For one thing, it was cheap. Customers search for restaurants from one centralized list and that search can be sorted to prioritize price. This produced the same effect that travel sites

Food delivery drivers outside a mall in Beijing.

had on the airline industry – a race to appear at the top of the list by being the cheapest, even if only by a tiny amount. Delivery charges were often more than offset by the promise of special discounts, loyalty programmes, VIP cards and so on. And the delivery costs themselves were not high. The new industry could rely on an army of low-paid scooter drivers who risked life and limb (both their own and those of anyone standing in their way) to get the product to the customer on time or risk paying the bill out of their own meagre salary.

Convenience was certainly the main draw. Fast food took off because it was novel and stuck around because it was easy. Delivery is no different. Data collected by the delivery services themselves reveal that the earliest and most consistent customers were either office workers who wanted to eat a quick meal at their desks or office workers who were tired after a day at their desks and wanted something fast and easy when they got home. But other groups soon started to catch on and catch up – the elderly, new parents and students. Surprisingly, variety was not much of a draw at all. Faced with a choice of every dish on the menu of every restaurant in the city, most people tended to order the same thing over and over, a behavioural tendency called 'choice fatigue'.

Restaurants in China didn't like delivery services any more than they did in other places and for the same reasons. The platform encourages cut-throat competition, with the service absorbing much of an already thin profit margin. Large chains could pay commissions to keep their stores at the top of the search list, but smaller ones were shut out. Faced with slimmer profits, most restaurants came to rely on volume. Especially at the height of the COVID-19 lockdown, you could walk into a mid-priced restaurant at lunchtime and see the entire dining room empty, except for a frantic stream of delivery drivers running in to grab their order from a table of wrapped-and-tagged plastic bags.

And we haven't even got to the issue of quality. Since most delivery customers are price-driven creatures of habit, it actually takes quite a lot to drive them away. If you order the same thing every day, you might be a little disappointed in today's lunch, but by tomorrow you will probably have forgotten. And if your main concern is convenience, your standards might not have been so high to begin with. Even the most carefully prepared meal will suffer significantly from being packed in a plastic box and allowed to cool to room temperature on the back of a scooter. The solution is the same one they use on aeroplanes – cram the food with strong tastes – chilli, vinegar, oil, salt and MSG. For those who retort that MSG can be found in nature, I agree but also note that the half teaspoon that gets casually chucked into each dish is the equivalent of half a kilo of umami-rich tomatoes. In other words, MSG may be fine, but the doses that we are getting are anything but natural. Cooks may not admit it (although many will), but far less care goes into a *waimai* order than does the exact same dish in a dining room. *Waimai* orders are made fast, spiked with salt and MSG and chucked into a container. That's how they can put out so many meals during a lunch rush and unless the food is so *memorably* awful, it won't matter much.

Taste of China

I don't want to give the impression that everyone deserted the kitchen en masse. Rather, that *waimai* ate away at certain habits and segments. For many office workers – the biggest consumers of delivery – *waimai* replaced a daily lunch of packaged food, especially instant ramen noodles. But instant noodles aren't going away, at least not in China, which remains by a large margin the world's largest consumer. (That's total sales; measured per capita, South Korea is nearly three times higher.) According to the World Instant Noodles Association, which I must emphasize is a thing that exists, Chinese demand declined significantly from 2013 to 2016, but then went right back up after 2017. What happened? At the low point of 2016, economists and observers saw the reason as the declining number of migrants, a main consumer of instant noodles, and rising incomes in rural areas. But since then, other groups have decided to cut back on food expenses – especially prepared food – in favour of a pot of cheap, filling instant noodles.[12] From a health perspective, instant noodles are unequivocally awful. Some of the worst offenders manage to pack a full day's allowance of sodium into a single serving.

But that hasn't dissuaded creative home cooks from inventing all manner of tasty enhancements. An Internet search for 'instant noodle upgrades' (升级版方便面) will open a whole world of questionably healthy delights, all variations on the theme of replacing the included flavour packet with something new: tomato sauce, a cube of Japanese curry roux, a spoon of peanut butter, Korean *gochujang* chilli paste or some combination of each. From there, you can add pre-cooked carrots, tofu, sliced ham, luncheon meat (aka Spam) or fish balls, and finish with a dusting of sliced green onions. Perfect for the many urban kitchens that come with a hotplate and little else. If anything sums up this trend of dormitory chic, it's the dish of instant noodles with processed cheese:

Cheese Instant Ramen

Add ¾ cup milk and ¾ cup water to a saucepan or clay pot, and bring to a boil over medium heat. Add a cake of dried instant noodles, and 1 teaspoon of chicken flavouring (powder or liquid, the original packet can be substituted). Lay 2 slices of processed cheese over the top, and crack 1 egg directly into the noodles (where they are not covered by the cheese). Turn off the heat and cover for 10 minutes, after which the egg yolk should still be soft. Sprinkle with *furikake* (dried seaweed) and serve.

(This is just one of many ways of preparing this dish. Others include using a toaster oven's grill to melt cheese over a dish of cooked noodles squirted with tomato ketchup. And yes, Cheese Ramen is sold in restaurants.)

Most convenience foods, like individually wrapped, shelf-stable snacks, are just mass-produced versions of foods that would once have been sold by a vendor. This is the case for the sad, plastic-wrapped tea eggs, or for the little chunks of spiced tofu that can sit for months on the shelves of convenience stores. But like so many foods that have gone the route of mass production, the healthier and tastier version is still the one made at home:

Spiced Dried Tofu

Cut 1 block of firm tofu into 1-cm-thick slices. Lay these flat on a steam tray or a stove-top steamer and steam for

10 minutes. When the slices are cool enough to handle, lay them in a single layer on top of some cheesecloth or a clean kitchen towel. If adding a second layer, separate these with another cloth. Cover with a third cloth and a large cutting board weighted down with a water-filled mixing bowl.

Leave to sit for about 1 hour, after which the tofu pieces will be thin and dense, and able to bend without breaking. If the tofu is not yet the right consistency, you can reheat and repeat the pressing with more weight. Cut the pieces in half lengthwise.

Heat 500 ml of water in a saucepan, add ½ cup large-cut onion pieces (sections of long onion, or ½ globe onion), 4 slices of ginger, 4 sliced cloves of garlic, 4 dried chillies, a handful of Sichuan peppercorns, 1 star anise and 1 bay leaf. Add 1 teaspoon of salt, and 3 tablespoons each of rock sugar (or ordinary sugar), dark soy sauce and oyster sauce. Bring to a simmer and add the sliced tofu.

After 15 minutes, the tofu should be brown and fragrant with spice. Remove and pat dry with a paper towel. These will be lovely sliced into strips and tossed with sesame oil, eaten as a snack with rice, or just on their own.

Other fad foods just took off on their own. Home cooks fell in love with a dish of pork ribs cooked in Coca-Cola, and then adapted the dish to chicken wings. Another was the craze for 'New Orleans' spice, especially after KFC added New Orleans-style chicken to its menus in the early 2000s. As of this writing, New Orleans-style chicken wings are available at KFC in China and absolutely nowhere else. You can buy New Orleans spice mix from any shop – I even know Chinese friends who ship it to their children living in the United States. What does this spice mix have to do with New Orleans? About as much as McDonald's Szechuan Sauce has to do with Sichuan – that is, nothing. In fact, both are based on essentially the same foundation of salt, sugar and onion powder. That hasn't stopped home cooks from falling in love with New Orleans chicken wings, cooked in their air fryers, the go-to gadget of the decade.

New Orleans Chicken Wings

Use any brand of packaged New Orleans spice mix, or if that is not available, make your own by mixing 3 teaspoons of mild chilli powder, 1 teaspoon each of onion powder, garlic powder and oyster sauce, and ½ teaspoon each of sugar, salt and five-spice powder.

Pat dry 1 package of chicken wings and pierce the skin of each one four or five times with the tip of a sharp knife. Toss the wings in a bowl first with a light coating of soy sauce and then with the spice mix. Let them rest for 15 minutes and then cook according to air fryer instructions.

Now, I am probably not making a lot of friends by closing this section not with romantic images of high cuisine, but with snack food. But this is a very big growth area, selling countless billions of units per year, and the fact is that someone is buying it. It's more than convenience; the normalization of snack foods also reflects changing tastes. If you eat a diet heavy in sugar and salt, you get accustomed to it. The strong tastes of *waimai* and pre-made restaurant food reflect this trend, none more so than *chuan*, the go-to snack of the 2000s.

Chuan 串 are precisely what the character suggests they would be: things on a stick. There are different types. Grilled *chuan* are beef or lamb kebabs dusted with cumin and chilli and cooked over charcoal. Originating in Central Asia, grilled *chuan* are a classic street food. Until recently every market, bus station and school entrance would have at least one vendor, manning a long thin grill. Grilled *chuan* are a world away from the watery, oversized cubes of beef that my part of the world tries to palm off on unsuspecting barbeque goers. Rather, these are cut thin so that the meat is grilled, rather than steamed internally, and skewered in a way to alternate lean and fat meat, like a *shawarma* rotated 90 degrees towards the horizon. *Chuan* are relatively easy to prepare, especially if you can muster up a bit of kitchen labour to help with the tedious task of threading the meat onto sticks. Some recipes make this process unnecessarily complex, calling for marinating the meat in pear juice, preparing a flavoured basting oil, or pre-smoking the spices that will end up being cooked over a charcoal grill. I see no need for any of that. A good piece of lamb is really all you need:

Grilled Lamb Chuan

Trim off the large pieces of fat from ½ kg lamb. Place the fat to one side: The ratio of lean meat to fat should be about 4:1. Cut both meat into roughly 2–3-cm cubes and the fat slightly smaller. Combine both in a bowl and add one small chopped onion and plenty of salt. If you are concerned about the meat being tough, you can add ¼ teaspoon of baking soda as a tenderizer. Mix thoroughly, add one teaspoon of flour and mix again. Add 2 tablespoons of oil, mix to coat, cover and set aside to rest for 20 minutes.

Prepare the spice mix by combining 1 tablespoon each of cumin and ground chilli, and 1 teaspoon each of sesame and salt.

Thread the rested meat onto pre-soaked bamboo skewers, alternating lean meat and fat and squeezing as you go to even things up. Take care not to crowd the skewers. Place flat in a tray, cover with plastic wrap and refrigerate for one hour. Start the charcoal at least half an hour before cooking.

Grill the kebabs over steady charcoal heat (or an electric grill), turning frequently and dusting repeatedly with the spice mix. Grabbing and turning whole handfuls at a time bastes the kebabs with spice and rendered fat and also looks quite fancy. Make sure to cook thoroughly; slightly overcooked is preferable to underdone.

The other type of *chuan* is cooked in broth. Instead of meat, these might be fishcake, meatballs, little sausages, imitation crab sticks, deep-fried tofu, potato slices, daikon radish, or cross-cut corn on the cob, each on its own little stick, bubbling away in a bath of soup. In theory, these all sound perfectly nice; in reality, the ingredients are often extremely processed. But in fact, that strong, salty, factory-fresh taste can be pretty attractive after a long day of work, and as if we needed more reason, it also goes great with beer.

As for the soup, there is the Guandong-style fish stock based on Japanese *oden*. Guandong (not Guangdong – different place) stock is traditionally made from umami-rich *kombu* seaweed and smoky dried bonito. But now it mostly comes from a powder, the main ingredients of which are salt, MSG and sugar.

The more popular and beer-friendly version cooks the skewers in spicy *mala* soup. This is essentially a convenient iteration of Chongqing hotpot – it uses basically the same stock, plus someone else has already gone to the trouble of cooking your food for you. Like Guandong-style, *mala* hotpot spans an immense range of quality. The traditional preparation is a glorious affair involving frying massive amounts of onions, chillies, bean paste and spices in a giant pot of melted beef tallow. This is really only for an industrial kitchen. Even if you did know how to make *mala* soup base from scratch, the smell of tallow-fried chillies would follow you for weeks and once-friendly neighbours would suddenly be neither. Instead, home cooks make this broth by dissolving a giant block of pre-made base in hot water. While far easier, that still requires you to go out and buy all the stuff that goes in it. Be it *chuan* or hotpot (both the same dish, essentially), it's just easier to have someone else to do the work.

Banquet on Demand

The hotpot restaurant Haidilao was started in 1994, making it a relatively new company. (We will keep calling Haidilao a restaurant, but since we're about to go full-on corporate, we might think of it as more of a 'restaurant concept'.)

The chain started in Sichuan, a place with no shortage of hotpot restaurants. Hotpot, as we have discussed, can be found in a lot of places and so can the myths about how it was invented. But the dish is common enough that many places have their own local style. Beijing hotpot is traditionally served in a samovar-style copper pot heated by a lump of hot coal in the middle. Sichuan hotpot is usually served with two broths, one very plain and one spicy. Once a favourite of boat pullers working along the Chongqing docks, hotpot was never a fancy food, but it was quick and provided a kick of salt and energy. While most home and many restaurant kitchens today will simply flavour their hotpot with a pre-made block of spices, the traditional method for making Chongqing hotpot is a fairly laborious multi-stage process of frying a long list of aromatics and spices – onions, fresh and pickled ginger, fermented black beans, cinnamon, star anise, fennel, bay leaves, Sichuan peppercorns and course piles and piles of pickled and dried chillies, all in a base of beef tallow. Whether made in batches of 1 kilogram or 100, that base can then store almost indefinitely.

As a restaurant owner, how do you stand out? If you're in a place that is known for the quality of its livestock, somewhere like the Hulunbuir grasslands in the far north of Inner Mongolia, you sell that. Hotpot restaurants in the Hulunbuir city of Hailar do exactly that, informing customers that their beef comes from Chenqi and the sheep are raised in Xiqi. To an in-the-know Hulunbuir diner, that speaks volumes, since the grazing in Chenqi suits cattle, while the grass in Xiqi is especially suited to producing excellent sheep. And locals are *very* much in the know. (I once asked a group of Mongol cattle herders about the quality of Hulunbuir beef, prompting everyone to take out their mobile phones to show me pictures of cut meat like they were treasured snaps of their child's first birthday.) Woe unto the restaurant that ever tried to pass off lot-raised beef to a Mongol herdsman.

The path of superb quality was not open to Haidilao. Mongolian hotpot is generally cooked in water, flavoured only with ginger, onion and a sprinkling of wolfberries. People who take meat seriously (as do my friends in Hulunbuir) find the idea of using a strong broth to mask the taste of meat offensive, almost insulting. Sichuan hotpot is numbingly hot and diners would balk at anything less, but it would be a waste to use the highest quality ingredients. Secondly, Haidilao started in the small industrial city of Jianyang, hardly a centre of fine dining. As a mid-range restaurant seeking a place among other mid-range restaurants, Haidilao was mostly concerned with maintaining competitive prices and consumer experience.

It was the latter that shot them to fame. During the 1990s, the original restaurant in Jianyang developed a reputation for extreme hospitality, offering unique services like giving manicures to sitting diners. The chain's own lore has it that upon seeing a customer with dirty shoes, founder Zhang Yong (a former welder) sent the shoes out to be cleaned at no charge. More than the food, which remained fairly ordinary, this sort of over-the-top service became their calling card. Customers waiting for a seat can still get their nails done and their shoes polished for free.

The chain started expanding in China during the late 1990s and overseas during the 2000s, also investing in its own supply-chain infrastructure and introducing home delivery service in 2010. All the while, rumours circulated that the company was preparing for a public listing. When it did finally launch its Hong Kong IPO in 2018, the listing attracted eager investment from private and institutional investors, including Hillhouse Capital and Morgan Stanley, as well as banks and sovereign wealth funds in China, Singapore and Norway. In one swoop, the value of the company rocketed to nearly U.S.$1 billion.[13]

So, what makes the chain so attractive? From an investor standpoint, Haidilao embodies much of what we have seen in this chapter. It operates its own stores, rather than franchising, a strategy that requires deep cash reserves but creates supply efficiencies.[14] It is also future-looking, especially as regards technology. Haidilao was an early pioneer of the 'chefless kitchen', with almost all food preparation done off-site. Other mid-level chains, such as the Sichuan restaurant Meizhou dongpo switched to this model during the COVID-19 squeeze, with little complaint from diners.

For customers, the attraction is still not about the food. A survey of 250 diners in Beijing confirms that customers associate the chain with quality, but when asked to specify what that means, most focused on the enthusiasm and professionalism of the employees. In other words, Haidilao is still known mostly for quality *service*. The food is consistent, but few view it as extraordinary.[15]

Social media brought the convenience of food delivery . . . and ushered in the era
of the distracted diner.

In this sense, Haidilao encapsulates as well as anyone the core
values of China's franchise age. Despite being currently over-
stretched (soon after the IPO, the chain ambitiously doubled its
number of outlets), Haidilao is a remarkably efficient earner.
Just like fast food, the chain delivers a reliably good product in a
cheerful setting.

Sometimes that setting is the most familiar of all. Like many
hotpot chains, Haidilao wanted to jump on the *waimai* band-
wagon, or at least get a space in the delivery box. The problem
is that hotpot is not exactly portable. The traditional set-up
involves a giant bronze samovar fired with a bucket of hot coals,
but even the more modern one requires a special table with an
inset heater. It's easy enough to make hotpot at home using a
pot over an electric burner, but there's still shopping and clean-
ing up afterwards. When you order online, everything arrives
together: food, sauces, paper tablecloth, disposable plates and
an electric chafing dish. When you're done, you return the pot

to the box it came in and leave it for pickup. Almost like ordering room service.

Haidilao wasn't the first to offer this service, and it isn't the only one. But for many, it is the first choice. What makes the chain a sales titan is that most valuable and elusive of all twenty-first-century qualities: Haidilao has name recognition.

7

And Beyond . . .

For our last banquet, we have some choices. We might be
going to a university coffee shop, a rebranded fast-food
chain or the campus of a food tech start-up. We might be
enjoying the produce of the world or just a small part of it.
We might never see our chef because there is none. We
might choose our food or it might be chosen for us.

Whatever shape our last banquet eventually ends up
taking, all the ingredients for China's different food futures
already exist.

As we have already travelled through 5,000 years of history,
who could resist a peek into China's food future?

In many ways, the seeds of this future have already been
planted. Politically, China has laid a strong foundation to protect
its food security and, barring any major global shocks, will become
ever more confident of its leverage in global markets. State and
private investment currently flowing into future food technologies
like plant-based meat, smart farms and blockchain sourcing will
begin to bear fruit and make their way to market. China's consumers have shown every sign of embracing this future, if only because
cost and convenience are likely to trump all other concerns.

What might a Chinese banquet look like in ten years' time?
Extrapolating from existing trends and from the state-of-the-art

technology that China had hoped to showcase at events such as Beijing's 2022 Winter Olympics, we close *Seven Banquets* with a few possible scenarios for the near future.

Before going any further, let's start with some of the lessons we've learned from our romp through five millennia of China's food history.

One myth that I hope will have been dispelled is the idea of 'traditional China'. This isn't to deny the deep well of culture that China still draws on. What I reject is a concept of tradition that takes a photograph of the past and freezes it in time. To a historian, this sort of tradition is a romantic ideal of a past that never really existed; it's a past without change or change that is so glacially slow that it doesn't affect anyone.

But if there is one constant in history, it is change. The sepia-toned image of China's so-called traditional cuisine, the sort of dishes praised by the eighteenth-century gastronome Yuan Mei, would have been impossibly foreign to previous generations of diners in the Tang court and even more so to the golden age of Confucius – not just the constantly changing list of ingredients, but dishes and techniques that didn't exist until a relatively late date.

The idea of tradition is inseparable from nostalgia and nostalgia is always a moving target. Everything old was new once – in many cases, shockingly or offensively so. Think of a classic sort of dining scene we might imagine for Shanghai in the 1930s – a line of women wearing tightly fitting silk *qipao* dresses carrying in dishes of food to a group of stylish diners seated around a large mahogany table, jazz music gently wafting in from an old-timey gramophone in the next room. Much of this romantic scene is new – the gramophone most obviously and let's get rid of those electric lights while we're at it. We'll even replace the Shanghai jazz with a performance of regional *kunqu* opera.

So, are we traditional yet? Not quite, since *kunqu* was itself a relatively new form of opera – purists at the time would have called it garish. How about the clothes? Obviously, the men need to change those 'swallow tail' dinner jackets for long gowns, but the serving women need to change as well, since the silk *qipao* was itself an invention of the early twentieth century, a modernized version of Manchu court dress. And even if the dishes are all scrupulously classical – let's even pretend that the restaurant itself is an homage to Yuan Mei – the ingredients had all been carried in by ship and railway, stored on ice, bottled, tinned and so on. We might see this as a quintessentially nostalgic scene, but to an old-timer, it all would have been distressingly modern.

But not all change is equal. Fads come and go – that's their job – but linear changes like advances in technology tend to move in one direction, transforming the ground beneath our feet. The key drivers of change – industrialization, globalization, franchising or social media – were revolutionary in the sense that the world could scarcely go back to how things had been before their arrival.

And now these changes are coming faster than ever.

What Might Be Coming

To envision the direction of change, let's start with the food challenges that China will face in the next decade. We can break the big challenges down into a few groups:

The first one is food security, meaning that China will have enough food. This is usually defined as staple grains, but because we can't expect people to return to a famine diet, we can also include the food necessities that people have either got used to or those that are needed to keep vital industries running.

The second is the limits of the natural environment. China will face the challenge of maintaining, expanding or substituting domestic food production while stemming or reversing the effects of decades of environmental degradation.

The third is food safety, which at one level means keeping food free of pesticides and poisons, but in a broader public health sense also means raising awareness of good nutrition and ensuring that ordinary people have access to wholesome food.

The last is maintaining livelihoods. Even after decades of breakneck urbanization, China is still a majority agrarian country, with hundreds of millions of families depending on farming to survive. Add to them the millions more who work in food industries and the fact that many of these industries have political significance at the national or local level.

For facing these issues, the decisive factor will be the direction of policy. This should not be surprising, and as China is both a single-party state and a planned economy, the policy makers in Beijing will naturally have the largest say. Technology comes in second and is itself a sub-category of policy. As the Chinese government is also the country's largest tech investor, any tech gains will have to pass through political considerations before reaching the public. Market trends will play an important role, but they won't determine the direction the country moves in.

For many of China's food challenges, the political directives have already been spelt out. Food security has long been a top concern of China's government. Each year since the mid-'90s, the top governing body has promulgated its agricultural plan as 'Document 1'. For a time, the direction wobbled back and forth between relying on the global market and encouraging China to grow its own grain, but that debate seems to have been settled firmly in favour of self-reliance.

Although the directive for China to supply its own grain puts a heavy strain on scarce land and water resources, the advantages are clear – no relying on market trends and no chance of being put into a corner by a trade war, a lesson that was no doubt deeply reinforced by the global isolation of Russia after the invasion of Ukraine.

To ensure domestic grain self-sufficiency, China has already invested huge sums into major terraforming projects, the diversion of water to the dry north and the opening of large tracts of the northeast to extensive agriculture. Even if much of this production (especially the massive expansion of corn) is eventually destined to feed animals, rather than people, the fact remains that for the first time in over a thousand years, more calories are moving from north to south than the reverse.[1] With grain sufficiency remaining a top concern, the country is likely to need new technology like water capture and GPS-guided automated farming to open areas of the country to extensive agriculture. These projects will be expensive, but the political will is likely to be there.

In other areas, China will seek to exert more control over global markets. More than just a massive importer of agricultural goods, China has aggressively sought a seat at the table to shape global markets. For soybeans, its largest import, China has already bought not just the beans but industry infrastructure like seed companies, oil processors and trading firms. It has also taken out leases on farmland across South America and Africa, expanding its agricultural footprint and arguably outsourcing the environmental costs of its own growing consumption of meat. I don't want to get into the question of whether this is just China playing the market game or whether it represents a new form of imperialism. That debate already has plenty of voices on either side. The point is simply that China has already taken significant steps to insulate itself from the risks of the global market and is not likely to move back from that position. This may be just as well since China has certainly come to understand the dangers of becoming economically dependent on the global market and especially on countries that are politically unfriendly. If a new Cold War were to turn off the tap of global trade, China would want to be ready.

On the other hand (since this is the future, we have to plan all of our scenarios at once), there is good reason to anticipate China becoming more engaged in the global food economy, especially in areas that don't affect its own security. China's food investments now span the globe, supplying the country both with food and with advanced food-production technology. Those future ventures in water-capture farming and GPS-guided automated agriculture are already being pioneered in places like Israel and Australia and it makes much more sense for China to simply buy the technology than to try to develop it from scratch. Even with the end of cheap government loans, new overseas investments are still breaking ground.

China is currently a major food exporter, especially of fruit and produce, but the long-term trend has been to move up the value chain. That means urging local producers to focus on making high-grade steel instead of raw iron ore, smart cars instead of bicycles or computers instead of plastic toys. For food, China's future exports may very well be in the area of infrastructure, such as building smart farming and food-processing systems. Just as China is now installing high-speed rail abroad, becoming a supplier of turnkey agriculture projects overseas would be a way of earning back some of the massive government spending in these areas.

Another area where politics and technology combine to affect food is in developing so-called 'future foods'. Some of these new foods are destined to be short-lived taste fads, but others have truly revolutionary potential. We'll focus on that second group.

The big one for China (and everyone else) is alternative protein. A viable alternative to current methods of producing meat, eggs, seafood and milk would transform the world. Globally, it would halt a major driver of climate change and deforestation. But for China, it would mean removing the need to grow all that corn or to import billions of dollars in soybeans and other feed crops like alfalfa hay, not to mention direct imports of meat and milk. It would be a substantial step towards solving China's persistent water shortage. Of course, this couldn't all take place at once, but given enough time, meat alternatives could start to make their way first into processed food – KFC and Burger King already have product lines using Beyond Meat – and then into semi-prepared products such as frozen dumplings or beef balls for home or restaurant use and finally to frozen mince. And China is keen to get in on the ground floor. Whichever new alternative protein – pea protein, cell-based, 3D printing or something we haven't yet thought of – finally comes out on top, there is reason to expect that China will be near the forefront of the technology. 'Green Biomanufacturing' was named a National Key R&D priority in 2020 and research hotspots in places like Nanjing cluster together expertise in research and manufacturing with generous state and private venture capital. Heavy investment in home-grown companies like Starfield and Hong Kong's Omnipork – currently producers of vegan pork mince – may allow China to produce the next big thing or at least be positioned to bring it quickly to market.[2]

But will people buy it? Pork will always have a place in special meals, but pricing and food safety issues have driven consumers to alternatives in the past and there's no reason to think that a truly acceptable alternative is that far away, and that a new generation wouldn't adopt the change quite quickly. Dairy would be a much easier transition, since China has only recently been won over to milk, and products like yogurt are already sold processed.

One of the unexpected effects of tech-based future foods is how they might affect China's food geography. Having invested trillions in infrastructure, China is able to move goods fast and cheaply. But what if food didn't need to move at all? Growing systems based on high-density hydroponics – a technological step up from the plastic-sheeted greenhouses that currently ring every city – could make urban areas essentially self-sufficient in fresh vegetables. If we're making a good many of our proteins in a laboratory as well, that now covers much of our fresh food supply.

Beyond just supplying cities with produce, we can think about the potential of combining the franchise model with delivery apps. Franchises work because they have found a way to outsource much of their food preparation to a central kitchen. Delivery apps are reaching towards (even if they're not quite there yet) a predictive algorithm that aims to know what you want before you want it. Put these together with a third innovation – a kitchen that is partially or completely automated – and you have all the ingredients for a profound transformation of the food industry.

Take a single dish, say something like fried noodles. At present, the dish is made by a cook, maybe well-trained or maybe not, using fresh ingredients that are cleaned and prepped in the downtime between meal services. Now think about all the ways that currently conceivable technologies could make that same dish more efficient. A truly smart algorithm would predict the day's orders by factoring a myriad of elements from the weather to who won yesterday's football match. That would mean that fresh materials could be ordered in with little or no waste and any emergency supplements could be dropped off by drone. Meat might come cut to order out of a food printer, possibly even one on-site. Preparation could be entirely automated, promising a completely standard taste every time, not to mention packing far more cooking capacity into the same amount of kitchen space. Orders might go to customers in a dining room or they might be delivered to homes and offices by driverless vehicles.

Here's the thing. Every single piece of that scenario already exists, possibly only in rudimentary form, but the technology is there. It only takes some enterprising soul to put it all together and make it work. Frozen and fast-food production is already largely mechanized, so why not other restaurant tasks? The savings – not least of all getting rid of most of your kitchen staff – would be too good to pass up. The change might come in bit by bit, maybe starting with those repetitive dishes that any cook could do with their eyes closed, and might get trialled in an institutional setting like a school or company cafeteria. But just like your smartphone or laptop computer, technology that started out expensive, bulky and exotic has a way of mainstreaming to the point that we eventually can't imagine living without it.

Note that I said more efficient, not better. If current trends are an indication, there will always be a special place for handicraft, if only as a function of scarcity. It's not hard to imagine a future where mass-produced food sits firmly in the middle, with handmade food occupying a place at the very top and another at the very bottom.

What about food at home? Here we have a couple of signposts. The first is just how completely Chinese consumers have been won over to delivery. In just a few years, hundreds of millions of households have taken to ordering delivery a few times a week or even more than once in a single day. Make food delivery easier, faster and cheaper, as automation promises to do, and there's every reason to expect that the curve will continue to trend up. There may be a backlash, but just like American households fell in love with processed food and haven't really dropped the habit, a convenience once adopted is not easily let go.

The second is that it could be getting harder to cook at home. This is for two reasons. Property prices are, in a word, nuts. In some Chinese cities, the price of an apartment is equivalent to eighty years of wages. As apartments get smaller, the first space to go on the chopping block is the kitchen – just ask anyone who has lived in Singapore. Second, many urban households consist of two exhausted parents, an exhausted child and one or more grandparents who hold the whole thing together. Visit a Chinese market at midday and nearly everyone you see will be retired, buying vegetables to take home for dinner. This generation will not be with us forever and it's entirely reasonable to imagine that their current caregiving capacity will not be replaced. The upcoming generation of grandparents might cook holiday meals, but be completely content to order out for much of everything else.

Which brings us to our big question: what will people eat and how will they eat it? Of course, we don't know, but keeping the big picture in mind, we can imagine a few scenarios.

Global Harvest

In this first scenario, China has continued along its current path of globalization, gradually becoming less a customer and more a shop owner. Years of wise investments and savvy diplomatic wrangling have placed China in a position to lead global food trends and prices. Enmeshed in a web of global financing and tie-ups, Chinese companies span the globe and are respected global citizens.

Nobody benefits more than China's food consumers. With the wheels of commerce greased by free trade agreements, Chinese consumers are in a position to enjoy all the benefits of globalization. More than just lowering prices, opening China to the world's food has also changed tastes.

Our banquet in this idealistic scenario consists of a snack at the Adam Smith café. On the table, we have milk from New Zealand, cherries from Europe and bread shipped in from Russia (don't forget that all this confidence in global trade also means that China has continued to invest in chains that can deliver food within hours). Cured ham comes from a small artisanal producer in China's southwest, an area that used to grow pork in vast factory farms, but has since switched up to higher-value, small-batch organic produce that fetches high prices in China and across the world.

Cold War

In the second, the world has been divided into political trade blocs. Food trade is a victim of global tensions, which include frequent conflicts over international resources like river water and oceanic fishing grounds. China has become a food fortress. It has invested in programmes to green its deserts and cultivate its northern forests. Hundred-year leases of farmland in Africa and South America secure supplies but leave the country open to charges of new colonialism. Many of China's food companies have been kicked out of global stock markets and rely heavily on state investment. In return, the country's vast market has been denied to unfriendly competitors.

In this scenario, our banquet is still international but in a Cold War sort of way. The 'Rising China' chain of fast food still uses imported ingredients, but the imports come from friends only: flour from Russia and beef from a Chinese state-owned farm in Angola. If the setting looks familiar, it is because Rising China took over 2,000 McDonald's outlets after that chain decided to leave the country. The outlets were already Chinese-owned, so the change simply meant rebranding the logo and nationalizing the supply chains. Name changes aside, the menu looks mostly the same, although the taste is somehow different and the prices are definitely higher than they used to be. The clown has been replaced with a CGI monkey, who greets children by name as they come in the door.

Technoteria

Our last scenario is lunch in the company cafeteria of WeEat, an imaginary food tech subsidiary of computer giant Tencent and China's state grain company COFCO. Like all of its tech competitors, WeEat attracts young graduates with high salaries and

Is this really the future of dining? Relax, that future's already here.

lavish perks, including free housing and food on the company's expansive campus.

Workers are tracked by cameras wherever they go on the manicured grounds: not just their identity, but basic health stats like heart rate and blood pressure. When they enter the cafeteria, the algorithm tracks these health stats against past purchases and a touchless touch screen (known as a point screen) greets each person with a choice of three individualized meal sets. Although they are free to order anything from the extensive menu, most people take the first algorithm choice, which today is seafood paella with lime juice.

After confirming the order, the kitchen gets to work. A serving of rice from an automated farm, one of the few fresh ingredients kept on site, is spread into a steam tray, followed by a series of cartridges that deliver a precise mix of real and manufactured spices into a pool of synthesized chicken stock (we're long past the point of simply mixing bagged ingredients). After a brief pass through a high-pressure steam oven, the dish is topped

266

with a generous serving of freshly printed shrimp and cross-cut squid and returned to the oven for a blast of heat. The first time any human sets eyes on the food is when a robot server wheels the completed dish directly to the table.

Yesterday Once More

Which of these scenarios will eventually resemble China's actual food future? Were I to venture a guess (and why wouldn't I?), it is that China will wobble back and forth between the first two, with the third rapidly working in the background to transform the stage where all of this plays out. Two things that are certain is that the world is so thoroughly connected that any change will send shocks rippling back and forth across the globe and that, whatever change comes our way, China will be an integral part of what comes next.

LIST OF FEATURED RECIPES

WEIGHTS AND MEASURES

	Before 1930	1930–59	After 1959
Weight			
jin 斤	0.6 kg	0.5 kg	0.5 kg
liang 兩	37 g	31 g	50 g
qian 錢	3.7 g	3.1 g	5 g
fen 分	.37 g	.31 g	.5 g
Length			
cun 寸	3.2 cm	3.3 cm	3.3 cm
fen 分	3.2 mm	3.3 mm	3.3 mm
Volume			
dou 斗	10.3 litre	10 litre	10 litre
sheng 升	1.03 litre	1 litre	1 litre
ge 合	103 ml	100 ml	100 ml

Cups and bowls: pre-twentieth-century recipes often give measurements in cups and bowls, which then as now came in different sizes. Readers seeking the comfort of an arbitrary standard could think of these as 200 ml and 300 ml, respectively. Modern recipes (including my own recreations) use the U.S. cup measure of 240 ml.

TIMELINE OF MAJOR DYNASTIES

(Some overlap due to concurrent regimes)

Prehistory	Xia	2070–1600 BCE
Ancient	Shang	1600–1046 BCE
	Zhou	1046–221 BCE
Early Imperial	Qin	221–206 BCE
	Han	206 BCE–220 CE
	Northern Wei	386–535
Medieval	Sui	581–618
	Tang	618–907
	Liao	916–1125
Late Imperial	Song	960–1279
	Yuan	1271–1368
	Ming	1368–1644
	Qing	1644–1911
Modern	Republic	1912–
	People's Republic	1949–

REFERENCES

INTRODUCTION: *What Is Food History?*

1 Margaret Visser, *Much Depends on Dinner: The Extraordinary History and Mythology, Allure and Obsessions, Perils and Taboos of an Ordinary Meal* (Toronto, 1986). Those interested in close-up studies of individual foods can see the more than one hundred titles in the Reaktion Books 'Edible' series.
2 Lizzie Collingham, *The Hungry Empire: How Britain's Quest for Food Shaped the Modern World* (London, 2017), pp. 57–70, 239–49; Patricia J. O'Brien, 'The Sweet Potato: Its Origin and Dispersal', *American Anthropologist*, LXXIV/3 (1972), pp. 342–65.
3 Veronica S. W. Mak, *Milk Craze: Body, Science, and Hope in China* (Honolulu, HI, 2021), pp. 85–7.
4 David Kessler and Peter Temin, 'The Organization of the Grain Trade in the Early Roman Empire', *The Economic History Review*, LX/2 (2007), pp. 313–32; G. E. Rickman, 'The Grain Trade under the Roman Empire', *Memoirs of the American Academy in Rome*, XXXVI (1980), pp. 261–75.
5 David Foster Wallace discussed the social rise of lobster in his iconic essay 'Consider the Lobster', *Gourmet*, VIII (2004), pp. 50–64. Diets are a specialty of the detail-loving *Annales* school of historians. To appreciate the complex interaction of forces that shape what food people ate, see Emmanuel Le Roy Ladurie's unequalled classic, *The Peasants of Languedoc* (Urbana, IL, 1976).
6 W. Jeffrey Bolster, *The Mortal Sea: Fishing the Atlantic in the Age of Sail* (Cambridge, MA, and London, 2014).
7 Paul Freedman, *Out of the East: Spices and the Medieval Imagination* (New Haven, CT, 2008). Kara Newman, *The Secret Financial Life of Food: From Commodities Markets to Supermarkets* (New York, 2012), pp. 17–26. Kevin H. O'Rourke and Jeffrey G. Williamson, 'Did Vasco Da Gama Matter for European Markets?', *Economic History Review*, LXII/3 (2009), pp. 655–84.
8 Martha Washington, transcribed by Karen Hess with historical notes and copious annotations, *Martha Washington's Booke of Cookery and Booke of Sweetmeats* (New York, 1995).
9 Anna Bryson, *From Courtesy to Civility: Changing Codes of Conduct in Early Modern England* (Oxford and New York, 1998); John Gillingham, 'From Civilitas to Civility: Codes of Manners in Medieval and Early Modern England', *Transactions of the Royal Historical Society*, XII (2002), pp. 267–89.

10 Patricia Monaghan, 'Calamity Meat and Cows of Abundance: Traditional Ecological Knowledge in Irish Folklore', *Anthropological Journal of European Cultures*, XIX/2 (2010), pp. 44–61.
11 Richard S. Rivlin, 'Historical Perspective on the Use of Garlic', *The Journal of Nutrition*, CXXXI/3 (2001), pp. 951–4.
12 Arjun Appadurai, 'How to Make a National Cuisine: Cookbooks in Contemporary India', *Comparative Studies in Society and History*, XXX/1 (1988), pp. 3–24.
13 Hannele Klemettilä, *The Medieval Kitchen: A Social History with Recipes* (London, 2012). For the novice, there is no better place to start than Stephen Schmidt's short blog post 'On Adapting Historical Recipes' at the Manuscript Cookbooks Survey, www.manuscriptcookbookssurvey. org, 20 November 2022.

1 OF MEAT AND MORALITY: *The Eight Treasures of Zhou*

1 Neolithic cultures like Houli are named after a modern village located near the dig site. We of course have no idea what the people actually called themselves.
2 Deliang He and Yun Zhang, 'Shandong shiqian jumin yinshi shenghuo de chubu kaocha' [Initial investigation into the diets of prehistoric Shandong], *Dongfang Bowu*, II (2006), pp. 50–61.
3 Li Liu et al., 'Paleolithic Human Exploitation of Plant Foods during the Last Glacial Maximum in North China', *Proceedings of the National Academy of Sciences of the United States of America*, CX/14 (2013), pp. 5380–85.
4 Dorian Q. Fuller and Michael Rowlands, 'Towards a Long-Term Macro-Geography of Cultural Substances: Food and Sacrifice Traditions in East, West and South Asia', *Chinese Review of Anthropology*, XII (2009), pp. 1–37. Dorian Q. Fuller and Michael Rowlands, 'Ingestion and Food Technologies: Maintaining Differences over the Long-Term in West, South and East Asia', in *Interweaving Worlds: Systematic Interactions in Eurasia, 7th to the 1st Millennium BC*, ed. T. C. Wilkinson et al. (Oxford, 2011), pp. 37–60.
5 Ye Wa and Anke Hein, 'A Buried Past: Five Thousand Years of (Pre) History on the Jing-Wei Floodplain', *Asian Archaeology*, IV (2020), pp. 1–15.
6 Gideon Shelach-Lavi, 'How Neolithic Farming Changed China', *Nature Sustainability*, V (2022), pp. 735–6.
7 *Huainanzi*, book 19, second century BCE.
8 Cheng Gao, *Shiwu jiyuan* [Origin of things], quoted in Zhao Jianmin, *Zhongguo caiyao wenhua shi* [History of China's Food Culture] (Beijing, 2017), pp. 29–30.
9 Just to clarify that Confucius was just one voice in a much larger school of thought, and that he was not especially influential during his own lifetime.
10 Roel Sterckx, 'Sages, Cooks and Flavours in Warring States and Han China', *Monumenta Serica*, LIV (2006), pp. 42–3.
11 Ibid., pp. 31–5.

12 Jean Levi, 'The Rite, the Norm and the Dao: Philosophy of Sacrifice and Transcendence of Power in Ancient China', in *Early Chinese Religion, Part One: Shang through Han (1250 BC–220 AD)*, ed. J. Lagerwey and M. Kalinowski (Leiden, 2009), pp. 645–748. Rongguang Zhao, *Zhongguo yinshi shilun* [Essays on China's food history] (Harbin, 1990), pp. 199–200; Sterckx, 'Sages', pp. 13–14.

13 These texts are the *Rites of Zhou (Zhouli)*, *Etiquette and Rites (Yili)* and the *Book of Rites (Liji)*. On aging, see *Book of Rites, Neize* 47.

14 Jiajing Wang et al., 'Revealing a 5,000-y-Old Beer Recipe in China', *Proceedings of the National Academy of Sciences of the United States of America*, CXIII/23 (2016), pp. 6444–8. Patrick E. McGovern et al., 'Chemical Identification and Cultural Implications of a Mixed Fermented Beverage from Late Prehistoric China', *Asian Perspectives*, XLIV/2 (2005), pp. 249–75. Solomon H. Katz, Fritz Maytag and Miguel Civil, 'Brewing an Ancient Beer', *Archaeology*, XLIV/4 (1991) pp. 24–33. Li Liu et al., 'The Origins of Specialized Pottery and Diverse Alcohol Fermentation Techniques in Early Neolithic China', *Proceedings of the National Academy of Sciences of the United States of America*, CXVI/26 (2019), pp. 12767–74. Jingwen Liao et al., 'A New Filtered Alcoholic Beverage: Residues Evidence from the Qingtai Site (ca. 5,500–4,750 cal. BP) in Henan Province, Central China', *Frontiers of Earth Science*, 9 May 2022.

15 Chi Han, *Nanfang caomu zhuang* [Botany of the South], quoted in Mu-Chou Poo, 'The Use and Abuse of Wine in Ancient China', *Journal of the Economic and Social History of the Orient*, XVII/2 (1999), pp. 123–51. *Ge* is a kind of wild taro.

16 The same starter is used in other Asian fermented foods, such as tempeh and Korean *doenjang* paste.

17 *Etiquette and Rites*, quoted in Poo, 'Use and Abuse', p. 136.

18 Tak Kam Chan, 'From Conservatism to Romanticism: Wine and Prose-Writing from Pre-Qin to Jin', in *Scribes of Gastronomy*, ed. Isaac Yue and Siufu Tang (Hong Kong, 2013), p. 16.

19 Sterckx, 'Sages', p. 38.

20 Poo, 'Use and Abuse'.

21 Adapted from Nicholas Morrow Williams, 'The Morality of Drunkenness in Chinese Literature of the Third Century CE', in *Scribes of Gastronomy*, eds Isaac Yue and Siufu Tang (Hong Kong, 2013), p. 27.

22 Yuan Chen, 'Legitimation Discourse and the Theory of the Five Elements in Imperial China', *Journal of Song-Yuan Studies*, XLIV (2014), pp. 325–64.

23 *Rites of Zhou, Tianguan zhongzai 100*. The last line refers to the diagnostic technique of observing the life force and complexion of the patient.

24 *Rites of Zhou, Tianguan zhongzai 98*.

25 Sterckx, 'Sages'.

26 Pangtong Qiu, *Zhongguo caiyao shi* [History of Chinese cuisine] (Qingdao, 2010), pp. 27–32. Sterckx, 'Sages', p. 6.

27 Lin Yu et al., 'Wo guo Shiji jizai de jiang ji jiangyou lishi qiyuan yanjiu' [Historical Origin of Chinese Pastes and Sauces as Recorded in the Shiji], *Shandong nongye daxue xuebao* (2015), pp. 14–22.

References

28 Zhao Jianmin, *Zhongguo caiyao wenhua*, pp. 37–8.
29 Qiu, *Zhongguo caiyao shi*, pp. 29–31.
30 *Book of Rites*, in Sterckx, 'Sages', p. 41.
31 Ibid., p. 42.
32 Zhao, *Zhongguo yinshi*, p. 194; Sterckx, 'Sages', pp. 18–19.
33 *Etiquette and Rites, Pinli 16*.
34 Adapted from David R. Knechtges and Jerry Swanson, 'Seven Stimuli for the Prince: The *Ch'i-Fa* of Mei Ch'eng', *Monumenta Serica*, XXIX/1 (1970), pp. 99–116; Sterckx, 'Sages', p. 7.
35 Adapted from Knechtges and Swanson, 'Seven Stimuli'. Yi Yin and Yi Ya are two historical figures associated with cuisine.
36 David R. Knechtges, 'A Literary Feast: Food in Early Chinese Literature', *Journal of the American Oriental Society*, CVI/1 (1986), pp. 49–63.
37 *Book of Rites, Neize 50–56*.
38 Ho Shun-yee, 'The Significance of Musical Instruments and Food Utensils in Sacrifices of Ancient China', *Monumenta Serica*, LI (2003), pp. 1–18.
39 This additional detail comes from an early fifteenth-century commentary called the *Complete Etiquette and Rites (Liji daquan)*.
40 *Essential Techniques*, recipe 75.
41 Ancient brewers had learned to concentrate alcohol by freezing or steaming fermented mash. See Constance A. Cook, 'Moonshine and Millet: Feasting and Purification Rituals in Ancient China', in *Of Tripod and Palate: Food, Politics and Religion in Traditional China*, ed. Roel Sterckx (New York and Basingstoke, 2005), pp. 9–33.
42 Sterckx, 'Sages', p. 13. Chung-lin Chiu, 'Jinglao shi suoyi jianlao – Mingdai xiangyin jiuli de bianqian jiqi yu difanghui de hudong' [Respecting the Elders to Despise the Elders: The Evolution and Local Interaction of the Ming Dynasty Wine Drinking Ritual], *Zhongyang yanjiuyuan lishi yuyansuo jikan*, LXXI/1 (2005), pp. 1–79.

2 BY SILK ROAD AND HIGH SEA: *New Foods Come to China*

1 Saishi Wang, *Tangdai yinshi* [Foods of the Tang Dynasty] (Jinan 2003), p. 38.
2 Ibid., pp. 1–5, 11–13.
3 *Flavouring the Pot*, pp. 294–5.
4 *Essential Techniques*, recipe 82.
5 Wang, *Tangdai yinshi*, pp. 6–8, 14–17, 32–4. Zhang Jing, *Canzhuoshang de zhongguo shi* [Tabletop History of China] (Beijing, 2022), pp. 64–71.
6 *Principles of Eating and Drinking*.
7 James Benn, *Tea in China: A Religious and Cultural History* (Honolulu, HI, 2015).
8 From 'Tasting Tea in a Western Hills Monastery', in Ronald Egan, 'The Interplay of Social and Literary History: Tea in the Poetry of the Middle Historical Period', in *Scribes of Gastronomy*, ed. Isaac Yue and Siufu Tang (Hong Kong, 2013), pp. 69–85.
9 Sun Pingzhong quoted in Yuemei Shi, 'Tangdai shaoweiyan kaoshi' [Study and Explanation of the Tang Dynasty Burning-Tail Banquet], *Xingtai xueyuan xuebao*, XXXIII/3 (2018), pp. 133–5.

277

10 Pangtong Qiu, *Zhongguo caiyao shi* [History of Chinese Cuisine] (Qingdao, 2010), especially p. 175. The original list and comments appear in the tenth-century *Qingyilu*.

11 This recipe appears in *Shi zhen lu* [Treasures of the Table] (fifth or sixth century).

12 *Essential Techniques*, recipe 80.

13 *Taiping yulan* [Readings of the Taiping Era] (tenth century).

14 Alain George, 'Direct Sea Trade between Islamic Iraq and Tang China: From the Exchange of Goods to the Transmission of Ideas', *Journal of the Royal Asiatic Society*, XXV/4 (2015), pp. 1–46.

15 Craig Lockard, '"The Sea Common to All": Maritime Frontiers, Port Cities and Chinese Traders in the Southeast Asian Age of Commerce, ca. 1400–1750', *Journal of World History*, XXI/2 (2010), pp. 219–47. Momoki Shiro, 'Dai Viet and the South China Sea Trade: From the 10th to the 15th Century', *Crossroads: An Interdisciplinary Journal of Southeast Asian Studies*, XII/1 (1998), pp. 1–34.

16 Xu, Guanmian, 'Junks to Mare Clausum: China-Maluku Connections in the Spice Wars, 1607–1622', *Itinerario*, XLIV/1 (2020), pp. 196–225.

17 Ping-Ti Ho, 'Early-Ripening Rice in Chinese History', *Economic History Review*, IX/2 (1956), p. 207.

18 Ibid. For a critical analysis of the Champa rice theory, see Kent Deng and Lucy Zheng, 'Economic Restructuring and Demographic Growth: Demystifying Growth and Development in Northern Song China, 960–1127', *Economic History Review*, LXVIII/4 (2015), pp. 1107–31.

19 Jennifer Downs, 'Survival Strategies in Ming Dynasty China: Planting Techniques and Famine Foods', *Food and Foodways*, VIII/4 (2000), pp. 273–88. Ping-Ti Ho, 'The Introduction of American Food Plants into China', *American Anthropologist*, LVII/2 (1955), pp. 191–201.

20 Brian R. Dott, *The Chile Pepper in China: A Cultural Biography* (New York, 2020); Cao Yu, *Zhongguo shila shi* [China's Spicy History] (Beijing, 2022), pp. 50–81.

21 Qiu, *Zhongguo caiyao*, p. 404.

22 The Mongol 'empire' was actually an overlapping mix of khanates and princedoms, of which the Chinese Yuan was just one part. Its numerous capitals and princely towns also included Qara Qorum, Shangdu and Khotan. Nancy Shatzman Steinhardt, 'Imperial Architecture along the Mongolian Road to Dadu', *Ars Orientalis*, XVIII (1988), pp. 59–93. Hodong Kim, 'Was "da Yuan" a Chinese Dynasty?', *Journal of Song-Yuan Studies*, XLV (2015), pp. 279–305.

23 Jingming Zhang and Jie Zhang, *Yinshi renleixue: Shiyuxia de Liaodai yinshi wenhua yanjiu* [Food Anthropology: Liao-Era Food Culture Beneath the Horizon] (Beijing, 2021), pp. 91–8.

24 Thomas David DuBois, 'Many Roads from Pasture to Plate: A Commodity Chain Approach to China's Beef Trade, 1732–1931', *Journal of Global History*, XIV/1 (2019), pp. 22–43.

25 Jianzhong Wan and Mingchen Li, *Zhongguo yinshi wenhua shi. Jingjin diqu juan* [Cultural History of Chinese food, Beijing and Tianjin] (Beijing, 2013), p. 135.

26 Jun Li, '"Zhama" kao' [Study of 'Zhama'], *Lishi yanjiu*, 1 (2005), pp. 179–83.

27 Jianxin Gao, 'Yuandai shiren bixia de "Zhamayan" lüe kao' [Initial Study of the 'Zhamayan' in Yuan poetry], *Nei Menggu daxue xuebao (Zhexue shehui kexue ban)*, XLVIII/2 (2016), pp. 5–8.

28 Jianxin Gao, 'Yuandai shiren'. Scholars have convincingly suggested that distilling might have been known earlier. See David R. Knechtges, 'Tuckahoe and Sesame, Wolfberries and Chrysanthemums, Sweet-Peel Orange and Pine Wines, Pork and Pasta: The Fu as a Source for Chinese Culinary History', *Journal of Oriental Studies*, XLV/1–2 (2012), pp. 1–26. In such cases, Yuan-era records may have been recording a better or more efficient method.

29 Imperial visits to Manchuria were costly and often dangerous but clearly very meaningful to the Qing rulers. Ruth Rogaski, *Knowing Manchuria: Environments, the Senses and Natural Knowledge on an Asian Borderland* (Chicago, IL, 2022).

30 Sources record these as 'meat-eating parties'.

31 Issac Yue, 'The Comprehensive Manchu–Han Banquet: History, Myth and Development, *Ming Qing Yanjiu*, XX/1 (2008), pp. 93–111.

32 Zhao Rongguang, *Man Han quanxi yuanliu kaoshu* [Study of the origins of the Manchu-Han Feast] (Beijing, 2003), pp. 206–28.

33 *Pleasure Boats of Yangzhou*, 4:60. Yuan Mei mentions this event but provides no detail.

34 Ingredients lists from *Guanglusi zeli* [Protocols of the Imperial Kitchen] 1839. See also Wang Renxing, *Man Han quanxi yuanliu* [Origins of the Manchu-Han Feast] (Beijing, 1986), pp. 19–25.

35 I base this on instructions in the *Protocols of the Imperial Kitchen* juan 47 to allocate tents, cooking utensils and funds for buying materials based on the unambiguous 'number of seated diners' (*xi shu*). The exaggerated largesse of the meals most likely found its way to the diner's retinue.

36 Wang Renxing, *Man Han quanxi*, p. 2.

37 The Chinese name *sanzi* is a transliteration from Uighur. An early twelfth-century source explains *sanzi* as a fried cake called *huanbing*, but by the Ming it is clearly identified as today's dish of crisp fried noodles.

38 Shaodan Zhang, 'Cattle Slaughter Industry in Qing China: State Ban, Muslim Dominance and the Western Diet', *Frontiers of History in China*, XVI/1 (2021), pp. 4–38.

39 *Zhaoshi* literally means 'bright style', but it more likely is a Manchu word written in Chinese characters.

40 *Flavouring the Pot*, p. 95.

41 This menu is further explained in Zhao, *Man Han*, pp. 244–5.

42 Meng Zhang, 'Knowing Exotica: Edible Birds' Nests and the Cultures of Knowledge in Early Modern China', *Harvard Journal of Asian Studies*, LXXXIV/2 (2024).

3 GARDENS OF DELIGHT: *Imperial China's High Cuisine*

1 Zhanghua Ding and Weibing Li, *Honglou shijing* [Foods of the Red Mansion] (Nanjing, 2019), pp. 255–65.
2 Kent Deng and Lucy Zheng, 'Economic Restructuring and Demographic Growth: Demystifying Growth and Development in Northern Song China, 960–1127', *Economic History Review*, LXVIII/4 (2015), pp. 1107–31.
3 For those interested in a more literal translation, the Master of Provisions is the 'Master of Measuring the Tea, Rice and Wine'; the 'grain burners' are 'lighters of the grain dregs' (probably referring to some sort of alcohol stove). The indigent young men were *xianhan* and *sibo*. The needles were 'guest needles', because they were so hard to dislodge. *Sazan* means a 'brief respite', most likely meaning that one was paying them to go away. *Dream of Splendour* (*juan* 2, Food and Produce).
4 The market for meat was even more elaborate in the coastal southern capital of Lin'an, today's Hangzhou, which also consumed large amounts of seafood. Weijie Yu, *Hangzhou Songdai shiliao shi* [History of Food Materials in Song Dynasty Hangzhou] (Beijing, 2018), pp. 142–79.
5 *Mrs Wu's Records from the Kitchen*, recipe 94.
6 *Old Records of Hangzhou* (*Wu lin jiushi*), quoted in Qiu Pangtong, *Zhongguo caiyao shi* [History of Chinese Cuisine] (Qingdao, 2010), pp. 222–3.
7 *Mrs Wu's Records from the Kitchen*, recipe 42. *Sharen* is the aromatic seed of *Wurfbainia villosa*.
8 Ibid., recipe 32.
9 Qiu, *Zhongguo caiyao*, p. 208.
10 *Dream of Splendour* (autumn sacrifice).
11 Strained bean paste (清酱) is made by cooking bean paste with salted water, while using a weight to compress bean solids at the bottom of the vat. This technique from wine making gave birth to liquid soy sauce.
12 Françoise Sabban, 'Court Cuisine in Fourteenth-Century Imperial China: Some Culinary Aspects of Hu Sihui's *Principles of Eating and Drinking*', *Food and Foodways*, I (1985), pp. 161–96.
13 *Principles of Eating and Drinking*. *Lao* could mean either yoghurt or cheese. Most versions of *Sheik al Mehshee* cook the aubergine in tomato, but the traditional recipe uses yoghurt.
14 The character 釀 usually means 'to ferment', but here it means 'chopped finely'. Qiu, *Zhongguo caiyao*, p. 326.
15 Paul D. Buell and Eugene Anderson have made stunning advances in tracing the global culinary and medical knowledge in the *Principles of Eating and Drinking* and more recently in their work the *Muslim Medicinal Recipes* (*Huihui yaofang*). Paul D. Buell and Eugene Anderson, *A Soup for the Qan: Chinese Dietary Medicine of the Mongol Era as Seen in Hu Szu-Hui's Yin-shan Cheng-yao* (London and New York, 2000) and *Arabic Medicine in China: Tradition, Innovation and Change* (Leiden, 2021).
16 See Livia Kohn, *Daoist Dietetics: Food for Immortality* (St Petersburg, FL, 2010).
17 *Dietetic Pharmacopeia* (persimmon).

18 Weijie Yu, *Hangzhou Songdai shi shiliao* [Materials on Diet in Song Dynasty Hangzhou] (Beijing, 2018), p. 46.
19 Conversely, 'not poisonous' also means that the medical benefits are not very potent. Vivienne Lo, 'Pleasure, Prohibition and Pain: Food and Medicine in Traditional China', in *Of Tripod and Palate: Food, Politics and Religion in Traditional China*, ed. Roel Sterckx (New York and Basingstoke, 2005), pp. 163–85.
20 *Principles of Eating and Drinking.* Instruction to 'eat as much as you like' means that there are no adverse side effects.
21 *Dream of Splendour (juan 6).*
22 Haitian Hu and Jianhui Liang, eds, *Yinshi liaofa* (Guangzhou, 1985), part 3, p. 30.
23 Timothy Brook, *Praying for Power: Buddhism and the Formation of Gentry Society in Late-Ming China* (Cambridge, MA, 1994).
24 Jin Feng's wonderful *Tasting Paradise on Earth* (Seattle, WA, 2020) is the first and last word on Jiangnan cuisine during this era.
25 *Tianmianjiang* is a salty, dark brown paste made from fermented wheat.
26 *Pleasure Boats of Yangzhou*, quoted in Qiu, *Zhongguo caiyao*, pp. 438–9.
27 Qiu, *Zhongguo caiyao*, p. 393.
28 Ibid., pp. 393–9. I am grateful to Wang Chengwei for his insight on China's cooking-fuel revolution.
29 Duosheng Zhu, 'Cong Qianlong dao Minguo: Sichuan haiwei cai 200 nian' [From Qianlong to Republic: 200 years of Sichuan seafood cuisine], *Shiyuan zatan*, 26 November 2022, pp. 42–5. Qiu, *Zhongguo caiyao*, pp. 452–4.
30 On the evolution of individual dishes, see Yong Lan, *Zhongguo Chuancai shi* [History of China's Sichuan Cuisine] (Chengdu, 2019), especially pp. 151–226.
31 *Mr Song's Book of Longevity*, quoted in Yong Lan, *Zhongguo Chuancai shi*, pp. 160–70.
32 Ibid., p. 175.
33 Charles Kwong, 'Making Poetry with Alcohol: Wine Consumption in Tao Qian, Li Bai and Su Shi', in *Scribes of Gastronomy*, ed. Isaac Yue and Siufu Tang (Hong Kong, 2013), pp. 45–68. Translations changed slightly from the original.
34 On culinary writing as an arena of cultural production, see Jin Feng, 'The Female Chef and the Nation: Zeng Yi's "Zhongkui lu" (Records from the kitchen)', *Modern Chinese Literature and Culture*, XXVII/1 (2016), pp. 1–37.
35 Cynthia J. Brokaw, *Commerce in Culture: The Sibao Book Trade in the Qing and Republican Periods* (Cambridge, MA, 2007).
36 Qiu, *Zhongguo caiyao*, p. 307.
37 Yuan Mei, *Recipes from the Garden of Contentment*. I draw on Sean Chen's artful translation. Sean J. S. Chen and Yuan Mei, *Recipes from the Garden of Contentment: Yuan Mei's Manual of Gastronomy* (Barrington, MA, 2018).
38 Henry Notaker, *A History of Cookbooks from Kitchen to Page over Seven Centuries* (Oakland, CA, 2017), especially pp. 58–64. Quote from p. 55.
39 秋油, the first extraction of sauce from a vat. Similar to extra virgin olive

oil.

40 Yan Liang, 'Beef, Fish and Chestnut Cake: Food for Heroes in the Late Imperial Chinese Novel', *Journal of Chinese Literature and Culture*, V/1 (2018), pp. 119–47.

41 Wankuan Shao, 'Cong Ming Qing shiqi shipu kanke de liuxing kan Ming Qing xiaoshuo Zhong de yinshi miaoxie – yi Jinpingmei Hongloumeng zhongde cai weili' [Descriptions of Food in Ming-Qing Literature as Seen from trends in Ming-Qing Food Literature: Example of *Plum in the Golden Lotus Vase* and *Dream of Red Mansions*], *Nongye kaogu*, IV (2014), pp. 270–75.

42 Cao Xueqin, *Dream of Red Mansions*, chapter 19.

43 Zhanghua Ding and Weibing Li, *Honglou shijing* [Foods of the Red Mansion] (Nanjing, 2019).

44 Chapter 52, from the Yang Hsien-yu and Gladys Yang translation of Cao Xueqin, *Dream of Red Mansions: (Hung Lou Meng)*, (Beijing, 1978).

45 *Secrets of the Table* quoted in Ding and Li, *Honglou shijing*, pp. 110–11.

46 Xueqin, *Dream of Red Mansions*, chapter 54.

4 FANCY FOODS AND FOREIGN FADS: *China Eats the World*

1 *The Travels of Marco Polo: The Complete Yule-Cordier Edition* (New York, 1993), pp. 338–9.

2 Ibid., pp. 123, 340.

3 D. Fernández Navarrete, *Tratados historicos, politicos, ethicos y religiosos de la monarchia de China* (Madrid, 1676), pp. 347–8. Quoted in Brian Lander and Thomas David DuBois, 'A History of Soy in China, from Weedy Bean to Global Commodity', in *The Age of Soybeans: An Environmental History of the Soyacene during the Great Acceleration*, ed. Claiton Marcio da Silva (Cambridge, 2022), pp. 29–47.

4 May-bo Ching, 'Chopsticks or Cutlery? How Canton Hong Merchants Entertained Foreign Guests in the Eighteenth and Nineteenth Centuries', in *Narratives of Free Trade: The Commercial Cultures of Early U.S.–China Relations*, ed. Kendall Johnson (Hong Kong, 2012), pp. 99–115.

5 'Macanese Cuisine Database', Macao, City of Gastronomy, www.gastronomy.gov.mo, 15 November 2022.

6 The 'sick man' moniker was applied fairly broadly, first in reference to the Ottoman Empire.

7 Edward East quoted in Jayeeta Sharma, 'Food and Empire', in *The Oxford Handbook of Food History*, ed. Jeffrey M. Pilcher (Oxford and New York, 2012), pp. 241–57.

8 Thomas David DuBois, 'Borden and Nestlé in East Asia, 1870–1929: Branding and Retail Strategy in the Condensed Milk Trade', *Business History* (2019).

9 On the actual state of meat eating in pre-Meiji Japan, see Hans Martin Krämer, '"Not Befitting Our Divine Country": Eating Meat in Japanese Discourses of Self and Other from the Seventeenth Century to the Present', *Food and Foodways*, XVI/1 (2008), pp. 33–62.

10 Kanagaki Robun, 'Aguranabe' [Sitting around the Stew-Pan], (1871),

in *Modern Japanese Literature: An Anthology*, ed. Donald Keene (New York, 1956), pp. 31–3.

11 Fukuzawa Yukichi, 'On Meat-Eating' (1870). Translation by Michael Bourdaghs, used with permission from www.bourdaghs.com.

12 From the 1927 speech 'Jianguo fanglüe zhiyi, xinli jianshe' [Psychological Construction, a Strategy for National Foundation].

13 *Minhai zhengbao*, 8 August 1948.

14 On restaurants in Beijing, see Jianzhong Wan and Mingchen Li, *Zhongguo yinshi wenhua shi. Jingjin diqu juan* [Cultural History of Chinese Food, Beijing and Tianjin] (Beijing, 2013), pp. 299–306; on culinary nostalgia in Nanjing, Jin Feng, *Tasting Paradise on Earth: Jiangnan Foodways* (Seattle, WA, 2019), pp. 129–55.

15 Isaac Taylor Headland, *Home Life in China* (London, 1914), p. 174. Quoted in the saintcavish WeChat blog, www.stcavish.com.

16 *300 Chinese Recipes for the Home* (n.p., 1933) pp. 167–8.

17 *Minguo ri bao*, 1 January 1921.

18 *Suzhou ming bao*, 9 November 1927.

19 *Nanjing wan bao*, 28 August 1934.

20 Thomas David DuBois, 'Counting the Carnivores: Who Ate Meat in Republican-Era China?', *Social Science History*, XLVI/4 (2022), pp. 751–75.

21 Joshua Specht, *Red Meat Republic: A Hoof-to-Table History of How Beef Changed America* (Princeton, NJ, 2019).

22 Thomas David DuBois, 'Many Roads from Pasture to Plate: A Commodity Chain Approach to China's Beef Trade, 1732–1931', *Journal of Global History*, XIV/1 (2019), pp. 22–43.

23 Mao Zedong, 'Report on an Investigation of the Peasant Movement in Hunan', 1927, www.marxists.org.

24 Frank Dikötter, *Mao's Great Famine* (London, 2011).

25 Karl Gerth, *Unending Capitalism: How Consumerism Negated China's Communist Revolution* (Cambridge, UK, 2020).

26 Jianhua Zhang, 'Beijing "Lao Mo canting" gonggong kongjian de Sulian xingxiang yu Zhong-Su guanxi bianqian de yingxiang' [Beijing 'Ol' Moscow Restaurant': Public Space Images of the Soviet Union as a Reflection of Changes in Sino-Soviet Relations], *Eluosi xuekan* XIII/46 (2017), pp. 80–94. *Beijing ribao*, 7 October 1954.

27 Beijing zhanlanguan Mosike canting, ed., *E-shi dacai liubai li* [600 Russian Dishes] (Beijing, 1987).

5 'LIFE'S A BANQUET': Food Culture in the Go-Go '90s

1 Xipeng Zhu, 'Huanfa xinguangcai de laozihao – Taifenglou fandian xiandaihua' [New Lustre on Old Brands – Modernization of Taifenglou Restaurant], *Fandian xiandaihua*, 4 (1994), pp. 19–20.

2 Yunxiang Yan, 'McDonald's in Beijing: The Localization of Americana', in *Golden Arches East: McDonald's in East Asia*, 2nd edition, ed. James L. Watson (Redwood City, CA, 2006), pp. 39–76. Thomas David DuBois, 'Fast Food for Thought: Finding Global History in a Beijing McDonald's', *World History Connected*, XVIII/2 (2021), https://

worldhistoryconnected.press.uillinois.edu.

3 CCP Central Committee, 'Decisions concerning People's Communes', in Youbao Wu, *Gonggong shitang caipu* [Cookbook for mass canteens] (Shanghai, 1959).

4 *Zhongguo shipin*, 4 (1988), p. 11.

5 Beer is an industry that naturally favours consolidation. See Kevin Hawkins and Rosemary Radcliffe, 'Competition in the Brewing Industry', *Journal of Industrial Economics*, XX/1 (1971), pp. 20–41. China's dairy industry followed a similar path. Thomas David DuBois, 'Milk from the Butterfly Spring: State and Enterprise in the Yunnan Dairy Industry', *Rural China*, XVII/1 (2020), pp. 87–110.

6 Mao Zedong, 'Report on an Investigation of the Peasant Movement in Hunan', 1927, www.marxists.org.

7 Eugene Cooper, 'Chinese Table Manners: You Are How You Eat', *Human Organization*, XLV/2 (1986), pp. 179–84. Mayfair Yang, *Gifts, Favors and Banquets: The Art of Social Relationships in China* (Ithaca, NY, 1994). Doug Guthrie, *Dragon in a Three-Piece Suit: The Emergence of Capitalism in China* (Princeton, NJ, 1999). Ellen Oxfeld, 'The Moral Registers of Banqueting in Contemporary China', *Journal of Current Chinese Affairs*, XLVIII/3 (2019), pp. 322–39.

8 Zu'an was a polite name used by the inventor of the dish, Hunan chef Tan Yankai.

6 FRANCHISE FEVER: *The Price of Efficiency*

1 Elizabeth Gooch and Fred Gale, 'China's Foreign Agriculture Investments', EIB-192, U.S. Department of Agriculture, Economic Research Service, www.ers.usda.gov (April 2018). Cecilia Tortajada and Hongzhou Zhang, 'When Food Meets BRI: China's Emerging Food Silk Road', *Global Food Security*, XXIX (2021), pp. 1–13.

2 Brian Lander and Thomas David DuBois, 'A History of Soy in China, from Weedy Bean to Global Commodity', in *The Age of Soybeans: An Environmental History of the Soyacene during the Great Acceleration*, ed. Claiton Marcio da Silva (Cambridge, 2022), pp. 29–47. Philip M. Fearnside, 'Soybean Cultivation as a Threat to the Environment in Brazil', *Environmental Conservation*, XXVII/1 (2011), pp. 23–38.

3 Thomas David DuBois, 'Behind China's Overseas Food Investments: A Tale of Two Dairies', *Asian Studies Review* (2019).

4 Thomas David DuBois, 'Milk from the Butterfly Spring: State and Enterprise in the Yunnan Dairy Industry', *Rural China*, XVII/1 (2020), pp. 87–110.

5 Globally, the supermarket revolution started in the United States and gradually spread outwards. Thomas Anthony Reardon and Ashok Gulati, 'The Supermarket Revolution in Developing Countries Policies for Competitiveness with Inclusiveness', *International Food Policy Research Institute (IFPRI), Policy Briefs*, www.ifpri.org (2008).

6 Shuwen Zhou, 'Formalisation of Fresh Food Markets in China: The

Story of Hangzhou', in *Integrating Food into Urban Planning*, ed. Yves
Cabannes and Cecilia Marocchino (London, 2018), pp. 247–63.

7 DuBois, 'Behind China's Overseas Food Investments'.

8 Changbai Xiu and K. K. Klein, 'Melamine in Milk Products in China:
Examining the Factors That Led to Deliberate Use of the Contaminant?',
Food Policy, XXXV (2010), pp. 463–70.

9 Yan Shi et al., 'Safe Food, Green Food, Good Food: Chinese Community
Supported Agriculture and the Rising Middle Class', *International
Journal of Agricultural Sustainability*, IX/4 (2011), pp. 551–8.

10 Thomas David DuBois, 'China's Old Brands: Commercial Heritage and
Creative Nostalgia', *International Journal of Asian Studies*, XVIII/1 (2021),
pp. 45–59.

11 Christopher St Cavish, 'KFC's Egg Tarts', *Smart Shanghai*, www.
smartshanghai.com, 27 February 2017.

12 World Instant Noodles Association, https://instantnoodles.org.

13 Laura He, 'Chinese Hotpot Chain Haidilao's U.S.$963 Million IPO Makes
It Hong Kong's Fifth Largest This Year', *South China Morning Post*,
www.scmp.com, 18 September 2018. Laura He, 'China's Biggest Hotpot
Chain Haidilao Taps Hillhouse, Morgan Stanley as Cornerstone
Investors in up to U.S.$963 Million IPO', *South China Morning Post*,
www.scmp.com, 18 September 2018.

14 Haidilao doubled its number of outlets in 2020, even as imitators
adopted a franchise model that passes the cost of expansion on to
licence owners. A franchise might cost between 700,000 and 2.5 million
yuan, depending on location.

15 Jing Wang and Lijuan Cheng, 'The Relationships among Perceived
Quality, Customer Satisfaction and Customer Retention: An Empirical
Research on Haidilao Restaurant', International Conference on Services
Systems and Services Management, ICSSSM (2012).

7 AND BEYOND . . .

1 Mindi Schneider and Shefali Sharma, 'China's Pork Miracle?
Agribusiness and Development in China's Pork Industry', *Institute for
Agriculture and Trade Policy*, iatp.org (2014).

2 Doris Lee and Thomas David DuBois, 'China's Quest for Alternative
Proteins', *Asia Global Online* (2022), www.asiaglobalonline.hku.hk.s

SELECT BIBLIOGRAPHY

CHINESE FOOD WRITING

This list only includes food writings mentioned in the text. English titles are loosely translated. For all other Chinese sources please reference the footnotes.

300 Chinese Recipes for the Home 家庭向支那料理三百種, 1933
Book of Tea 茶經, Lu Yu 陸羽, eighth century
China Food 中国食品, 1978–
Chongqing Famous Recipes 重庆名菜, 1960
Cooking for Commune Canteens 公共食堂烹饪, 1959
Dietetic Pharmacopeia 食療本草, *Meng Shen* 孟詵, early eighth century
Dream of Splendour in the Eastern Capital 東京夢華錄, Meng Yuanlao 孟元老, 1127
Essential Techniques for the Common People 齊民要術, Jia Sixie 賈思勰, early sixth century
Family Cookbook 家庭菜谱, 1956
Flavouring the Pot 調鼎集, 1868
Food and Drink of the Cloud Forest Hall 雲林堂飲食制度集, Ni Zan 倪瓚, fourteenth century
Foreign Pharmacopoeia 海要本草, Li Xun 李珣, tenth century
Garden of Enlightenment 醒園錄, Li Huanan 李化楠, 1785
Mr Song's Book of Longevity 宋氏養生部, Song Xu 宋詡, 1504
Mrs Wu's Records from the Kitchen 宋浦江吳氏中饋錄, twelfth century (Not to be confused with other books also called *Records from the Kitchen* 中饋錄 from the late Qing)
People's Cookbook 大众菜谱, 1966
Pleasure Boats of Yangzhou 揚州畫舫錄, Li Dou 李斗, 1764
Practical Collection of Vital Home Skills 居家必用事類全集, Yuan dynasty
Protocols of the Imperial Kitchen 光祿寺則例, 1839
Principles of Eating and Drinking 飲膳正要, Hu Sihui 忽思慧, 1330
Recipes from the Garden of Contentment 隨園食單, Yuan Mei 袁枚, 1792
Secrets of the Table 食憲鴻秘, Zhu Yizun 朱彝尊, 1731
Secrets of Western Cooking 西餐烹飪秘訣, 1925
Sichuan Cuisine 四川菜谱, 1977
Thoughts on a Vegetarian Diet 素食說略, Xue Baochen 薛寶辰, late nineteenth–early twentieth century
Yi Ya's Recorded Thoughts 易牙遺意, Han Yi 韓奕, fourteenth century

USEFUL REFERENCE

These are some of the classic books on the history and culture of food in China.

GENERAL

Anderson, Eugene, *The Food of China* (New Haven, CT, 1988). The classic.

Chang, Kwang-chih, *Food in Chinese Culture: Anthropological and Historical Perspectives* (New Haven, CT, 1977)

Dunlop, Fuchsia, *Land of Fish and Rice: Recipes from the Culinary Heart of China* (New York and London, 2016)

Höllmann, Thomas O., *The Land of the Five Flavours: A Cultural History of Chinese Cuisine* (New York, 2013)

Lin, Hsiang Ju, *Slippery Noodles: A Culinary History of China* (London, 2015)

Yuan, Mei, trans. Sean Jy-Shyang Chen, *The Way of Eating: Yuan Mei's Manual of Gastronomy* (Great Barrington, MA, 2019). This outstanding translation also has a companion volume devoted specifically to recipes.

TECHNOLOGY

Bray, Francesca, *Science and Civilisation in China*, vol. VI, part II: *Agriculture* (Cambridge, 1984)

Huang, H. T., *Science and Civilisation in China*, vol. VI, part V: *Fermentations and Food Science* (Cambridge, 2001)

CULTURE AND POLITICS

Feng, Jin, *Tasting Paradise on Earth: Jiangnan Foodways* (Seattle, WA, 2019)

Sterckx, Roel, *Of Tripod and Palate: Food Politics and Religion in Traditional China* (New York, 2005)

Swislocki, Marc, *Culinary Nostalgia: Regional Food Culture and the Urban Experience in Shanghai* (Stanford, CA, 2009)

FOOD IN SOCIETY

Oxfeld, Ellen, *Bitter and Sweet: Food Meaning and Modernity in Rural China* (Oakland, CA, 2017)

Watson, James, *Golden Arches East: McDonald's in East Asia* (Stanford, CA, 2006). Especially Yunxiang Yan's classic chapter on McDonald's in Beijing.

ACKNOWLEDGEMENTS

At a very low point, Misa and my family swooped in to save my career and my self-esteem.

Emei, Huanghou and my lovely colleagues at Beijing Normal University helped me become a new person in China.

Xiao Kunbing and Liu Maoli cheered me through culinary trade school in Chengdu. Two of that city's outstanding restaurants, Xiaoya 小雅, founded by Li Jieren in 1930, and Zhang Yuanfu's Michelin-starred Song Yunze 松云泽, generously welcomed me into their kitchens.

Laura Kenney, Michael Leaman and the outstanding production team at Reaktion helped turn my half-baked idea into a book – possibly even a *good* book.

Finally, let's not forget the friendship and insight of thousands of Chinese meals in hundreds of kitchens across three decades.

Illustrations are by Chengdu artist Xu Ke.

PHOTO ACKNOWLEDGEMENTS

The author and publishers wish to express their thanks to the sources listed below for illustrative material and/or permission to reproduce it. Some locations of artworks are also given below, in the interest of brevity:

Art Institute of Chicago: pp. 42, 66, 67; chineseposters.net (Landsberger collection): pp. 198 (BG E15/829), 209 (BG E13/933); collection of the author: pp. 174, 201; Thomas David DuBois: pp. 8, 32 (after Chris J. Stevens and Dorian Q. Fuller, 'The spread of agriculture in eastern Asia: Archaeological bases for hypothetical farmer/language dispersals', *Language Dynamics and Change*, VII/2 (2017)), 72 (Liaoshangjing Museum, Inner Mongolia), 156, 223, 228, 237, 242; courtesy Historical Photographs of China, University of Bristol/ www.hpcbristol.net: pp. 73 (photo Malcolm Rosholt, © 2012 Mei-Fei Elrick and Tess Johnston), 134 (photo Charles Wheeler, © 2014 Alison Brooke), 179 (photo Malcolm Rosholt, © 2012 Mei-Fei Elrick and Tess Johnston); Harvard-Yenching Library, Harvard University, Cambridge, MA (Hedda Morrison photograph collection), photos © 2024 Presidents and Fellows of Harvard College: pp. 75, 137, 233; The Metropolitan Museum of Art, New York: p. 140; National Diet Library, Tokyo: p. 69; National Library of China, Beijing, photos World Digital Library: p. 87; National Palace Museum, Taipei: pp. 33, 116; drawing after Ren Rixin, 'Shandong Zhucheng Han mu huaxiang shi', *Wenwu*, no. 10 (1981): p. 53 (original carving at Zhucheng Museum, Shandong); illustrations by Xiao Ke, Chengdu artist: pp. 62, 82, 157, 178, 218, 253, 266.

INDEX

Page numbers in *italics* indicate illustrations